MW00655242

BaZi The Destiny Code

八字命理

BaZi - The Destiny Code

First edition February 2005
Third Print August 2006

The author can be reached at:

Mastery Academy of Chinese Metaphysics Sdn. Bhd. (611143-A)
19-3, The Boulevard, Mid Valley City,
59200 Kuala Lumpur, Malaysia.
Tel: +603-2284 8080, +603-2284 8318
Fax: +603-2284 1218
Email: info@masteryacademy.com
Website: www.masteryacademy.com

DISCLAIMER:

The author, Joey Yap, and the publisher, JY Books Sdn. Bhd., have made their best efforts to produce this high quality, informative and helpful book. They make no representation or warranties of any kind with regard to the completeness or accuracy of the contents of the book, and accept no liability of any kind for any losses or damages caused or alleged to be caused directly or indirectly from using the information contained herein.

Published by JY Books Sdn. Bhd. (659134-T)

INDEX

PREFACE

During my school days, learning BaZi on my own was a difficult, daunting and nearly impossible task. There were no books on BaZi in English and no formal classes on the subject. Chinese books available on the subject were often mainly classical texts which required the assistance of Masters to interpret and understand them. These Chinese books after all had been written by Masters for the Masters. Advancing my own knowledge in BaZi required undertaking studies with Masters in Hong Kong.

Today, as a Master Trainer and Consultant teaching BaZi in various English speaking countries, I find the challenge that I faced remains for those with an interest in BaZi when it comes to reading and reference materials. My students often ask if I can refer them to an English text that could be helpful in their BaZi studies or to help them understand BaZi better. Much of the motivation behind writing this book was to afford individuals from all walks of life, both English and Chinese-educated, the opportunity to learn more about BaZi. You see, those who can read and write Chinese are not necessarily more advantaged than those who can read and write only English where BaZi studies are concerned. This is because often the texts or books available are written in an archaic language. I hope this book will be able to remove some of the barriers and obstacles that people in the past have encountered in seeking to learn more about BaZi.

I was further spurred on to write this book by the tremendous success of my BaZi Beginners DVD, which has been an instant best-seller since it hit the market! This convinced me of the need for a good informative beginner's text on the subject.

Writing this beginner's book has been a great challenge – I knew the text has to be practical but at the same time not too technical, entertaining and yet informative. I am confident that readers will find this book helpful, practical and easy to digest as I have taken great pains to ensure that this book satisfied the standards I have set for myself.

I've also viewed the writing of this book as an opportunity to establish a benchmark for the respect that the practice of BaZi rightfully deserves. In recent years, Feng Shui has been over commercialised to the extent that today it suffers an image problem. A once respectable ancient science has become the stuff of hoo-hah and superstition. A misinformed public is not the way forward for any field of study. Accordingly, I feel it is important to write this book to help put people on the right footing about BaZi and to prevent needless commercialisation of the subject.

One of the early challenges I faced, when pioneering the teaching of BaZi to westerners was the accurate translation of key BaZi terminology from Chinese to English. The challenge was to translate the terms without losing any of the original essence. As Chinese BaZi terminology is very much couched in a pictorial language, the selection of the correct English words required much consideration. I therefore had to coin several English terms for BaZi references. Over the years that I have been teaching BaZi, these terms have grown to become almost a language of its own, which all my students use when they talk about BaZi. You will be introduced to these terms, or BaZi Language as I like to call it, throughout this (and future) books. I hope they will be helpful in your journey towards understanding BaZi and your Destiny Code.

BaZi (pronounced Bhat Ji in Cantonese – Baa Z in Mandarin) means eight characters. These eight characters are translated from our birth information – Year, Month, Day and Hour – into four pairs of distinct Chinese Characters. Four pairs make Eight Characters (or BaZi), and each pair is known as a pillar, hence the name "Four Pillars of Destiny" as is sometimes known. Through just these Eight Characters, the potential, the mysteries, the ups and downs of life, are revealed to us in full technicolour! (BaZi after all is a pictorial art!). By decoding a person's BaZi, we can unlock and reveal everything there is to know about a person's life and destiny.

I chose the title 'The Destiny Code' because I felt it encapsulates the essence of what BaZi is all about. To a layperson, these eight characters have no meaning. But to those who have the key, it holds vast and tremendous insights. Just as a person's DNA holds the key to the scientific make-up and the secrets of the human body, so a person's BaZi holds the key to his or her Destiny and the 'secrets' of what is in store for him or her in this life. I hope the title 'The Destiny Code' also conveys to my readers a sense of BaZi being a Chinese science, a 'technology' (not in the sense of computers and gadgets, but in the context of the application of a science) that helps guide us and improve our lives.

Readers of The Destiny Code who already have my BaZi Beginners Workshop DVD will find this book an invaluable companion. For newcomers to the subject, I am sure this book will be an informative and invaluable introduction to your BaZi (Chinese Astrology) studies.

Do drop by at the Mastery Academy website and try out the BaZi Ming Pan Calculator. You can also participate in the online forums where you can broaden your knowledge of BaZi and have your questions answered online.

Destiny awaits beyond this page!

Joey Yap
Feb 15, 2005
www.masteryacademy.com | www.joeyyap.com

MASTERY ACADEMY
OF CHINESE METAPHYSICS™

At www.masteryacademy.com, you will find some useful tools to ascertain key information about the Feng Shui of a property or for study of Astrology.

To learn more about your personal Destiny, you can use the Joey Yap BaZi Ming Pan Calculator to plot your Four Pillars of Destiny – you just need to have your date of birth (day, month, year) and time of birth. The Joey Yap Flying Star Calculator can be utilised to plot your home or office Flying Star chart. To find out your personal best directions, use the 8 Mansions Calculator.

For more information about BaZi, Xuan Kong or Flying Star Feng Shui, or if you wish to learn more about these subjects with Joey Yap, logon to the Mastery Academy of Chinese Metaphysics website at **www.masteryacademy.com**.

Chapter One:

What is Destiny All About?

一命，二運，三風水

First Destiny, Second Luck, Third Feng Shui – Chinese saying

Most people are aware that Feng Shui is extensively used by business tycoons, largely in Asia, to enhance their wealth. But few people know of the presence of Masters who work behind the scenes for some of Asia's most powerful and wealthy tycoons, advising on everything from suitable businesses to acquire, where and what positions to place key managerial staff, stock market investments to make, the best time to sign contracts, logo designs, and even accurate, almost prescient, economic forecasts.

Like the Emperors of ancient times, who had Imperial Astronomers at their disposal to select dates for warfare or peace treaties, today's Tycoon Emperors have in their employ, in-house BaZi and Feng Shui Masters, tasked with everything from date selection of official openings to

selecting suitable CEOs to manage individual businesses in their empire. It is not enough that a person be capable and qualified – he/she must also have the luck that ensures he/she will be able to execute a plan.

Even the seemingly early retirement of certain tycoons, superstars or politicians from public life is often planned and deliberate, based on advice from their in-house BaZi Masters.

The work of Feng Shui is often obvious and seen by all, but BaZi is often unseen and hidden, an invisible hand working behind the scenes. For many Asian tycoons, when it comes to business, nothing is left to chance, then it is certainly not 'left' to luck or destiny. Feng Shui and BaZi are used synergistically, as they should be.

Feng Shui is the Prescription, BaZi is the Diagnosis

The public has yet to understand this synergy between BaZi and Feng Shui.

In May 2003, a journalist in Kuala Lumpur interviewed me during the launch of my new Feng Shui video course, the Xuan Kong 10-Day Video coaching program. The journalist in question had an opportunity to review my Xuan Kong 10-Day Video Coaching program prior to the interview. The opening salvo of his interview was a formidable question indeed.

風水

"If Feng Shui was so easy, then everybody should be rich".

But who said Feng Shui is only about wealth creation?

If Feng Shui could create millionaires or billionaires, as so many think, then it must be the world's most amazing get-rich scheme ever. And all Feng Shui masters in the world should be billionaires.

Allow me to let you in on a little secret: have you had a look at Forbes magazine lately? It's NOT a Feng Shui master who is at the top of the Forbes wealthiest individuals list.

What CAN Feng Shui do for a person?

Feng Shui only helps hasten and magnify what a person's capacity in life is. If a person's capacity is extensive, then Feng Shui can help yield greater effects. If his capacity is limited, then there's little scope as to what Feng Shui can change for this person.

A person's capacity in life is what we term Destiny in Chinese Metaphysics. Every person is born with certain capacity in life, a life path. This capacity governs his or her potential, outcomes and achievements in life. When an individual's capacity is properly analysed and understood, then it is possible to assist him or her appropriately. This assistance can either be advice through BaZi on how to act and when to act, or through Feng Shui on how to enhance his or her ability to fulfill his or her potential to its limits or to avoid perils and downfalls in life.

Destiny can be analogised to a map of one's life. This map is unchanging and static - the destinations upon it are already fixed at the time of a person's birth.

Destiny is a guideline to your personal limits in life. We often hear the phrase 'the sky's the limit', which suggests that with effort, determination, positive thinking (and a dash of luck), a person can achieve anything he or she wants. In Chinese Metaphysics, a person's Destiny is essentially his limit – it's how far you can go and what you can expect to achieve in life.

Feng Shui cannot change a person's Destiny. Yet Destiny is controlled by the actions and inactions of an individual. Now you might be wondering: how can my actions influence my Destiny and yet my Destiny is fixed?

Let's just say today, a person was born with the Destiny to be the next Bill Gates. This individual will not find he becomes Bill Gates by simply sitting around and twiddling his thumbs. But yet, even actions or inactions have their limits. Truly, if it was possible to 'motivate' or 'positively will' oneself into great wealth or achievement, we would see motivational coaches and life coaches jostling with Feng Shui masters for the Number One position on the Forbes list of richest people in the world. But this is not so!

How many Bill Gates are there? One. How many Warren Buffetts? One. How many Richard Branson? One. And the reason for this is Destiny.

But a person's life is not just about Destiny. Destiny (Ming 命) cannot change, but Fortunes (Yun 運) can. The term "Fortunes" is synonymous with the term "Luck" in BaZi. Fortunes are dynamic and ever changing and can be analogised to paths upon the map of your life. Fortunes or luck cycles refer to the quality of the roads in this map of life. Thus, when Fortunes are favourable, the destination is reached more quickly and more efficiently and the path is smooth. When Fortunes are unfavourable, then the path to a destination is fraught with challenges and obstacles, even failure to reach the destination. Hence, the Chinese often talk of Destiny and Fortunes (Ming Yun 命運).

Issues of Destiny

"Men at some times are masters of their fates"
– William Shakespeare

In the course of my experiences as a Master Trainer teaching Chinese Astrology, I have often found that Destiny is something that people have lots of hang-ups about!

Many people believe that their lives are 100 percent within their control and that individuals have the ability, if they so wish, to achieve anything in this lifetime.

Yet, one must acknowledge that there are few areas of human experiences that are entirely untouched by the question of Destiny. Whether you are religious (it doesn't matter what religion) or an atheist, there will always be a point, a moment, when one realises, there are greater forces at work in our lives and that things sometimes happen that are beyond our control.

The Chinese say: "that which you are not meant to have, you can never have". Your Destiny sets out broadly what in this lifetime you will be able to have and what you will not be able to have. Destiny does not mean that you cease to be in control of your own life. Destiny does not mean that you cannot (through effort, hard work, persistence, industriousness) achieve or improve things in life. The study of Destiny is about knowing what is within your control and ability, and what is not.

The Fated Problem

I find that when the subject of Destiny comes up, it becomes inexplicably associated with fate and the concept of a person being 'fated' to do or not do something. Understandably and rightly so, there is a great deal of resistance to the concept of fate in the modern society that we live in today.

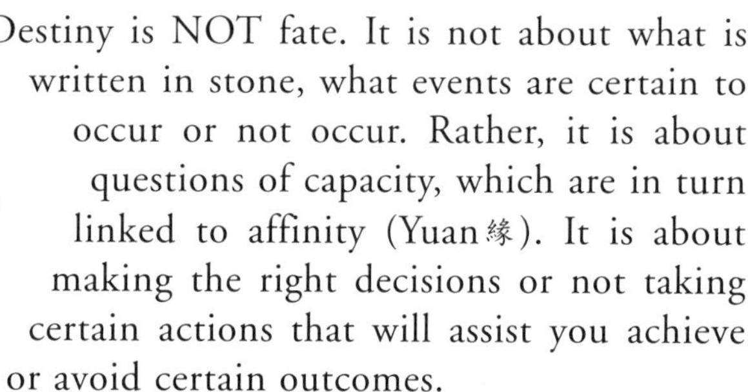

Destiny is NOT fate. It is not about what is written in stone, what events are certain to occur or not occur. Rather, it is about questions of capacity, which are in turn linked to affinity (Yuan 緣). It is about making the right decisions or not taking certain actions that will assist you achieve or avoid certain outcomes.

Limitations? What Limitations?

Many people ask - what is the point in trying to or making an effort to do anything if everything is pre-destined? Equally, many people today believe that with changes in society such as the removal of class-based systems and concepts like meritocracy, equality and equal access to education, anyone who makes enough of an effort and tries hard enough can achieve all that he or she wishes to achieve.

We live in a society today where it is considered not politically correct to label people 'limited' or to tell people that they have limitations (never mind that in large corporations, an entire department called Human Resources is devoted to finding out just what employees can and cannot do and to ensure they are equipped with the right skills – the question of 'capacity'). And generally, nobody likes to be told that they're not capable of doing something.

Now, I have to be a bit harsh here. Wake up and smell the coffee. **Life is not always fair**.

The higher powers of this universe did not make every person equal. By equal I mean not every person is DESTINED to achieve greatness to become President of the USA or a multi-millionaire. There is only one Bill Gates. Only one Donald Trump. Only one Warren Buffett.

And Destiny is the reason for this.

Now, it's not all bad news. While the Chinese believe that life is pre-destined, they do not believe in a fatalistic outlook on life. Destiny is akin to the famous saying "It's not about the hand you're dealt, but how you play it".

Heaven

Earth

Man

In the study of Chinese Metaphysics, the ancient sages believed that the universe is made up of a triumvirate of Heaven, Earth and Man, known as the Cosmic Trinity. Each of the elements of the Cosmic Trinity – Heaven, Earth, Man – controls or exerts an influence equivalent to 33%. The path of our life and a certain degree of our fortunes are set out by Heaven, the environment or Feng Shui magnifies our fortunes or luck, but Man's own action (or inaction) is what makes an outcome swing one way or the other.

Hence, a person with a limited capacity may have many achievements thanks to his hard work and positive thinking attitude, while a person with the capacity to do great things may squander his potential by choosing to sleep all day at home.

Now, you might be wondering: if it's all pre-destined, what is the point in knowing?

The truth is that it is good to know one's limits in life. The English have a saying 'You cannot make a silk purse out of a sow's ear'. Think about it: knowing the limits, knowing the no-go's, knowing what could never be achieved would save many people a lot of heartbreak, disappointment, unhappiness and frustration – surely life would be so much more pleasant and enjoyable, without the pressure to achieve something that may well be impossible? Surely there would be more happy people in this world if people focused on the can dos rather than getting upset over the can't dos?

There are many ways in which Destiny can be viewed in a positive light. Knowing your limits is just one aspect of Destiny – the other aspect of Destiny is knowing your true abilities and hidden talents, understanding yourself better. An entire industry has been spawned in the last 20 years, aimed at helping people understand themselves better, make better use of their talents, discover their true 'inner selves' – all this (and more!) are revealed through the study of one's Destiny. So what's not to know?

We all believe we are special. We all believe we are unique. And we all believe that because we are special and unique, we are destined for something. The question is WHAT?

Decoding your Destiny Code

Like most forms of Astrology, Chinese Astrology has 4 types of applications.

- **Personality Analysis** – Discovering a person's character, nature, behaviour and potential.
- **Destiny Analysis** – Investigating the life path or destiny of a person.
    a. Static Chart – Investigating the potential of wealth, relationships, career and health
    b. Dynamic Chart – Exploring the future through 10-year cycles, annual and monthly cycles

- **Event Analysis** – Studying of a particular event that occurs or will occur at a place and time
- **General Analysis** – Exploring the astrology of a country, or city, economic and political cycles

There are two major systems of Chinese Astrology which can be used to ascertain a person's Destiny Code: BaZi (Eight Characters 八字 or Four Pillars 四柱) and Zi Wei Dou Shu (Purple Star Astrology 紫微斗數). Both systems are equally potent and fascinating.

Finding out what Destiny has in-store for you is a bit like finding out your DNA. First, you need to be able to find the code, then you need to be able to read the code. Both these systems utilise distinct techniques to decode an individual's Destiny Code.

BaZi's most useful feature is its use in helping us understand the personality traits, character, behaviour and potential of a person. It is also a technique for Destiny Analysis which is used to evaluate a person's life path. Generally, BaZi is relatively easier to learn than Zi Wei Dou Shu 紫微斗數 because there are fewer "star names" to memorise. BaZi is a system that centers on the concept of "balance" between the "elements" while Zi Wei uses many "stars" to classify events, personalities and outcomes. This is a book on BaZi so I will keep the discussion brief - Zi Wei will be covered in another book.

BaZi Basics

A literal translation of the words BaZi 八字 means 'Eight 八 Characters 字'. In the West, BaZi is sometimes known as 'Four Pillars of Destiny'. As these Eight Characters are derived from 4 pairs of characters, BaZi is sometimes called Si Zhu 四柱 or Four Pillars.

Hour 時	Day 日	Month 月	Year 年	
印 Direct Resource	日元 Day Master	才 Indirect Wealth	傷 Hurting Officer	Heavenly Stems 天干
辛 *Xin* Yin Metal	壬 *Ren* Yang Water	丙 *Bing* Yang Fire	乙 *Yi* Yin Wood	
亥 *Hai* **Pig** Yin Water	戌 *Xu* **Dog** Yang Earth	戌 *Xu* **Dog** Yang Earth	未 *Wei* **Goat** Yin Earth	Earthly Branches 地支
壬 甲	丁 戊 辛	丁 戊 辛	乙 己 丁	

87	77	67	57	47	37	27	17	7	
財 丁 *Ding* Yin Fire	殺 戊 *Wu* Yang Earth	官 己 *Ji* Yin Earth	卩 庚 *Geng* Yang Metal	印 辛 *Xin* Yin Metal	比 壬 *Ren* Yang Water	劫 癸 *Gui* Yin Water	食 甲 *Jia* Yang Wood	傷 乙 *Yi* Yin Wood	Luck Pillars 大運
丑 *Chou* **Ox** Yin Earth	寅 *Yin* **Tiger** Yang Wood	卯 *Mao* **Rabbit** Yin Wood	辰 *Chen* **Dragon** Yang Earth	巳 *Si* **Snake** Yin Fire	午 *Wu* **Horse** Yang Fire	未 *Wei* **Goat** Yin Earth	申 *Shen* **Monkey** Yang Metal	酉 *You* **Rooster** Yin Metal	

Now, BaZi is much more sophisticated and precise than the daily newspaper forecasts that are based on the 12 celestial animal signs. Do bear in mind that these Sunday horoscopes are mainly for entertainment purposes. It is not possible to generalise entire swaths of people born in Dragon Years as 'bold, fierce and ambitious' – honestly, how many people are born in a Dragon year? Can they all be bold, fierce and ambitious? I think not. By all means read them and have a chuckle but remember, they are NOT true examples of Chinese Astrology or BaZi applications.

BaZi is a complete system of astrology that consists of hundreds and thousands of possible combinations. It is a classical study, with texts that go as far back as the Tang Dynasty. Amongst the notable texts on the subject are Di Tian Sui 滴天髓, Zi Ping Zhen Quan 子平真詮 and Yuan Hai Zi Ping 淵海子平.

Grand Master Xu Zi Ping is credited as the founding father of the BaZi systems practiced today. Grand Master Xu Zi Ping lived during the Five Dynasty era (AD907 – 978). He revolutionised the BaZi system then and formulated the Zi Ping BaZi system that is widely practiced today by many renowned masters of the subject.

BaZi translates our birth information – a person's Year, Month, Day and Hour of birth - into four pairs of distinct chinese characters called Jia Zi 甲子. Four pairs make Eight Characters or BaZi. Each pair is also known as a pillar, hence the name Four Pillars.

The Eight Characters are made up of Yin and Yang variations of the Five Elements (Wood, Water, Metal, Fire and Earth). By analysing the structure of a person's BaZi (which reveals compatibility, clashes, combinations and the interplay between these Eight Characters) we can determined, with significant accuracy and great detail, a person's character, nature and life path. By decoding a person's BaZi, we can unveil his or her Destiny Code.

An individual can make use of the information contained in his or her Destiny Code to accelerate performance at work, strengthen relationships with others, overcome weaknesses, maximise talents and potential, and make informed decisions based on forecasts of his or her upcoming cycle of luck.

The Basis of BaZi

天有不測之風雲，人有旦夕之禍福

"The sky has its randomness in terms of weather, and a person's life has its fluctuation in terms of fortune" - Chinese Saying

What are the origins of BaZi as a scientific study? And why do we need to know where BaZi originates from? It is important to understand the source of BaZi so that it can be viewed in its proper context – as a scientific study – and not as fortune telling or some kind of religious or superstitious practice.

Science, even in its modern high technology form today, remains an accumulation of experiences and observations. Modern science and its discoveries are a result of observation and recording of the results from experiments. Meteorology or the study of weather is a good example of how seemingly random events can be developed into a science through observation.

Accordingly, BaZi and Chinese Metaphysical studies such as Feng Shui were developed in a similar fashion – through observation. In the case of BaZi, these observations were recorded in philosophical studies.

The Chinese Five Arts 五術

Legendary, mystical and historical incidents were often used as a reference to study and formulate patterns of determining one's destiny in the early days. The legendary sage, Fu Xi's *Early Heaven Ba Gua,* King Wen's *Later Heaven Theory* and Confucius's *Yi-Jing* (*I-Ching*) contained such developed and profound observations that during the Han dynasty, these texts were commonly used by destiny analysts for decoding a person's Destiny Code.

As early as the era of the Huang Di (Yellow Emperor 2700BC – 2150BC), there were Imperial astronomers responsible for observing the stars and heavens and advising the Emperor on the well-being of the country and nation based on their observations.

During those ancient times, Imperial astronomers also served as strategists and advisors to the Emperor as they were supposed to be well-versed in the secrets of Heaven and Earth. By analysing the stars and using the secrets of Heaven and Earth, the Imperial Astronomer advised the Emperor on timing and opportunities for warfare and other important actions.

The records these astrologers or strategists kept later become sources of reference for astrologers of the later dynasties in China. For example, the text *River Map Lo Book* (He Tu Luo Shu 河圖洛書) was studied and later re-invented into *Numerology and Divination of Early and Later Heaven*(He Luo Li Shu 河洛理數).

Ming

Ancient sages spent much time studying, researching and understanding the meaning of life by observation of men's destiny. Through this, they were able to develop methodologies for forecasting a person's destiny, a subject known as Destiny Studies (Ming Xue 命學). In order to study a person's destiny, several methods of assessment are used and this includes Chinese Astrology systems like Purple Star Astrology 紫微斗數 and BaZi 八字.

Bu

To complement the Destiny Studies and in order to predict the outcome of incidents and events, the sages developed the *Science of Divination* (Bu Shi 卜筮). In modern terms, the Science of Divination can be akin to the Mathematics of Probability.

By accumulating experiences and empirical data on the observations of physical appearances such as the shape and appearances of the human body, facial features, lines on the palm, location of stars in the heavens, the Study of Physiognomy (Xiang Xue 相學) was developed. This field of study consists of the study of facial features and appearances, palms, grave-sites and residential sites. '*Xiang*' (*Fortune-telling through Physiognomy*) includes methods based on observation of appearance, physiognomy, symbolic imagery and mathematical science of the Ba Gua, and time and space to determine our life or character and possible outcomes in life. In this category, we have techniques like Face-Reading, Palm Reading and Feng Shui. Feng Shui is equivalent to the fortune telling of the house through observation of its appearance, direction and location in the environment.

相
Xiang

Yi

By observing the human body and through theories of the Yi Jing (I-Ching) and Ba Gua, the Study of Medicine (Yi Xue 醫學) was developed. This field includes the study of herbs and how they react to the human body, how meridians of Qi flow in the anatomy and how to harness the invisible forces in nature to vitalize oneself. Chinese medical studies are largely based on concepts of the Yi Jing (I-Ching), Ba Gua, Five Elements and most of all, the Yin and Yang.

Shan

Through investigation of men's emotional boundaries and energy patterns, the Study of Alchemy (Shan 山 or Xian Xue 仙學) was established. This includes the study of magic, spells, rituals, exercises for prolonging life, and physical conditioning that enhance the quality of health. This study mainly converges on ways to maintain and develop personal physical and emotional health.

The ancient Chinese termed these five types of studies - 命，卜，相，醫，山 – as the Five Techniques or Five Arts (Wu Shu 五術). Today, we refer to them as Chinese Metaphysics. Very loosely translated these Five Arts are "Mountain, Medical, Fate, Physiognomy and Divination".

BaZi is part of the Destiny Studies (Ming Xue 命學) category.

The Study of Ming 命 - The Study of Life

命，卜，相，醫，山

The Study of Destiny (Ming Xue 命學) is focused on '**people**' and, it can be said, is about achieving a greater understanding of human beings. For in order to improve one's fortune, one must first understand all there is to know about the person.

Forecasting a person's destiny is much like a weatherman using data collected from the environment to forecast the weather.

Every person is affected by certain types of energies from the universe at the time of their birth. By tracking these energies in that person's life at that time of birth, and tracking the changes in the decades and years to come, we can forecast a possible pattern. A person's BaZi, which is derived from the date and time of birth, encapsulates all this information.

Here's what we can ascertain with the information derived from a person's BaZi:

- Characteristics and talents
- Family relationships with his/her parents and siblings
- Life with his/her spouse
- Children and their well-being
- The ability to amass, accumulate, manage and/or to save wealth

- Outcomes of certain actions and decisions in life
- Physical conditions and common illnesses
- Issues that are created by him or herself
- Judgment and relationships with his community and friends
- Relationship with superiors and subordinates
- Working capabilities and career prospects
- Opportunities to enjoy one's life

BaZi analysis is about using the information contained in the person's BaZi to unlock information on the person's in-born and potential talents. A person's BaZi, in essence, contains his or her DESTINY CODE.

Many Asian businesses make use of BaZi to determine which senior managers should be placed in what positions at which time. This is to ensure that the person's capabilities are not just properly utilised but that his or her luck is suitable and beneficial to the company's endeavours. This is a tremendously sophisticated form of management that is more than just basic Human Resource management. The Human Resource department may be able to tell a company what an individual is capable of but it cannot tell if a person's personal life is likely to be affected in the next six to twelve months before a big merger deal (e.g. by a divorce, the death of a family member, or illness). The HR department cannot tell if a person will be able to effectively deal with certain problems that a business is facing or if a person will have difficulties with staff or legal difficulties when moved to a certain department. But a good professional BaZi master can!

BaZi also has tremendous benefits when it comes to domestic affairs. Parents can set their children's education path according to their talents and potential and pave a better foundation for them to maximise their true innate talent and gifts. Relationships between couples would be less stressful if parties had no reason to suspect their spouses, based on their BaZi. Alternatively, difficult times or trying moments in a relationship can be more easily worked out if the parties understood the source of the conflict or tension.

BaZi can help you make use of talents that you have or seek out opportunities which maximise your inherent abilities and avoid entering into a field which appears to be suitable but in fact will not bring you any achievement or success. It is like planting the seeds in an area of the field that is already fertile rather than attempting cultivation in an area that cannot yield anything.

BaZi can also be used to forecast:

- The general fortune of a person in one decade (Big Limits of 10 Years)
- The Yearly Cycles
- The Monthly Cycles

Forecasting your luck cycles helps you understand what to expect in your life path. Knowing what's in store is a great advantage in life. If you like your destination, follow through and enjoy the journey. If you don't like it – go the other way!

八字命理

Often BaZi is a tool largely associated with Fortune Telling. I think this is not an appropriate term to describe the capabilities of this art. BaZi helps you understand yourself, the external factors that influence you and helps guide you in making better decisions and improving your life.

BaZi is about possibilities, a better future and better fortunes. That is why I don't think the term "Fortune Telling" does BaZi any justice. The art of BaZi has much more than meets the eye. A BaZi practitioner is like a Life Coach or counselor. Their role is to help you understand the path of your life and to guide you to a better living.

By the time you finish this book, you will understand what I mean. Your Destiny Code is your BaZi. Now is the time to decode your destiny and improve your future!

Your BaZi reveals your road ahead.

Chapter Two:
The Heavenly Stems and Earthly Branches

In the introduction, I explained how BaZi enables extremely accurate forecasting of a person's destiny from only an individual's birth data – their Year, Month, Day and Hour of Birth.

The reason why BaZi is sometimes called Four Pillars of Destiny is because when viewed together, a person's BaZi data or Year, Month, Day and Hour of birth generate 4 pairs of characters. These characters, one on top, one below, are read together as one Pillar. Hence the term, Four Pillars.

Hour 時	Day 日	Month 月	Year 年	
印 Direct Resource	日元 Day Master	才 Indirect Wealth	傷 Hurting Officer	Heavenly Stems 天干
辛 *Xin* Yin Metal	壬 *Ren* Yang Water	丙 *Bing* Yang Fire	乙 *Yi* Yin Wood	
亥 *Hai* **Pig** Yin Water	戌 *Xu* **Dog** Yang Earth	戌 *Xu* **Dog** Yang Earth	未 *Wei* **Goat** Yin Earth	Earthly Branches 地支
壬 甲	丁 戊 辛	丁 戊 辛	乙 己 丁	

87	77	67	57	47	37	27	17	7	
財 丁 *Ding* Yin Fire	殺 戊 *Wu* Yang Earth	官 己 *Ji* Yin Earth	卩 庚 *Geng* Yang Metal	印 辛 *Xin* Yin Metal	比 壬 *Ren* Yang Water	劫 癸 *Gui* Yin Water	食 甲 *Jia* Yang Wood	傷 乙 *Yi* Yin Wood	Luck Pillars 大運
丑 *Chou* **Ox** Yin Earth	寅 *Yin* **Tiger** Yang Wood	卯 *Mao* **Rabbit** Yin Wood	辰 *Chen* **Dragon** Yang Earth	巳 *Si* **Snake** Yin Fire	午 *Wu* **Horse** Yang Fire	未 *Wei* **Goat** Yin Earth	申 *Shen* **Monkey** Yang Metal	酉 *You* **Rooster** Yin Metal	

Like all of the Chinese Five Arts, the Five Element theory is an extremely important component of BaZi. A BaZi chart, which is plotted from the BaZi data (Year, Month, Day, Hour of Birth), is essentially an expression of these four pieces of information in the form of the Five Elements (Fire, Water, Wood, Earth, Metal).

A BaZi chart is a code, one which when decoded, tells us what is the strength of the various elements at the time of a person's birth. As each of the elements represents a particular aspect of a person's life (i.e. Wealth, Career, Relationships), by examining the individual elements, a BaZi practitioner is able to ascertain the outcomes, the potential and the events in a person's life.

BaZi has many complex layers, much like an onion. I have simplified many of the ideas in order to make the subject more accessible and understandable for a beginner. However, as your understanding of BaZi grows, you will begin to 'see' the many layers within a BaZi chart.

Getting BaZi: A few thoughts on learning BaZi

In my experience as a Master Trainer, teaching BaZi to many students around the world of all cultural origins, descent and nationalities, I have found that the most important thing that students must remember is to keep an open mind.

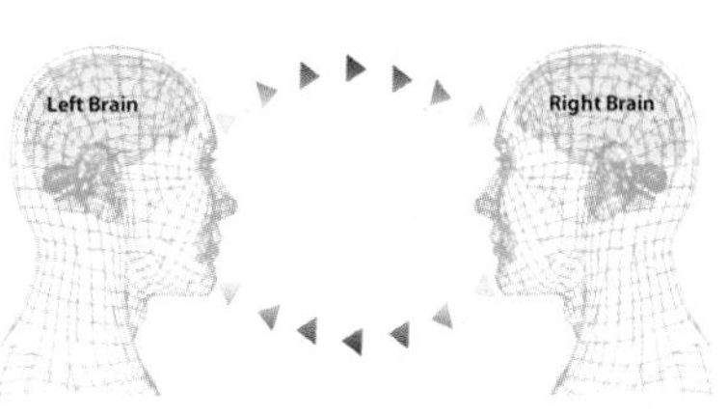

It does require a measure of retooling your thinking processes – from how you look at the concept of destiny and luck to whether you're a right brain or left brain person. You need a certain amount of logical deduction alongside a measure of creativity, the ability to look at the micro situation as well as the big picture. Now, I realise this is a lot to think about - so just remember to focus on two things: think pictorially and always relate your thoughts back to the Five Elements and Yin and Yang.

At the start, you can expect to only see very obvious or apparent information. Remember, BaZi is a bit like art appreciation – as your skill and understanding develops, so will your ability to 'see' the picture in the BaZi with greater clarity.

Let's get started!

Understanding the BaZi Chart

A BaZi chart comprises of Four Pillars. Each pillar consists of two characters – one at the top, one at the bottom. The top character is known as a Heavenly Stem (Tian Gan 天干) and the bottom character is known as the Earthly Branch (Di Zhi 地支). To avoid confusion, don't think stem or branch – think Heavenly (as in above) and Earthly (as in below) to guide you as to which is what.

A complete BaZi chart has four sets of characters – Four Heavenly Stems and Four Earthly Branches.

	Hour 時	**Day** 日	**Month** 月	**Year** 年
Heavenly Stems 天干	丁 *Ding* Yin Fire	辛 *Xin* Yin Metal	庚 *Geng* Yang Metal	甲 *Jia* Yang Wood
Earthly Branches 地支	酉 *You* **Rooster** Yin Metal	酉 *You* **Rooster** Yin Metal	午 *Wu* **Horse** Yang Fire	申 *Shen* **Monkey** Yang Metal
	辛	辛	丁 己	戊 庚 壬

This is what a BaZi chart looks like.

What does the BaZi practitioner look for in a BaZi chart?

Remember the Five Elements and Yin and Yang? Like in the practice of Feng Shui, a BaZi chart should have balance. The Qi must flow well and not be disrupted and the chart should have a balance of all the Five Elements: Metal, Wood, Water, Fire and Earth.

A good BaZi chart has harmony between the elements, whilst a bad chart is elementally imbalanced. If a chart is good, then the person will enjoy good fortune and the bumps in life will just be bumps. If a chart is bad, then a person's fortune will not be smooth and bumps in life will seem more like mountains.

Learning BaZi begins with learning a few basic Chinese characters. Now, before you hit the panic button, I urge you to bear in mind this little fact: you only need to learn 22 characters in total. The Roman alphabet comprises of 26 characters – most of us seem to have managed that without too much trouble! So let me assure you, learning the BaZi characters will not be difficult.

Once you've learnt the BaZi characters, you would already have begun to learn the language of BaZi. The next step after that is to plot your own BaZi chart using your own birth data. To do this, you'll convert your BaZi data into Chinese Characters, comprising the Heavenly Stems and Earthly Branches.

The BaZi Language: The Ten Heavenly Stems天干

The Heavenly Stems are known as prevailing Qi or surface Qi. In the context of BaZi, the Heavenly Stems represent external perceptions of a person – in other words, what a person shows on the surface, in terms of character, personality or outlook. The Heavenly Stems show characteristics, personality or outlook that everyone - friends, family, acquiantances - can see and perceive.

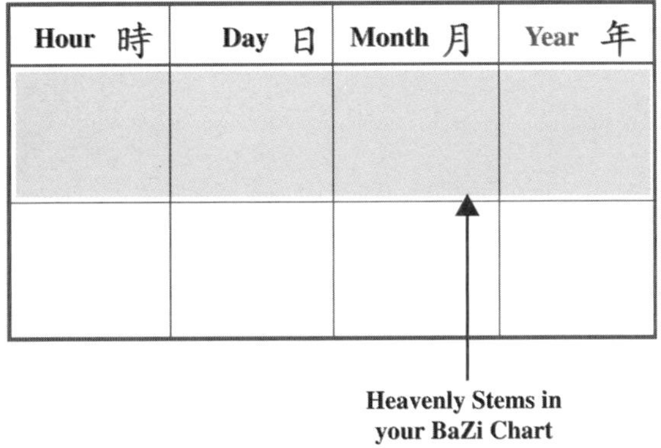

For example, if a person's Wealth Element appears in the Heavenly Stems only, this denotes a person who likes people to know that he or she is wealthy. These people are likely to be ostentatious in showing off their wealth so everyone knows that they have money! (whether they actually have any wealth or not, is another matter!)

Hour 時	Day 日	Month 月	Year 年
		Wealth Element	

Example of Wealth element ONLY appearing in Heavenly Stem

By contrast, an individual with Wealth Elements that appear only on the Earthly Branch does not make his wealth readily apparent and will be modest with showing his wealth – he may for example, keep a low profile, drive a simple Japanese car rather than a Mercedes and not be readily known by many people to be wealthy.

Hour 時	Day 日	Month 月	Year 年
		Wealth Element	

Example of Wealth element ONLY appearing in Earthly Branch

Heavenly Stems	Element and Polarity
甲 *Jia*	Yang Wood
乙 *Yi*	Yin Wood
丙 *Bing*	Yang Fire
丁 *Ding*	Yin Fire
戊 *Wu*	Yang Earth
己 *Ji*	Yin Earth
庚 *Geng*	Yang Metal
辛 *Xin*	Yin Metal
壬 *Ren*	Yang Water
癸 *Gui*	Yin Water

There are Ten Heavenly Stems and they comprise of the Yin and Yang polarities of the Five Elements: Wood, Fire, Earth, Metal and Water.

Now, I realise that often people associate the concepts of Yin and Yang with weak and strong. While this is broadly correct, it is best at this point not to make judgments based on whether an element is Yin or Yang. Yes, there are concepts of weak and strong in BaZi but they are not based on the polarity but other factors which will be discussed later in this book. For now, just treat the Stems as Yin and Yang versions of the Five Elements and nothing more.

Getting to Know the Ten Heavenly Stems

A little pointer before we begin to learn more about the Ten Heavenly Stems. The study of BaZi is one that requires a little bit of imaginative capability and a little bit of logical deduction. It is a right brain and left brain study – you need to be able to 'picture' a BaZi (you'll understand why in a minute) and see the elements in pictorial form.

So as you go through this section, don't just focus on the text. Remember also to try and get a mental picture of the Ten Heavenly Stems as they are described to you. To help you along, I've included some pictures.

甲 (pronounced as 'Ji' + 'Ark') represents Yang Wood. Jia Wood should be visualised as a great big tree – think California Redwoods, think teak trees, think towering solid oaks. These trees are hard and unyielding.

乙 (pronounced as 'yiii' or the letter 'e') represents Yin Wood. If Jia Wood is a great solid redwood tree, then Yi Wood are the leaves, flowers, small bushes, twines and vines and grass. It is flexible and malleable.

丙 (easy – pronounced as it appears!) Bing represents Yang Fire and is the fire of the sun – it is bright, vibrant, warm, life-giving. Its function is to bring sunshine and brightness to the world.

丁 (easy also – pronounced as it appears!) Ding fire is Yin Fire and is the fire of the candle – a small flame but illuminating in the darkness.

戊 (pronounced 'Woo') Wu is Yang Earth and represents large boulders, big rocks or large stones. It is solid, heavy and unmoving.

己 (pronounced with the same tone as the letter 'G') Ji is Yin Earth and represents soil, sand or soft earth. It is fine and porous.

庚 (pronounced 'Gh-ung') Geng is Yang Metal and represents raw iron or a large axe. It is hard, tough and unfinished.

辛 (pronounced 'Sin') Xin is Yin Metal and represents fine jewellery, necklaces and beautiful rings. It is shiny, sparkling and glamorous.

壬 (pronounced 'R-urn') Ren is Yang Water and represents the waters of the ocean, waters of the lake or the powerful gushing waters of a river.

癸 (pronounced 'Kway') Gui is Yin Water and represents water from rain clouds, mist, dew or frost.

Sneak Preview: Using the Elements

Remember what we said about a pictorial approach? Okay, here's a sneak preview of how the Ten Heavenly Stems and their pictorial representations help us understand a person's character. A person who is the element of Gui 癸 (Yin Water) will be harder to pin down or is more elusive than a person who is Wu 戊 (Yang Earth). Why? Because Gui 癸 (Yin Water), that of the rain clouds or mist, is always moving. By contrast, Wu 戊, being a great big boulder, isn't going anywhere unless someone forcibly (and with great effort) moves it! We've all heard the saying about a rolling stone gathering no moss but when was the last time you saw a boulder actually move on its own accord?

Now, think about some of the other Heavenly Stems and their characteristics. These will give you a general picture about the inherent characteristics of a person's chart. To help you along the way, here are a few questions to get you thinking!

Which of the two Woods, Jia 甲 Wood or Yi 乙 Wood do you think is more stubborn? Is a Xin 辛 Metal or Geng 庚 Metal person likely to be showy and vain?

If you haven't figured it out, don't worry. Keep thinking in pictures, asking yourself questions and you'll figure it out soon enough.

More BaZi Language: The 12 Earthly Branches 地支

When it comes to the 12 Earthly Branches, DO NOT think about the conventional understanding that most people have about the Chinese Zodiac - you know, the one which says Dragons are fierce and ambitions, Dogs are loyal and Snakes are sly.

Earthly Branches		Animal Sign	Element
子 Zi	Pronounced as 'Zh-er'	Rat	Yang Water
丑 Chou	Pronounced as 'Ch-o' as in the word 'go'	Ox	Yin Earth
寅 Yin	Pronounced as 'Yeen' as in the word 'seen'	Tiger	Yang Wood
卯 Mao	Pronounced as 'Mow' as in the word 'how'	Rabbit	Yin Wood
辰 Chen	Pronounced as 'Ch-earn' with a silent 'r'	Dragon	Yang Earth
巳 Si	Pronounced as 'Sir' with a silent 'r'	Snake	Yin Fire
午 Wu	Pronounced as Woo	Horse	Yang Fire
未 Wei	Pronounced as Way	Goat	Yin Earth

Branch	Pronunciation	Animal	Element
申 Shen	Pronounced as 'Sh-earn' with a silent 'r'	Monkey	Yang Metal
酉 You	Pronounced as YOU	Rooster	Yin Metal
戌 Xu	Pronounced as 'Shoot' with a silent 't'	Dog	Yang Earth
亥 Hai	Pronounced as 'Hi' as in hi !	Pig	Yin Water

Not only are these stereotypes really unacceptable, they are also not relevant or even truthful! The 12 Animal Signs are layman terminology used to help us understand the Qi of the 12 Earthly Branches. Never had they come up with 'personality traits' all alone.

How many people born in the same year as you have the same traits as you do? Probably not more than a handful. My point exactly.

The use of the animals in the Earthly Branches is largely due to the fact that in the old days when BaZi was developed, it was too difficult to explain the Earthly Branches to laypersons other than by using animals commonly found in the household.

Furthermore, anyone who knows Chinese or Mandarin will realise that the Chinese characters and pronunciations for the words used to describe the Earthly Branches are not the actual words used to describe the animal. For example, Rat in the Chinese language is Shu鼠 but in the Earthly Branches, Rat is Zi子.

I think a better way of looking at the Earthly Branches is as codes for the Yin and Yang versions of the Five Elements. So remember, when you're thinking about the Earthly Branches, think of the animals as simply codes for the Five Elements and their Yin and Yang manifestations.

Once again, don't let the Yin or Yang nature confuse you into thinking they refer to strength or weakness. Yin is Yin, Yang is Yang – don't peg any meanings to this at this point in time!

Stems vs Branches

"One in Branch is better than three in Stem"
– ancient Chinese BaZi saying

Now that you understand the Heavenly Stems and Earthly Branches, you might be wondering: which is better or which is stronger?

Let's think pictorially again. This time, imagine the BaZi pillars as a tree with roots underneath and towering leaves above. Like an iceberg, a tree may appear small on the surface, but its roots may run deep into the earth or many miles around the tree.

The Earthly Branches are like the roots of a tree – they are the foundation of the pillar. The Branches are what the pillar sits on and relies on for its strength and to hold it up, just like the roots of a tree anchor it and keep it stable. Earthly Branches carry the main Qi – the Heavenly Stems simply show the Qi on the surface that is usually weaker.

Hence it is often said in the ancient Classic that "one in Branch is stronger than three on Stem".

Heavenly Stems are obvious or prevailing Qi while Earthly Branches are less obvious but carry more strength, just like the roots of the tree give the tree its ability to stand upright.

Later on, you will learn that the Earthly Branches play a more important part in BaZi analysis because not only do they carry the force of time but they represent the seasons and tell us about the strength of the elements. Also, a clash in the Earthly Branch is more severe than a clash in the Heavenly Stem.

In BaZi, a Pillar which comprises of one Heavenly Stem one Earthly Branch should be solid and steady, similar to a sturdy tree. We like the elements in the Pillar to be harmonious with each other. Otherwise, the BaZi is not balanced and the Qi does not flow well (between Heaven and Earth). A well-balanced chart is one that has harmonious flow of Qi between Heaven (Stems) and Earth (Branches). These are usually charts belonging to people with superior fortunes.

Chapter Three: Unveiling the Code of Heaven

To know what's in store for you at the time of your birth, you need to first learn how to plot your BaZi chart. Unfortunately, decoding the secrets of Heaven from your Destiny Code is not as easy as flashing a wand - so we do have to do a little bit of work in order to get to substance that we're interested in.

Now, obviously we are in the age of technology, computers and the Internet – of course you don't have to learn to plot your own BaZi chart manually. My website, **www.masteryacademy.com** has a BaZi Ming Pan calculator that does the job fine.

BUT...

Manual plotting has its advantages. Firstly, it is unlikely to be wrong. Secondly, it assists you in learning the BaZi Destiny Code language, notably the Chinese characters that are used in BaZi (remember what I said earlier about a little bit of effort? This is it!).

Finally, ALL forms of Astrology studies require their students to do chart plotting manually. Be it in Western or Vedic Astrology, every student must learn to plot charts by hand.

So, let's get plotting!

The Ten Thousand Year Calendar – An Essential BaZi Reference Book

To plot your chart, you need to translate your Western (Gregorian) Date of Birth into the Chinese (Solar) Date of Birth. The chief reference guide you will need to achieve this is the book called - The Ten Thousand Year Calendar, also known as the Wan Nian Li (萬年曆).

The Chinese had a sophisticated calendaring system, so much so that they had two Calendars. Most Chinese people know of the existence of the Chinese Lunar Calendar, which is used to determine the date of Chinese New Year; but running parallel to this Lunar Calendar is the Chinese Solar Calendar. It is this Solar Calendar that is used for many of the important calculations in Feng Shui and Four Pillars of Destiny or BaZi . These two calendars merge into what is known as the Farmer's Calendar or Nong Li.

The Lunar Calendar (which is usually the reference point for important Chinese festivals such as Chinese New Year, the Winter Festival and Mid-Autumn Festival) follows the cycle of the Moon.

The Solar calendar is based on the twelve months and four seasons of the year. The Lunar calendar varies yearly, has a leap month every three years and the transit of the year (celebrated as Chinese New Year) changes each year. By contrast, the transit of the year in the Solar calendar is like clockwork: February 4th of every year is the transition point into a new year. There are no leap months or missing months.

A Brief Note About Spring

There has been a lot of hoo-hah regarding "Li Chun" (literally meaning the "Coming of Spring") or the lack of it in certain years. Some people say when a year has no Li Chun or 'Coming of Spring', the year is called a "blind year" and that is likely to be difficult because there is no growth. They associate "Spring" with "Growth" and with no "Coming of Spring" there is no growth. Thus, many people unknowingly believe that getting married in a "blind year" is bad fortune.

This misconception must be corrected.

Li Chun is a term derived from the Chinese Solar Calendar and is used to describe the first month of the Chinese Solar Calendar. It does not refer to the first month of the Chinese Lunar calendar. So, in fact, every year has a Li Chun or a Coming of Spring because the Solar Calendar, unlike the Lunar Calendar, does not have 'missing months' and the start of every year in the Solar Calendar falls more or less on the same day, which is 4th of February. There is no such concept in Chinese Astrology as a bad year due to the absence of Spring!

Chinese Feng Shui and Chinese BaZi are based on the Chinese Solar Calendar. Since most people's date of birth today is recorded in the form of Western Gregorian dates rather than the Chinese Lunar Calendar date, the Ten Thousand Year Calendar enables the plotting of a BaZi chart easily since it shows the dates of the Chinese Solar and Lunar Calendar, side by side their corresponding Western Gregorian dates.

This is important particularly for BaZi because it determines whether a person is born under the previous year's animal sign or the next year's animal sign. For example, if a person is born in the month of January of 2004 (supposedly the Year of the Monkey), they are still considered to have been born in the Year of the Goat (2003). To be considered as born in the Year of the Monkey, the person must have arrived in this world after February 4, 2004.

Lest you wonder how enormous or heavy this Ten Thousand Year calendar is, take heart that it doesn't really have ten thousand years of dates – its probably only got about 100 - 150 years of dates! The Ten Thousand Year Calendar is available in most Chinese bookstores – it is published by a variety of publishers mostly in Chinese. However, those who have difficulty with the Chinese characters and numerals may want to get my bi-lingual version of the Ten Thousand Year Calendar – check in major bookstores near you or the online store in our academy's website www.masteryacademy.com for details on getting your copy.

A Quick lesson on the Ten Thousand Year Calendar.

Most Ten Thousand Year Calendars will have the year printed numerically and the BaZi pillar for the year printed beneath it. Yes, every year has a 'Year Pillar'. It is from this Year Pillar that astrologers derive information such as 'Wood Monkey year' or 'Metal Rooster year'. It is using this Year Pillar that many astrologers provide annual predictions on everything from the state of the economy to which industries will perform well in a given year.

二月大 2nd Mth Big				正月小 1st Mth Small				月別 Month
丁 卯 Ding Mao				丙 寅 Bing Yin				干支 Branches and Stems
一白 One White				二黑 Two Black				九星 Nine Star
春分 Spring Equinox		驚蟄 Awakening of Worms		雨水 Rain Water		立春 Coming of Spring		節氣 Season
三十 30th day		十五 15th day		二十九 29th day		十四 14th day		
14時 50 分 14hr 50min		13時 57 分 13hr 57min		15時 51 分 15hr 51min		19時 58 分 19hr 58min		朔 Constellation
未 Wei		未 Wei		申 Shen		戌 Xu		
國曆 Gregorian		干支 Branches and stems	星 Star	國曆 Gregorian		干支 Branches and stems	星 Star	農曆 Solar Calender
2	20	己 巳 Ji Si	6	1	22	庚 子 Geng Zi	4	初一 1st day
2	21	庚 午 Geng Wu	7	1	23	辛 丑 Xin Chou	5	初二 2nd day
2	22	辛 未 Xin Wei	8	1	24	壬 寅 Ren Yin	6	初三 3rd day
2	23	壬 申 Ren Shen	9	1	25	癸 卯 Gui Mao	7	初四 4th day
2	24	癸 酉 Gui You	1	1	26	甲 辰 Jia Chen	8	初五 5th day
2	25	甲 戌 Jia Xu	2	1	27	乙 巳 Yi Si	9	初六 6th day
2	26	乙 亥 Yi Hai	3	1	28	丙 午 Bing Wu	1	初七 7th day
2	27	丙 子 Bing Zi	4	1	29	丁 未 Ding Wei	2	初八 8th day
2	28	丁 丑 Ding Chou	5	1	30	戊 申 Wu Shen	3	初九 9th day
2	29	戊 寅 Wu Yin	6	1	31	己 酉 Ji You	4	初十 10th day
3	1	己 卯 Ji Mao	7	2	1	庚 戌 Geng Xu	5	十一 11th day
3	2	庚 辰 Geng Chen	8	2	2	辛 亥 Xin Hai	6	十二 12th day
3	3	辛 巳 Xin Si	9	2	3	壬 子 Ren Zi	7	十三 13th day
3	4	壬 午 Ren Wu	1	2	4	**癸 丑 Gui Chou**	8	十四 14th day
3	5	**癸 未 Gui Wei**	2	2	5	甲 寅 Jia Yin	9	十五 15th day
3	6	甲 申 Jia Shen	3	2	6	乙 卯 Yi Mao	1	十六 16th day
3	7	乙 酉 Yi You	4	2	7	丙 辰 Bing Chen	2	十七 17th day
3	8	丙 戌 Bing Xu	5	2	8	丁 巳 Ding Si	3	十八 18th day
3	9	丁 亥 Ding Hai	6	2	9	戊 午 Wu Wu	4	十九 19th day
3	10	戊 子 Wu Zi	7	2	10	己 未 Ji Wei	5	二十 20th day
3	11	己 丑 Ji Chou	8	2	11	庚 申 Geng Shen	6	二十一 21st day
3	12	庚 寅 Geng Yin	9	2	12	辛 酉 Xin You	7	二十二 22nd day
3	13	辛 卯 Xin Mao	1	2	13	壬 戌 Ren Xu	8	二十三 23rd day
3	14	壬 辰 Ren Chen	2	2	14	癸 亥 Gui Hai	9	二十四 24th day
3	15	癸 巳 Gui Si	3	2	15	甲 子 Jia Zi	1	二十五 25th day
3	16	甲 午 Jia Wu	4	2	16	乙 丑 Yi Chou	2	二十六 26th day
3	17	乙 未 Yi Wei	5	2	17	丙 寅 Bing Yin	3	二十七 27th day
3	18	丙 申 Bing Shen	6	2	18	丁 卯 Ding Mao	4	二十八 28th day
3	19	丁 酉 Ding You	7	2	19	戊 辰 Wu Chen	5	二十九 29th day
3	20	戊 戌 Wu Xu	8					三十 30th day

2004 甲申 Jia Shen

Wood Monkey

Grand Duke 方公

2004 is the Year of the Wood Monkey. Now, if you look at 2004 in the Ten Thousand Year Calendar, you will find it is the year of Jia Shen 甲申. *If you are using the Joey Yap bi-lingual Ten Thousand Year Calendar, it is on page 334.*

二月大 2nd Mth Big				正月大 1st Mth Big				月別 Month
乙卯 Yi Mao				甲寅 Jia Yin				干支 Branches and Stems
四綠 Four Green				五黃 Five Yellow				九星 Nine Star
春分 Spring Equinox		驚蟄 Awakening of Worms		雨水 Rain Water		立春 Coming of Spring		節氣 Season
十九 19th day		初四 4th day		十九 19th day		初四 4th day		
9時 1 分 9hr 1min		8時 6 分 8hr 6min		10時 2 分 10hr 2min		14時 7 分 14hr 7min		朔 Constellation
巳 Si		辰 Chen		巳 Si		未 Wei		
國曆 Gregorian		干支 Branches and stems	星 Star	國曆 Gregorian		干支 Branches and stems	星 Star	農曆 Solar Calender
3	3	乙亥 Yi Hai	9	2	1	乙巳 Yi Si	6	初一 1st day
3	4	丙子 Bing Zi	1	2	2	丙午 Bing Wu	7	初二 2nd day
3	5	丁丑 Ding Chou	2	2	3	丁未 Ding Wei	8	初三 3rd day
3	**6**	**戊寅 Wu Yin**	3	**2**	**4**	**戊申 Wu Shen**	9	初四 4th day
3	7	己卯 Ji Mao	4	2	5	己酉 Ji You	1	初五 5th day
3	8	庚辰 Geng Chen	5	2	6	庚戌 Geng Xu	2	初六 6th day
3	9	辛巳 Xin Si	6	2	7	辛亥 Xin Hai	3	初七 7th day
3	10	壬午 Ren Wu	7	2	8	壬子 Ren Zi	4	初八 8th day
3	11	癸未 Gui Wei	8	2	9	癸丑 Gui Chou	5	初九 9th day
3	12	甲申 Jia Shen	9	2	10	甲寅 Jia Yin	6	初十 10th day
3	13	乙酉 Yi You	1	2	11	乙卯 Yi Mao	7	十一 11th day
3	14	丙戌 Bing Xu	2	2	12	丙辰 Bing Chen	8	十二 12th day
3	15	丁亥 Ding Hai	3	2	13	丁巳 Ding Si	9	十三 13th day
3	16	戊子 Wu Zi	4	2	14	戊午 Wu Wu	1	十四 14th day
3	17	己丑 Ji Chou	5	2	15	己未 Ji Wei	2	十五 15th day
3	18	庚寅 Geng Yin	6	2	16	庚申 Geng Shen	3	十六 16th day
3	19	辛卯 Xin Mao	7	2	17	辛酉 Xin You	4	十七 17th day
3	20	壬辰 Ren Chen	8	2	18	壬戌 Ren Xu	5	十八 18th day
3	21	癸巳 Gui Si	9	2	19	癸亥 Gui Hai	6	十九 19th day
3	22	甲午 Jia Wu	1	2	20	甲子 Jia Zi	7	二十 20th day
3	23	乙未 Yi Wei	2	2	21	乙丑 Yi Chou	8	二十一 21st day
3	24	丙申 Bing Shen	3	2	22	丙寅 Bing Yin	9	二十二 22nd day
3	25	丁酉 Ding You	4	2	23	丁卯 Ding Mao	1	二十三 23rd day
3	26	戊戌 Wu Xu	5	2	24	戊辰 Wu Chen	2	二十四 24th day
3	27	己亥 Ji Hai	6	2	25	己巳 Ji Si	3	二十五 25th day
3	28	庚子 Geng Zi	7	2	26	庚午 Geng Wu	4	二十六 26th day
3	29	辛丑 Xin Chou	8	2	27	辛未 Xin Wei	5	二十七 27th day
3	30	壬寅 Ren Yin	9	2	28	壬申 Ren Shen	6	二十八 28th day
3	31	癸卯 Gui Mao	1	3	1	癸酉 Gui You	7	二十九 29th day
4	1	甲辰 Jia Chen	2	3	2	甲戌 Jia Xu	8	三十 30th day

2003 癸未 Gui Wei

Water Goat

Grand Duke 魏明

2003 was the year of Gui Wei 癸未 or Water Goat. See page 332 of the Joey Yap bi-lingual Ten Thousand Year Calendar.

二月大 2nd Mth Big				正月小 1st Mth Small				月别 Month
己卯 Ji Mao				戊寅 Wu Yin				干支 Branches and Stems
七赤 Seven Red				八白 Eight White				九星 Nine Star
清明 Clear and Bright		春分 Spring Equinox		驚蟄 Awakening of Worms		雨水 Rain Water		節氣 Season
二十七 27th day		十一 11th day		二十五 25th day		初十 10th day		
0時 36 分 0hr 36min		20時 35 分 20hr 35min		19時 47 分 19hr 47min		21時 33 分 21hr 33min		朔 Constellation
子 Zi		戌 Xu		戌 Xu		戌 Xu		
國曆 Gregorian		干支 Branches and stems	星 Star	國曆 Gregorian		干支 Branches and stems	星 Star	農曆 Solar Calender
3	10	癸巳 Gui Si	3	2	9	甲子 Jia Zi	1	初一 1st day
3	11	甲午 Jia Wu	4	2	10	乙丑 Yi Chou	2	初二 2nd day
3	12	乙未 Yi Wei	5	2	11	丙寅 Bing Yin	3	初三 3rd day
3	13	丙申 Bing Shen	6	2	12	丁卯 Ding Mao	4	初四 4th day
3	14	丁酉 Ding You	7	2	13	戊辰 Wu Chen	5	初五 5th day
3	15	戊戌 Wu Xu	8	2	14	己巳 Ji Si	6	初六 6th day
3	16	己亥 Ji Hai	9	2	15	庚午 Geng Wu	7	初七 7th day
3	17	庚子 Geng Zi	1	2	16	辛未 Xin Wei	8	初八 8th day
3	18	辛丑 Xin Chou	2	2	17	壬申 Ren Shen	9	初九 9th day
3	19	壬寅 Ren Yin	3	2	18	癸酉 Gui You	1	初十 10th day
3	20	癸卯 Gui Mao	4	2	19	甲戌 Jia Xu	2	十一 11th day
3	21	甲辰 Jia Chen	5	2	20	乙亥 Yi Hai	3	十二 12th day
3	22	乙巳 Yi Si	6	2	21	丙子 Bing Zi	4	十三 13th day
3	23	丙午 Bing Wu	7	2	22	丁丑 Ding Chou	5	十四 14th day
3	24	丁未 Ding Wei	8	2	23	戊寅 Wu Yin	6	十五 15th day
3	25	戊申 Wu Shen	9	2	24	己卯 Ji Mao	7	十六 16th day
3	26	己酉 Ji You	1	2	25	庚辰 Geng Chen	8	十七 17th day
3	27	庚戌 Geng Xu	2	2	26	辛巳 Xin Si	9	十八 18th day
3	28	辛亥 Xin Hai	3	2	27	壬午 Ren Wu	1	十九 19th day
3	29	壬子 Ren Zi	4	2	28	癸未 Gui Wei	2	二十 20th day
3	30	癸丑 Gui Chou	5	3	1	甲申 Jia Shen	3	二十一 21st day
3	31	甲寅 Jia Yin	6	3	2	乙酉 Yi You	4	二十二 22nd day
4	1	乙卯 Yi Mao	7	3	3	丙戌 Bing Xu	5	二十三 23rd day
4	2	丙辰 Bing Chen	8	3	4	丁亥 Ding Hai	6	二十四 24th day
4	3	丁巳 Ding Si	9	**3**	**5**	**戊子 Wu Zi**	7	二十五 25th day
4	4	戊午 Wu Wu	1	3	6	己丑 Ji Chou	8	二十六 26th day
4	**5**	**己未 Ji Wei**	2	3	7	庚寅 Geng Yin	9	二十七 27th day
4	6	庚申 Geng Shen	3	3	8	辛卯 Xin Mao	1	二十八 28th day
4	7	辛酉 Xin You	4	3	9	壬辰 Ren Chen	2	二十九 29th day
4	8	壬戌 Ren Xu	5					三十 30th day

2005 乙酉 Yi You

Wood Rooster

Grand Duke 蔣嵩

The year 2005 is the year of Yi You 乙酉 *or the Wood Rooster. See page 336 of the Joey Yap bi-lingual Ten Thousand Year Calendar.*

Plotting a BaZi chart

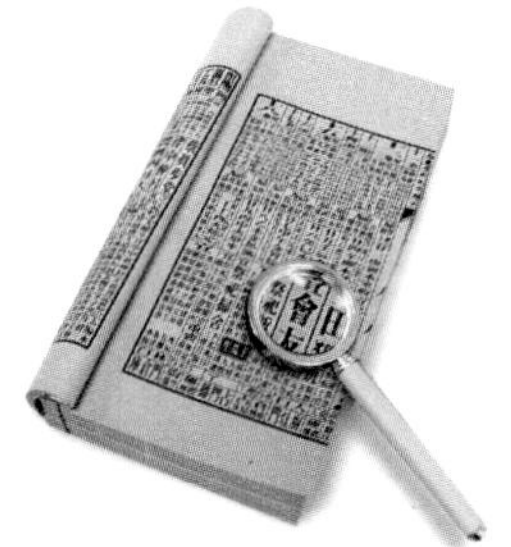

Okay, now that we have an understanding of the Ten Thousand Year Calendar, it's time to learn how to plot a BaZi chart.

Each BaZi chart contains two aspects: a static BaZi chart which comprises of the Four Pillars, and the dynamic aspect of the chart, which is the Luck Pillars. We'll start with the static chart first.

First, you will need to have the relevant birth data to plot your BaZi chart. This would be your date of birth (year, month and day), your time of birth and gender.

Here's the check list:

1. Name:
2. Sex: M / F
3. Date of Birth: Day_____ Month_____ Year_____
4. Time of Birth:

Fill in the Western (Gregorian) birth details. The following section will show you how to convert the data into the Chinese Solar equivalent.

Step 1: Preparation

4.30pm	20	2	1967
Hour 時	Day 日	Month 月	Year 年

Draw the diagram above. This will provide you with guidance when filling in the BaZi characters and ensure no mistakes are made. Each BaZi comprises of Four Pillars – a Year Pillar, Month Pillar, Day Pillar and Hour Pillar. Using this diagram, fill in the birth data so that you plot the chart sequentially and in a systematic manner. Write the Month in numerical figures on top to help you remember the date you are plotting. (ie: February 20, 1967 at 4.30pm.)

Step 2: Check the year

In the Western Gregorian calendar, a new year is celebrated on the 1st of January of each year. The Chinese Xia calendar also has the same tradition of transiting each year at the same date, which is February 4. Contrary to popular misconception, you do not use the Chinese New Year as the transition date for each year. That is because we do not use the Chinese Lunar calendar for BaZi. We only use the Chinese Solar Calendar.

So, if a person is born on February 6, 2004 he or she is definitely born in the Year of the Jia Shen 甲申 (Wood Monkey). However, if he or she is born on February 3, 2004 then he or she is born in the Year of the Gui Wei 癸未 (Water Goat).

Step 3: Identify the Year Pillar

Once you have ascertained the correct year of birth, copy down the Year Pillar in the Year Box of the Diagram.

Using our example of February 20, 1967 at 4.30pm, this person's Year Pillar would be Ding Wei 丁未 or Fire Goat. So, write Ding Wei丁未in the Year Pillar.

二月大 2nd Mth Big				正月大 1st Mth Big				月別 Month
癸卯 Gui Mao				壬寅 Ren Yin				干支 Branches and Stems
四綠 Four Green				五黃 Five Yellow				九星 Nine Star
清明 Clear and Bright		春分 Spring Equinox		驚蟄 Awakening of Worms		雨水 Rain Water		節氣 Season
二十六 26th day		十一 11th day		二十六 26th day		十一 11th day		
19時 45 分 19hr 45min		15時 37 分 15hr 37min		14時 42 分 14hr 42min		16時 24 分 16hr 24min		朔 Constellation
戌 Xu		申 Shen		未 Wei		申 Shen		
國曆 Gregorian		干支 Branches and stems	星 Star	國曆 Gregorian		干支 Branches and stems	星 Star	農曆 Solar Calender
3	11	甲戌 Jia Xu	8	2	9	甲辰 Jia Chen	5	初一 1st day
3	12	乙亥 Yi Hai	9	2	10	乙巳 Yi Si	6	初二 2nd day
3	13	丙子 Bing Zi	1	2	11	丙午 Bing Wu	7	初三 3rd day
3	14	丁丑 Ding Chou	2	2	12	丁未 Ding Wei	8	初四 4th day
3	15	戊寅 Wu Yin	3	2	13	戊申 Wu Shen	9	初五 5th day
3	16	己卯 Ji Mao	4	2	14	己酉 Ji You	1	初六 6th day
3	17	庚辰 Geng Chen	5	2	15	庚戌 Geng Xu	2	初七 7th day
3	18	辛巳 Xin Si	6	2	16	辛亥 Xin Hai	3	初八 8th day
3	19	壬午 Ren Wu	7	2	17	壬子 Ren Zi	4	初九 9th day
3	20	癸未 Gui Wei	8	2	18	癸丑 Gui Chou	5	初十 10th day
3	21	甲申 Jia Shen	9	2	19	甲寅 Jia Yin	6	十一 11th day
3	22	乙酉 Yi You	1	2	20	乙卯 Yi Mao	7	十二 12th day
3	23	丙戌 Bing Xu	2	2	21	丙辰 Bing Chen	8	十三 13th day
3	24	丁亥 Ding Hai	3	2	22	丁巳 Ding Si	9	十四 14th day

1967

丁未

Ding Wei

Fire Goat

Page 260 of Joey Yap's Ten Thousand Year Calendar

Hour 時	Day 日	Month 月	Year 年
			丁 Ding Yin Fire
			未 Wei Goat

Step 4: Identify the Month Pillar

The Chinese Xia calendar also has a monthly transition point. Although this date does vary, it does not vary significantly, usually it is plus or minus a day. Use the table below as a rough guide but always refer back to the actual Ten Thousand Year Calendar to be sure.

Transition Date	Earthly Branch of the month		Seasons
February 4th	寅 Yin	Tiger	Spring
March 6th	卯 Mao	Rabbit	
April 5th	辰 Chen	Dragon	
May 6th	巳 Si	Snake	Summer
June 6th	午 Wu	Horse	
July 7th	未 Wei	Goat	
August 8th	申 Shen	Monkey	Autumn
September 8th	酉 You	Rooster	
October 8th	戌 Xu	Dog	
November 7th	亥 Hai	Pig	Winter
December 7th	子 Zi	Rat	
January 6th	丑 Chou	Ox	

It's well worth committing the information in this table to memory. Once you know the information by heart, you will be able to ascertain almost immediately what is the Earthly Branch of the Month Pillar. So, if it is a person born on October 23, you immediately know that this person is born in the month of the Xu 戌 (Dog). If a person is born on August 16, you will immediately be able to tell that this person is born in the month of the Shen 申 (Monkey).

At this point you might be wondering, why the emphasis on the Month Branch? This is a good question and once we move on to reading, analysing and decoding a chart, you will see why knowing the Month Branch at first glance is important.

For the purposes of plotting a complete BaZi chart, you need the Month Pillar of course. To get the complete Month Pillar, with the Heavenly Stems and Earthly Branches, you will need to refer to the Ten Thousand Year Calendar.

Going back to our example of the person born February 20 1967 - to get the month pillar, first, turn to the page for the year 1967. If you are using the Joey Yap Ten Thousand Year Calendar, it is on page 260. (Note: The page number is correct based on the 3rd Reprint edition of the Ten Thousand Year Calendar.)

Now, from our little quick Monthly Transition Dates table above, we know that this person is born in Tiger Month. But what is in the Heavenly Stem of this Month Pillar? Look down the columns till you find February 20. If you look at the top of the column, you will see the Month Pillar for that Month. It is Ren Yin 壬寅.

二月大 2nd Mth Big				正月大 1st Mth Big				月別 Month
癸卯 Gui Mao				壬寅 Ren Yin				干支 Branches and Stems
四綠 Four Green				五黃 Five Yellow				九星 Nine Star
清明 Clear and Bright		春分 Spring Equinox		驚蟄 Awakening of Worms		雨水 Rain Water		節氣 Season
二十六 26th day		十一 11th day		二十六 26th day		十一 11th day		
19時 45 分 19hr 45min		15時 37 分 15hr 37min		14時 42 分 14hr 42min		16時 24 分 16hr 24min		朔 Constellation
戌 Xu		申 Shen		未 Wei		申 Shen		
國曆 Gregorian		干支 Branches and stems	星 Star	國曆 Gregorian		干支 Branches and stems	星 Star	農曆 Solar Calender
3	11	甲戌 Jia Xu	8	2	9	甲辰 Jia Chen	5	初一 1st day
3	12	乙亥 Yi Hai	9	2	10	乙巳 Yi Si	6	初二 2nd day
3	13	丙子 Bing Zi	1	2	11	丙午 Bing Wu	7	初三 3rd day
3	14	丁丑 Ding Chou	2	2	12	丁未 Ding Wei	8	初四 4th day
3	15	戊寅 Wu Yin	3	2	13	戊申 Wu Shen	9	初五 5th day
3	16	己卯 Ji Mao	4	2	14	己酉 Ji You	1	初六 6th day
3	17	庚辰 Geng Chen	5	2	15	庚戌 Geng Xu	2	初七 7th day
3	18	辛巳 Xin Si	6	2	16	辛亥 Xin Hai	3	初八 8th day
3	19	壬午 Ren Wu	7	2	17	壬子 Ren Zi	4	初九 9th day
3	20	癸未 Gui Wei	8	2	18	癸丑 Gui Chou	5	初十 10th day
3	21	甲申 Jia Shen	9	2	19	甲寅 Jia Yin	6	十一 11th day
3	22	乙酉 Yi You	1	2	20	乙卯 Yi Mao	7	十二 12th day
3	23	丙戌 Bing Xu	2	2	21	丙辰 Bing Chen	8	十三 13th day
3	24	丁亥 Ding Hai	3	2	22	丁巳 Ding Si	9	十四 14th day
3	25	戊子 Wu Zi	4	2	23	戊午 Wu Wu	1	十五 15th day
3	26	己丑 Ji Chou	5	2	24	己未 Ji Wei	2	十六 16th day
3	27	庚寅 Geng Yin	6	2	25	庚申 Geng Shen	3	十七 17th day
3	28	辛卯 Xin Mao	7	2	26	辛酉 Xin You	4	十八 18th day

1967 丁未 Ding Wei Fire Goat

Write the characters for Ren Yin 壬寅 in the Month Pillar column.

Hour 時	Day 日	Month 月	Year 年
		壬 *Ren* Yang Water	丁 *Ding* Yin Fire
		寅 *Yin* **Tiger**	未 *Wei* **Goat**

Step 5: Identify the Day Pillar

Finding the Day Pillar is quite easy. Just look up February 20 in the February month column. On the right hand column is listed the BaZi for that day.

1967 丁未 Ding Wei Fire Goat

二月大 2nd Mth Big				正月大 1st Mth Big				月別 Month
癸卯 Gui Mao				壬寅 Ren Yin				干支 Branches and Stems
四綠 Four Green				五黃 Five Yellow				九星 Nine Star
清明 Clear and Bright		春分 Spring Equinox		驚蟄 Awakening of Worms		雨水 Rain Water		節氣 Season
二十六 26th day		十一 11th day		二十六 26th day		十一 11th day		
19時 45 分 19hr 45min		15時 37 分 15hr 37min		14時 42 分 14hr 42min		16時 24 分 16hr 24min		朔 Constellation
戌 Xu		申 Shen		未 Wei		申 Shen		
國曆 Gregorian		干支 Branches and stems	星 Star	國曆 Gregorian		干支 Branches and stems	星 Star	農曆 Solar Calender
3	11	甲戌 Jia Xu	8	2	9	甲辰 Jia Chen	5	初一 1st day
3	12	乙亥 Yi Hai	9	2	10	乙巳 Yi Si	6	初二 2nd day
3	13	丙子 Bing Zi	1	2	11	丙午 Bing Wu	7	初三 3rd day
3	14	丁丑 Ding Chou	2	2	12	丁未 Ding Wei	8	初四 4th day
3	15	戊寅 Wu Yin	3	2	13	戊申 Wu Shen	9	初五 5th day
3	16	己卯 Ji Mao	4	2	14	己酉 Ji You	1	初六 6th day
3	17	庚辰 Geng Chen	5	2	15	庚戌 Geng Xu	2	初七 7th day
3	18	辛巳 Xin Si	6	2	16	辛亥 Xin Hai	3	初八 8th day
3	19	壬午 Ren Wu	7	2	17	壬子 Ren Zi	4	初九 9th day
3	20	癸未 Gui Wei	8	2	18	癸丑 Gui Chou	5	初十 10th day
3	21	甲申 Jia Shen	9	2	19	甲寅 Jia Yin	6	十一 11th day
3	22	乙酉 Yi You	1	2	20	乙卯 Yi Mao	7	十二 12th day
3	23	丙戌 Bing Xu	2	2	21	丙辰 Bing Chen	8	十三 13th day
3	24	丁亥 Ding Hai	3	2	22	丁巳 Ding Si	9	十四 14th day
3	25	戊子 Wu Zi	4	2	23	戊午 Wu Wu	1	十五 15th day
3	26	己丑 Ji Chou	5	2	24	己未 Ji Wei	2	十六 16th day
3	27	庚寅 Geng Yin	6	2	25	庚申 Geng Shen	3	十七 17th day
3	28	辛卯 Xin Mao	7	2	26	辛酉 Xin You	4	十八 18th day
3	29	壬辰 Ren Chen	8	2	27	壬戌 Ren Xu	5	十九 19th day

You will find that February 20 is a day of Yi Mao 乙卯. Yi 乙 is Yin Wood, while Mao 卯 is Rabbit. So this is a day of the Wood Rabbit.

Fill in Yi Mao 乙卯 into the Day Pillar of your diagram.

Hour 時	Day 日	Month 月	Year 年
	乙 Yi Yin Wood	壬 Ren Yang Water	丁 Ding Yin Fire
	卯 Mao Rabbit	寅 Yin Tiger	未 Wei Goat

The Heavenly Stem of the Day Pillar in every chart is known in BaZi terminology as the "Day Master". In this case, the Day Master is 乙 Yi Wood.

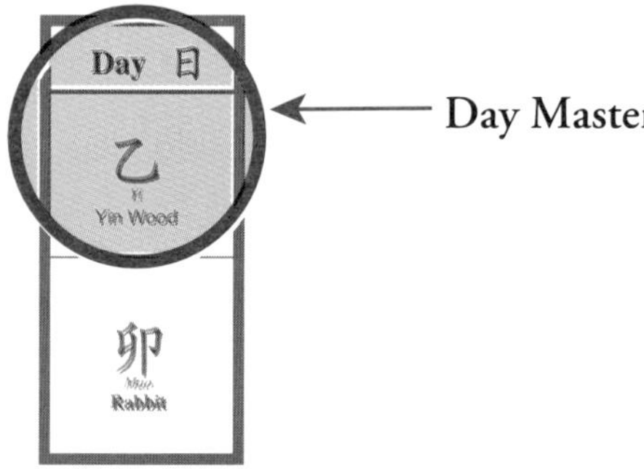

Different charts will have different Day Masters. As you progress through this book, you will learn the significance of the Day Master. But for now, just learn to identify the Day Master.

Step 6: Identify the Hour Pillar

Next, to ascertain the Hour Pillar, you have to do a little bit of cross-referencing. The table below is known as the Five Rat Chasing Day Establishing Hour Table. (This table is found on page 18 of the Joey Yap Ten Thousand Year Calendar). It is duplicated here for your easy reference.

戊 *Wu* **Yang Earth** 癸 *Gui* **Yin Water**	丁 *Ding* **Yin Fire** 壬 *Ren* **Yang Water**	丙 *Bing* **Yang Fire** 辛 *Xin* **Yin Metal**	乙 *Yi* **Yin Wood** 庚 *Geng* **Yang Metal**	甲 *Jia* **Yang Wood** 己 *Ji* **Yin Earth**	日 **Day** / 時 **Hour**	
甲子 *Jia Zi*	壬子 *Ren Zi*	庚子 *Geng Zi*	戊子 *Wu Zi*	丙子 *Bing Zi*	夜子 *Ye Zi* **Late Rat**	11 pm - 11.59 pm
壬子 *Ren Zi*	庚子 *Geng Zi*	戊子 *Wu Zi*	丙子 *Bing Zi*	甲子 *Jia Zi*	子 *Zi* **Early Rat**	12 am - 12.59 am
癸丑 *Gui Chou*	辛丑 *Xin Chou*	己丑 *Ji Chou*	丁丑 *Ding Chou*	乙丑 *Yi Chou*	丑 *Chou* **Ox**	1 am - 2.59 am
甲寅 *Jia Yin*	壬寅 *Ren Yin*	庚寅 *Geng Yin*	戊寅 *Wu Yin*	丙寅 *Bing Yin*	寅 *Yin* **Tiger**	3 am - 4.59 am
乙卯 *Yi Mao*	癸卯 *Gui Mao*	辛卯 *Xin Mao*	己卯 *Ji Mao*	丁卯 *Ding Mao*	卯 *Mao* **Rabbit**	5 am - 6.59 am
丙辰 *Bing Chen*	甲辰 *Jia Chen*	壬辰 *Ren Chen*	庚辰 *Geng Chen*	戊辰 *Wu Chen*	辰 *Chen* **Dragon**	7 am - 8.59 am
丁巳 *Ding Si*	乙巳 *Yi Si*	癸巳 *Gui Si*	辛巳 *Xin Si*	己巳 *Ji Si*	巳 *Si* **Snake**	9 am -10.59 am
戊午 *Wu Wu*	丙午 *Bing Wu*	甲午 *Jia Wu*	壬午 *Ren Wu*	庚午 *Geng Wu*	午 *Wu* **Horse**	11 am - 12.59 pm
己未 *Ji Wei*	丁未 *Ding Wei*	乙未 *Yi Wei*	癸未 *Gui Wei*	辛未 *Xin Wei*	未 *Wei* **Goat**	1pm - 2.59 pm
庚申 *Geng Shen*	戊申 *Wu Shen*	丙申 *Bing Shen*	甲申 *Jia Shen*	壬申 *Ren Shen*	申 *Shen* **Monkey**	3 pm - 4.59 pm
辛酉 *Xin You*	己酉 *Ji You*	丁酉 *Ding You*	乙酉 *Yi You*	癸酉 *Gui You*	酉 *You* **Rooster**	5 pm - 6.59 pm
壬戌 *Ren Xu*	庚戌 *Geng Xu*	戊戌 *Wu Xu*	丙戌 *Bing Xu*	甲戌 *Jia Xu*	戌 *Xu* **Dog**	7 pm - 8.59 pm
癸亥 *Gui Hai*	辛亥 *Xin Hai*	己亥 *Ji Hai*	丁亥 *Ding Hai*	乙亥 *Yi Hai*	亥 *Hai* **Pig**	9 pm - 10.59 pm

To ascertain the Hour Pillar of a BaZi, you will need to reference two pieces of information: the time of birth and the Day Master.

Take note that the Chinese Day has 12 hours only so each 'hour' comprises of two Western hours. So a person born at 7.30am and a person born at 8.30am both would be considered born in the Hour of the Chen辰 (Dragon).

From our example of February 20, 1967, 4.30pm, we can, using the table, in page 53 ascertain that this person was born in the Shen申 (Monkey) Hour. So fill in the Hour Branch as Shen申 or (Monkey) Hour .

Day Master

Hour 時	**Day 日**	**Month 月**	**Year 年**
	乙 *Yi* Yin Wood	壬 *Ren* Yang Water	丁 *Ding* Yin Fire
申 *Shen* **Monkey**	卯 *Mao* **Rabbit**	寅 *Yin* **Tiger**	未 *Wei* **Goat**

Now, ascertain the Day Master by looking at the Day Stem. In the case of our example, the Day Master is Yi乙.

From the Shen 申 (Monkey) Hour, slide your finger vertically across the columns until you come to the Pillar for Yi 乙. You will find that the Hour Stem is Jia 甲 (Yang Wood). Fill in Jia 甲 into the Stem of the Hour Pillar.

戊 Wu Yang Earth 癸 Gui Yin Water	丁 Ding Yin Fire 壬 Ren Yang Water	丙 Bing Yang Fire 辛 Xin Yin Metal	乙 Yi Yin Wood 庚 Geng Yang Metal	甲 Jia Yang Wood 己 Ji Yin Earth	日 Day / 時 Hour	
甲子 Jia Zi	壬子 Ren Zi	庚子 Geng Zi	戊子 Wu Zi	丙子 Bing Zi	夜子 Ye Zi Late Rat	11 pm - 11.59 pm
壬子 Ren Zi	庚子 Geng Zi	戊子 Wu Zi	丙子 Bing Zi	甲子 Jia Zi	子 Zi Early Rat	12 am - 12.59 am
癸丑 Gui Chou	辛丑 Xin Chou	己丑 Ji Chou	丁丑 Ding Chou	乙丑 Yi Chou	丑 Chou Ox	1 am - 2.59 am
甲寅 Jia Yin	壬寅 Ren Yin	庚寅 Geng Yin	戊寅 Wu Yin	丙寅 Bing Yin	寅 Yin Tiger	3 am - 4.59 am
乙卯 Yi Mao	癸卯 Gui Mao	辛卯 Xin Mao	己卯 Ji Mao	丁卯 Ding Mao	卯 Mao Rabbit	5 am - 6.59 am
丙辰 Bing Chen	甲辰 Jia Chen	壬辰 Ren Chen	庚辰 Geng Chen	戊辰 Wu Chen	辰 Chen Dragon	7 am - 8.59 am
丁巳 Ding Si	乙巳 Yi Si	癸巳 Gui Si	辛巳 Xin Si	己巳 Ji Si	巳 Si Snake	9 am -10.59 am
戊午 Wu Wu	丙午 Bing Wu	甲午 Jia Wu	壬午 Ren Wu	庚午 Geng Wu	午 Wu Horse	11 am - 12.59 pm
己未 Ji Wei	丁未 Ding Wei	乙未 Yi Wei	癸未 Gui Wei	辛未 Xin Wei	未 Wei Goat	1pm - 2.59 pm
庚申 Geng Shen	戊申 Wu Shen	丙申 Bing Shen	甲申 Jia Shen	壬申 Ren Shen	申 Shen Monkey	3 pm - 4.59 pm
辛酉 Xin You	己酉 Ji You	丁酉 Ding You	乙酉 Yi You	癸酉 Gui You	酉 You Rooster	5 pm - 6.59 pm
壬戌 Ren Xu	庚戌 Geng Xu	戊戌 Wu Xu	丙戌 Bing Xu	甲戌 Jia Xu	戌 Xu Dog	7 pm - 8.59 pm
癸亥 Gui Hai	辛亥 Xin Hai	己亥 Ji Hai	丁亥 Ding Hai	乙亥 Yi Hai	亥 Hai Pig	9 pm - 10.59 pm

Hour 時	Day 日	Month 月	Year 年
甲 *Jia* Yang Wood	乙 *Yi* Yin Wood	壬 *Ren* Yang Water	丁 *Ding* Yin Fire
申 *Shen* **Monkey**	卯 *Mao* **Rabbit**	寅 *Yin* **Tiger**	未 *Wei* **Goat**

This is the BaZi chart for someone born on February 20, 1967 at 4.30pm.

Practice makes perfect so I'll run through a few more examples here, to help you understand more about plotting the chart.

Example 2: March 26, 1956 at 9.30am.

Step 1:
Draw the BaZi diagram below on a piece of paper.

Hour 時	Day 日	Month 月	Year 年

Step 2:
Check for the correct Animal year – since this person is born well past February 4, there is no problem with the Year Pillar.

Step 3:

Look up the year 1956 in the Ten Thousand Year Calendar. If you are using the Joey Yap Ten Thousand Year Calendar Book, 1956 is on page 238. You will see that 1956 is the year of Bing Shen 丙申, the year of the Fire Monkey Shen 申.

二月大 2nd Mth Big				正月小 1st Mth Small				月別 Month
辛卯 Xin Mao				庚寅 Geng Yin				干支 Branches and Stems
一白 One White				二黑 Two Black				九星 Nine Star
清明 Clear and Bring		春分 Spring Equinox		驚蟄 Awakening of Worms		雨水 Rain Water		節氣 Season
二十五 25th day		初九 9th day		二十三 23th day		初九 9th day		
3時 32 分 3hr 32min		23時 21 分 23hr 21min		22時 25 分 22hr 25min		0時 5 分 0hr 5min		朔 Constellation
寅 Yin		子 Zi		亥 Hai		子 Zi		
國曆 Gregorian		干支 Branches and stems	星 Star	國曆 Gregorian		干支 Branches and stems	星 Star	農曆 Solar Calender
3	12	戊寅 Wu Yin	3	2	12	己酉 Ji You	1	初一 1st day
3	13	己卯 Ji Mao	4	2	13	庚戌 Geng Xu	2	初二 2nd day
3	14	庚辰 Geng Chen	5	2	14	辛亥 Xin Hai	3	初三 3rd day
3	15	辛巳 Xin Si	6	2	15	壬子 Ren Zi	4	初四 4th day
3	16	壬午 Ren Wu	7	2	16	癸丑 Gui Chou	5	初五 5th day
3	17	癸未 Gui Wei	8	2	17	甲寅 Jia Yin	6	初六 6th day
3	18	甲申 Jia Shen	9	2	18	乙卯 Yi Mao	7	初七 7th day
3	19	乙酉 Yi You	1	2	19	丙辰 Bing Chen	8	初八 8th day
3	20	丙戌 Bing Xu	2	2	20	丁巳 Ding Si	9	初九 9th day
3	21	丁亥 Ding Hai	3	2	21	戊午 Wu Wu	1	初十 10th day
3	22	戊子 Wu Zi	4	2	22	己未 Ji Wei	2	十一 11th day
3	23	己丑 Ji Chou	5	2	23	庚申 Geng Shen	3	十二 12th day
3	24	庚寅 Geng Yin	6	2	24	辛酉 Xin You	4	十三 13th day
3	25	辛卯 Xin Mao	7	2	25	壬戌 Ren Xu	5	十四 14th day
3	26	壬辰 Ren Chen	8	2	26	癸亥 Gui Hai	6	十五 15th day
3	27	癸巳 Gui Si	9	2	27	甲子 Jia Zi	7	十六 16th day
3	28	甲午 Jia Wu	1	2	28	乙丑 Yi Chou	8	十七 17th day

1956 丙申 Bing Shen Fire Monkey

Page 238 of Joey Yap's Ten Thousand Year Calendar

So, write Bing Shen 丙申 in the Year Pillar of your diagram.

Hour 時	Day 日	Month 月	Year 年
			丙 Bing Yang Fire
			申 Shen Monkey

Step 4: Identify the Month Pillar.

Since this person was born March 26, we know that they are born in the Month of Mao 卯 (Rabbit). Now, check the month of March 1956 to determine what the Heavenly Stem of this Rabbit Month is.

二月大 2nd Mth Big				正月小 1st Mth Small				月別 Month
辛卯 Xin Mao				庚寅 Geng Yin				干支 Branches and Stems
一白 One White				二黑 Two Black				九星 Nine Star
清明 Clear and Bring		春分 Spring Equinox		驚蟄 Awakening of Worms		雨水 Rain Water		節氣 Season
二十五 25th day		初九 9th day		二十三 23th day		初九 9th day		
3時 32 分 3hr 32min		23時 21 分 23hr 21min		22時 25 分 22hr 25min		0時 5 分 0hr 5min		朔 Constellation
寅 Yin		子 Zi		亥 Hai		子 Zi		
國曆 Gregorian		干支 Branches and stems	星 Star	國曆 Gregorian		干支 Branches and stems	星 Star	農曆 Solar Calender
3	12	戊寅 Wu Yin	3	2	12	己酉 Ji You	1	初一 1st day
3	13	己卯 Ji Mao	4	2	13	庚戌 Geng Xu	2	初二 2nd day
3	14	庚辰 Geng Chen	5	2	14	辛亥 Xin Hai	3	初三 3rd day
3	15	辛巳 Xin Si	6	2	15	壬子 Ren Zi	4	初四 4th day
3	16	壬午 Ren Wu	7	2	16	癸丑 Gui Chou	5	初五 5th day
3	17	癸未 Gui Wei	8	2	17	甲寅 Jia Yin	6	初六 6th day
3	18	甲申 Jia Shen	9	2	18	乙卯 Yi Mao	7	初七 7th day
3	19	乙酉 Yi You	1	2	19	丙辰 Bing Chen	8	初八 8th day
3	20	丙戌 Bing Xu	2	2	20	丁巳 Ding Si	9	初九 9th day
3	21	丁亥 Ding Hai	3	2	21	戊午 Wu Wu	1	初十 10th day
3	22	戊子 Wu Zi	4	2	22	己未 Ji Wei	2	十一 11th day
3	23	己丑 Ji Chou	5	2	23	庚申 Geng Shen	3	十二 12th day
3	24	庚寅 Geng Yin	6	2	24	辛酉 Xin You	4	十三 13th day
3	25	辛卯 Xin Mao	7	2	25	壬戌 Ren Xu	5	十四 14th day
3	26	壬辰 Ren Chen	8	2	26	癸亥 Gui Hai	6	十五 15th day
3	27	癸巳 Gui Si	9	2	27	甲子 Jia Zi	7	十六 16th day
3	28	甲午 Jia Wu	1	2	28	乙丑 Yi Chou	8	十七 17th day

1956 丙申 Bing Shen Fire Monkey

It is the month of Xin Mao 辛卯 (Metal Rabbit). Fill in Xin Mao 辛卯 in the Month Pillar.

Hour 時	**Day** 日	**Month** 月	**Year** 年
		辛 *Xin* Yin Metal	丙 *Bing* Yang Fire
		卯 *Mao* **Rabbit**	申 *Shen* **Monkey**

Step 5: Identify the Day Pillar

Next, find the Day Pillar. Look up March 26 in the Ten Thousand Year Calendar and check the corresponding BaZi for the date. You will see it is Ren Chen 壬辰 or Water Dragon.

二月大 2nd Mth Big				正月小 1st Mth Small				月別 Month
辛卯 Xin Mao				庚寅 Geng Yin				干支 Branches and Stems
一白 One White				二黑 Two Black				九星 Nine Star
清明 Clear and Bring		春分 Spring Equinox		驚蟄 Awakening of Worms		雨水 Rain Water		節氣 Season
二十五 25th day		初九 9th day		二十三 23th day		初九 9th day		
3時 32 分 3hr 32min		23時 21 分 23hr 21min		22時 25 分 22hr 25min		0時 5 分 0hr 5min		朔 Constellation
寅 Yin		子 Zi		亥 Hai		子 Zi		
西曆 Gregorian		干支 Branches and stems	星 Star	西曆 Gregorian		干支 Branches and stems	星 Star	農曆 Solar Calender
3	12	戊寅 Wu Yin	3	2	12	己酉 Ji You	1	初一 1st day
3	13	己卯 Ji Mao	4	2	13	庚戌 Geng Xu	2	初二 2nd day
3	14	庚辰 Geng Chen	5	2	14	辛亥 Xin Hai	3	初三 3rd day
3	15	辛巳 Xin Si	6	2	15	壬子 Ren Zi	4	初四 4th day
3	16	壬午 Ren Wu	7	2	16	癸丑 Gui Chou	5	初五 5th day
3	17	癸未 Gui Wei	8	2	17	甲寅 Jia Yin	6	初六 6th day
3	18	甲申 Jia Shen	9	2	18	乙卯 Yi Mao	7	初七 7th day
3	19	乙酉 Yi You	1	2	19	丙辰 Bing Chen	8	初八 8th day
3	20	丙戌 Bing Xu	2	2	20	丁巳 Ding Si	9	初九 9th day
3	21	丁亥 Ding Hai	3	2	21	戊午 Wu Wu	1	初十 10th day
3	22	戊子 Wu Zi	4	2	22	己未 Ji Wei	2	十一 11th day
3	23	己丑 Ji Chou	5	2	23	庚申 Geng Shen	3	十二 12th day
3	24	庚寅 Geng Yin	6	2	24	辛酉 Xin You	4	十三 13th day
3	25	辛卯 Xin Mao	7	2	25	壬戌 Ren Xu	5	十四 14th day
3	26	壬辰 Ren Chen	8	2	26	癸亥 Gui Hai	6	十五 15th day
3	27	癸巳 Gui Si	9	2	27	甲子 Jia Zi	7	十六 16th day
3	28	甲午 Jia Wu	1	2	28	乙丑 Yi Chou	8	十七 17th day
3	29	乙未 Yi Wei	2	2	29	丙寅 Bing Yin	9	十八 18th day
3	30	丙申 Bing Shen	3	3	1	丁卯 Ding Mao	1	十九 19th day

1956 丙申 Bing Shen Fire Monkey

Write Ren Chen 壬辰 in the Day Pillar.

Hour 時	Day 日	Month 月	Year 年
	壬 *Ren* Yang Water	辛 *Xin* Yin Metal	丙 *Bing* Yang Fire
	辰 *Chen* **Dragon**	卯 *Mao* **Rabbit**	申 *Shen* **Monkey**

Step 6: Identify the Hour Pillar

戊 *Wu* **Yang Earth** 癸 *Gui* **Yin Water**	丁 *Ding* **Yin Fire** 壬 *Ren* **Yang Water**	丙 *Bing* **Yang Fire** 辛 *Xin* **Yin Metal**	乙 *Yi* **Yin Wood** 庚 *Geng* **Yang Metal**	甲 *Jia* **Yang Wood** 己 *Ji* **Yin Earth**	日 **Day** / 時 **Hour**	
甲子 *Jia Zi*	壬子 *Ren Zi*	庚子 *Geng Zi*	戊子 *Wu Zi*	丙子 *Bing Zi*	夜子 *Ye Zi* **Late Rat**	11 pm - 11.59 pm
壬子 *Ren Zi*	庚子 *Geng Zi*	戊子 *Wu Zi*	丙子 *Bing Zi*	甲子 *Jia Zi*	子 *Zi* **Early Rat**	12 am - 12.59 am
癸丑 *Gui Chou*	辛丑 *Xin Chou*	己丑 *Ji Chou*	丁丑 *Ding Chou*	乙丑 *Yi Chou*	丑 *Chou* **Ox**	1 am - 2.59 am
甲寅 *Jia Yin*	壬寅 *Ren Yin*	庚寅 *Geng Yin*	戊寅 *Wu Yin*	丙寅 *Bing Yin*	寅 *Yin* **Tiger**	3 am - 4.59 am
乙卯 *Yi Mao*	癸卯 *Gui Mao*	辛卯 *Xin Mao*	己卯 *Ji Mao*	丁卯 *Ding Mao*	卯 *Mao* **Rabbit**	5 am - 6.59 am
丙辰 *Bing Chen*	甲辰 *Jia Chen*	壬辰 *Ren Chen*	庚辰 *Geng Chen*	戊辰 *Wu Chen*	辰 *Chen* **Dragon**	7 am - 8.59 am
丁巳 *Ding Si*	乙巳 *Yi Si*	癸巳 *Gui Si*	辛巳 *Xin Si*	己巳 *Ji Si*	巳 *Si* **Snake**	9 am -10.59 am
戊午 *Wu Wu*	丙午 *Bing Wu*	甲午 *Jia Wu*	壬午 *Ren Wu*	庚午 *Geng Wu*	午 *Wu* **Horse**	11 am - 12.59 pm
己未 *Ji Wei*	丁未 *Ding Wei*	乙未 *Yi Wei*	癸未 *Gui Wei*	辛未 *Xin Wei*	未 *Wei* **Goat**	1pm - 2.59 pm
庚申 *Geng Shen*	戊申 *Wu Shen*	丙申 *Bing Shen*	甲申 *Jia Shen*	壬申 *Ren Shen*	申 *Shen* **Monkey**	3 pm - 4.59 pm
辛酉 *Xin You*	己酉 *Ji You*	丁酉 *Ding You*	乙酉 *Yi You*	癸酉 *Gui You*	酉 *You* **Rooster**	5 pm - 6.59 pm
壬戌 *Ren Xu*	庚戌 *Geng Xu*	戊戌 *Wu Xu*	丙戌 *Bing Xu*	甲戌 *Jia Xu*	戌 *Xu* **Dog**	7 pm - 8.59 pm
癸亥 *Gui Hai*	辛亥 *Xin Hai*	己亥 *Ji Hai*	丁亥 *Ding Hai*	乙亥 *Yi Hai*	亥 *Hai* **Pig**	9 pm - 10.59 pm

This person was born at 9.30am which, as we can see from the table above, is the Si 巳 (Snake) Hour. To find out the Heavenly Stem of the Hour Pillar, look at the Day Master, which is the Day Pillar's Heavenly Stem. It is Yi 乙.

Now, run your finger vertically across the columns till you get to Ren 壬 you will see it is Yi Si 乙巳. Write Yi Si 乙巳 in your BaZi diagram.

Hour 時	Day 日	Month 月	Year 年
乙 *Yi* Yin Wood	壬 *Ren* Yang Water	辛 *Xin* Yin Metal	丙 *Bing* Yang Fire
巳 *Si* **Snake**	辰 *Chen* **Dragon**	卯 *Mao* **Rabbit**	申 *Shen* **Monkey**

This is the BaZi chart for someone born on March 26 at 9.30am.

Example 3: May 18, 1940 at 11.58pm.

Step 1: Draw the guide diagram.

Hour 時	Day 日	Month 月	Year 年

Step 2:
Check for the correct Animal year – since this person is born well past February 4, there is no problem with the Year Pillar.

Step 3:
Look up the year 1940 in the Ten Thousand Year Calendar. If you are using the Joey Yap Ten Thousand Year Calendar, 1940 is on page 206. You will see that 1940 is the year of Geng Chen 庚辰, the year of the Metal Dragon.

命運密碼

1940 庚辰 Geng Chen Metal Dragon

二月大 2nd Mth Big				正月大 1st Mth Big				月别 Month
己卯 Ji Mao				戊寅 Wu Yin				干支 Branches and Stems
四綠 Four Green				五黃 Five Yellow				九星 Nine Star
清明 Clear and Bring		春分 Spring Equinox		驚蟄 Awakening of Worms		雨水 Rain Water		節氣 Season
二十八 28th day		十三 13th day		二十八 28th day		十三 13th day		
6時35分 6hr 35min		2時24分 2hr 24min		1時24分 1hr 24min		3時4分 3hr 4min		朔 Constellation
卯 Mao		丑 Chou		丑 Chou		寅 Yin		
國曆 Gregorian		干支 Branches and stems	星 Star	國曆 Gregorian		干支 Branches and stems	星 Star	農曆 Solar Calender
3	9	辛亥 Xin Hai	3	2	8	辛巳 Xin Si	9	初一 1st day
3	10	壬子 Ren Zi	4	2	9	壬午 Ren Wu	1	初二 2nd day
3	11	癸丑 Gui Chou	5	2	10	癸未 Gui Wei	2	初三 3rd day
3	12	甲寅 Jia Yin	6	2	11	甲申 Jia Shen	3	初四 4th day
3	13	乙卯 Yi Mao	7	2	12	乙酉 Yi You	4	初五 5th day
3	14	丙辰 Bing Chen	8	2	13	丙戌 Bing Xu	5	初六 6th day
3	15	丁巳 Ding Si	9	2	14	丁亥 Ding Hai	6	初七 7th day
3	16	戊午 Wu Wu	1	2	15	戊子 Wu Zi	7	初八 8th day
3	17	己未 Ji Wei	2	2	16	己丑 Ji Chou	8	初九 9th day
3	18	庚申 Geng Shen	3	2	17	庚寅 Geng Yin	9	初十 10th day
3	19	辛酉 Xin You	4	2	18	辛卯 Xin Mao	1	十一 11th day
3	20	壬戌 Ren Xu	5	2	19	壬辰 Ren Chen	2	十二 12th day
3	21	癸亥 Gui Hai	6	2	20	癸巳 Gui Si	3	十三 13th day
3	22	甲子 Jia Zi	7	2	21	甲午 Jia Wu	4	十四 14th day
3	23	乙丑 Yi Chou	8	2	22	乙未 Yi Wei	5	十五 15th day
3	24	丙寅 Bing Yin	9	2	23	丙申 Bing Shen	6	十六 16th day
3	25	丁卯 Ding Mao	1	2	24	丁酉 Ding You	7	十七 17th day
3	26	戊辰 Wu Chen	2	2	25	戊戌 Wu Xu	8	十八 18th day
3	27	己巳 Ji Si	3	2	26	己亥 Ji Hai	9	十九 19th day
3	28	庚午 Geng Wu	4	2	27	庚子 Geng Zi	1	二十 20th day
3	29	辛未 Xin Wei	5	2	28	辛丑 Xin Chou	2	二十一 21st day
3	30	壬申 Ren Shen	6	2	29	壬寅 Ren Yin	3	二十二 22nd day

Page 206 of Joey Yap's Ten Thousand Year Calendar

Write Geng Chen 庚辰 in the YEAR PILLAR of your chart.

Hour 時	Day 日	Month 月	Year 年
			庚 *Geng* Yang Metal
			辰 *Chen* **Dragon**

Step 4: Identify the Month Pillar.

Since this person was born May 18, we know that this person is born in the Month of the Si 巳 (Snake). Now, check the month of May 1940 to determine what the Heavenly Stem of the Snake Month is.

It is the month of Xin Si 辛巳(Metal Snake). Fill in Xin Si in the Month Pillar.

四月大 4th Mth Big				三月小 3rd Mth Small				二月大 2nd Mth Big			
辛巳 Xin Si				庚辰 Geng Chen				己卯 Ji Mao			
二黑 Two Black				三碧 Three Jade				四綠 Four Green			
		小滿 Small Sprout		立夏 Coming of Summer		穀雨 Grain Rain		清明 Clear and Bring		春分 Spring Equinox	
		十五 15th day		二十九 29th day		十三 13th day		二十八 28th day		十三 13th day	
		13時 23 分 13hr 23min		0時 16 分 0hr 16min		13時 51 分 13hr 51min		6時 35 分 6hr 35min		2時 24 分 2hr 24min	
		未 Wei		子 Zi		未 Wei		卯 Mao		丑 Chou	
國曆 Gregorian		干支 Branches and stems	星 Star	國曆 Gregorian		干支 Branches and stems	星 Star	國曆 Gregorian		干支 Branches and stems	星 Star
5	7	庚戌 Geng Xu	8	4	8	辛巳 Xin Si	6	3	9	辛亥 Xin Hai	3
5	8	辛亥 Xin Hai	9	4	9	壬午 Ren Wu	7	3	10	壬子 Ren Zi	4
5	9	壬子 Ren Zi	1	4	10	癸未 Gui Wei	8	3	11	癸丑 Gui Chou	5
5	10	癸丑 Gui Chou	2	4	11	甲申 Jia Shen	9	3	12	甲寅 Jia Yin	6
5	11	甲寅 Jia Yin	3	4	12	乙酉 Yi You	1	3	13	乙卯 Yi Mao	7
5	12	乙卯 Yi Mao	4	4	13	丙戌 Bing Xu	2	3	14	丙辰 Bing Chen	8
5	13	丙辰 Bing Chen	5	4	14	丁亥 Ding Hai	3	3	15	丁巳 Ding Si	9
5	14	丁巳 Ding Si	6	4	15	戊子 Wu Zi	4	3	16	戊午 Wu Wu	1
5	15	戊午 Wu Wu	7	4	16	己丑 Ji Chou	5	3	17	己未 Ji Wei	2
5	16	己未 Ji Wei	8	4	17	庚寅 Geng Yin	6	3	18	庚申 Geng Shen	3
5	17	庚申 Geng Shen	9	4	18	辛卯 Xin Mao	7	3	19	辛酉 Xin You	4
5	18	辛酉 Xin You	1	4	19	壬辰 Ren Chen	8	3	20	壬戌 Ren Xu	5
5	19	壬戌 Ren Xu	2	4	20	癸巳 Gui Si	9	3	21	癸亥 Gui Hai	6
5	20	癸亥 Gui Hai	3	4	21	甲午 Jia Wu	1	3	22	甲子 Jia Zi	7
5	21	甲子 Jia Zi	4	4	22	乙未 Yi Wei	2	3	23	乙丑 Yi Chou	8
5	22	乙丑 Yi Chou	5	4	23	丙申 Bing Shen	3	3	24	丙寅 Bing Yin	9
5	23	丙寅 Bing Yin	6	4	24	丁酉 Ding You	4	3	25	丁卯 Ding Mao	1
5	24	丁卯 Ding Mao	7	4	25	戊戌 Wu Xu	5	3	26	戊辰 Wu Chen	2
5	25	戊辰 Wu Chen	8	4	26	己亥 Ji Hai	6	3	27	己巳 Ji Si	3
5	26	己巳 Ji Si	9	4	27	庚子 Geng Zi	7	3	28	庚午 Geng Wu	4
5	27	庚午 Geng Wu	1	4	28	辛丑 Xin Chou	8	3	29	辛未 Xin Wei	5
5	28	辛未 Xin Wei	2	4	29	壬寅 Ren Yin	9	3	30	壬申 Ren Shen	6
5	29	壬申 Ren Shen	3	4	30	癸卯 Gui Mao	1	3	31	癸酉 Gui You	7
5	30	癸酉 Gui You	4	5	1	甲辰 Jia Chen	2	4	1	甲戌 Jia Xu	8

You might notice that there is a 'blank space' in the Month Column of the Ten Thousand Year Calendar. This is known as a leap month in the Chinese Lunar Calendar. It has NOTHING to do with BaZi because BaZi is not based on the Lunar Calendar. So don't worry. The blank space does not mean a "missing" month. It is referring to the Lunar months.

四月大 4th Mth Big				三月小 3rd Mth Small				二月大 2nd Mth Big			
辛巳 Xin Si				庚辰 Geng Chen				己卯 Ji Mao			
二黑 Two Black				三碧 Three Jade				四綠 Four Green			
		小滿 Small Sprout		立夏 Coming of Summer		穀雨 Grain Rain		清明 Clear and Bring		春分 Spring Equinox	
		十五 15th day		二十九 29th day		十三 13th day		二十八 28th day		十三 13th day	
		13時 23 分 13hr 23min		0時 16 分 0hr 16min		13時 51 分 13hr 51min		6時 35 分 6hr 35min		2時 24 分 2hr 24min	
		未 Wei		子 Zi		未 Wei		卯 Mao		丑 Chou	
國曆 Gregorian		干支 Branches and stems	星 Star	國曆 Gregorian		干支 Branches and stems	星 Star	國曆 Gregorian		干支 Branches and stems	星 Star
5	7	庚戌 Geng Xu	8	4	8	辛巳 Xin Si	6	3	9	辛亥 Xin Hai	3
5	8	辛亥 Xin Hai	9	4	9	壬午 Ren Wu	7	3	10	壬子 Ren Zi	4
5	9	壬子 Ren Zi	1	4	10	癸未 Gui Wei	8	3	11	癸丑 Gui Chou	5
5	10	癸丑 Gui Chou	2	4	11	甲申 Jia Shen	9	3	12	甲寅 Jia Yin	6
5	11	甲寅 Jia Yin	3	4	12	乙酉 Yi You	1	3	13	乙卯 Yi Mao	7
5	12	乙卯 Yi Mao	4	4	13	丙戌 Bing Xu	2	3	14	丙辰 Bing Chen	8
5	13	丙辰 Bing Chen	5	4	14	丁亥 Ding Hai	3	3	15	丁巳 Ding Si	9
5	14	丁巳 Ding Si	6	4	15	戊子 Wu Zi	4	3	16	戊午 Wu Wu	1
5	15	戊午 Wu Wu	7	4	16	己丑 Ji Chou	5	3	17	己未 Ji Wei	2
5	16	己未 Ji Wei	8	4	17	庚寅 Geng Yin	6	3	18	庚申 Geng Shen	3
5	17	庚申 Geng Shen	9	4	18	辛卯 Xin Mao	7	3	19	辛酉 Xin You	4
5	18	辛酉 Xin You	1	4	19	壬辰 Ren Chen	8	3	20	壬戌 Ren Xu	5
5	19	壬戌 Ren Xu	2	4	20	癸巳 Gui Si	9	3	21	癸亥 Gui Hai	6
5	20	癸亥 Gui Hai	3	4	21	甲午 Jia Wu	1	3	22	甲子 Jia Zi	7
5	21	甲子 Jia Zi	4	4	22	乙未 Yi Wei	2	3	23	乙丑 Yi Chou	8
5	22	乙丑 Yi Chou	5	4	23	丙申 Bing Shen	3	3	24	丙寅 Bing Yin	9
5	23	丙寅 Bing Yin	6	4	24	丁酉 Ding You	4	3	25	丁卯 Ding Mao	1
5	24	丁卯 Ding Mao	7	4	25	戊戌 Wu Xu	5	3	26	戊辰 Wu Chen	2
5	25	戊辰 Wu Chen	8	4	26	己亥 Ji Hai	6	3	27	己巳 Ji Si	3
5	26	己巳 Ji Si	9	4	27	庚子 Geng Zi	7	3	28	庚午 Geng Wu	4
5	27	庚午 Geng Wu	1	4	28	辛丑 Xin Chou	8	3	29	辛未 Xin Wei	5
5	28	辛未 Xin Wei	2	4	29	壬寅 Ren Yin	9	3	30	壬申 Ren Shen	6
5	29	壬申 Ren Shen	3	4	30	癸卯 Gui Mao	1	3	31	癸酉 Gui You	7
5	30	癸酉 Gui You	4	5	1	甲辰 Jia Chen	2	4	1	甲戌 Jia Xu	8

Continuing on, let's fill in Xin Si 辛巳 into the Month Pillar of your diagram.

Hour 時	Day 日	Month 月	Year 年
		辛 *Xin* Yin Metal	庚 *Geng* Yang Metal
		巳 *Si* **Snake**	辰 *Chen* **Dragon**

Step 5: Identify the Day Pillar

Next is the Day Pillar. To find the Day Pillar, look up May 18 in the Ten Thousand Year Calendar and check the corresponding pillar for the date. You will see it is Xin You 辛酉 or Metal Rooster.

四月大 4th Mth Big				三月小 3rd Mth Small				二月大 2nd Mth Big			
辛巳 Xin Si				庚辰 Geng Chen				己卯 Ji Mao			
二黑 Two Black				三碧 Three Jade				四綠 Four Green			
		小滿 Small Sprout		立夏 Coming of Summer		穀雨 Grain Rain		清明 Clear and Bring		春分 Spring Equinox	
		十五 15th day		二十九 29th day		十三 13th day		二十八 28th day		十三 13th day	
		13時 23 分 13hr 23min		0時 16 分 0hr 16min		13時 51 分 13hr 51min		6時 35 分 6hr 35min		2時 24 分 2hr 24min	
		未 Wei		子 Zi		未 Wei		卯 Mao		丑 Chou	
國曆 Gregorian		干支 Branches and stems	星 Star	國曆 Gregorian		干支 Branches and stems	星 Star	國曆 Gregorian		干支 Branches and stems	星 Star
5	7	庚戌 Geng Xu	8	4	8	辛巳 Xin Si	6	3	9	辛亥 Xin Hai	3
5	8	辛亥 Xin Hai	9	4	9	壬午 Ren Wu	7	3	10	壬子 Ren Zi	4
5	9	壬子 Ren Zi	1	4	10	癸未 Gui Wei	8	3	11	癸丑 Gui Chou	5
5	10	癸丑 Gui Chou	2	4	11	甲申 Jia Shen	9	3	12	甲寅 Jia Yin	6
5	11	甲寅 Jia Yin	3	4	12	乙酉 Yi You	1	3	13	乙卯 Yi Mao	7
5	12	乙卯 Yi Mao	4	4	13	丙戌 Bing Xu	2	3	14	丙辰 Bing Chen	8
5	13	丙辰 Bing Chen	5	4	14	丁亥 Ding Hai	3	3	15	丁巳 Ding Si	9
5	14	丁巳 Ding Si	6	4	15	戊子 Wu Zi	4	3	16	戊午 Wu Wu	1
5	15	戊午 Wu Wu	7	4	16	己丑 Ji Chou	5	3	17	己未 Ji Wei	2
5	16	己未 Ji Wei	8	4	17	庚寅 Geng Yin	6	3	18	庚申 Geng Shen	3
5	17	庚申 Geng Shen	9	4	18	辛卯 Xin Mao	7	3	19	辛酉 Xin You	4
5	18	辛酉 Xin You	1	4	19	壬辰 Ren Chen	8	3	20	壬戌 Ren Xu	5
5	19	壬戌 Ren Xu	2	4	20	癸巳 Gui Si	9	3	21	癸亥 Gui Hai	6
5	20	癸亥 Gui Hai	3	4	21	甲午 Jia Wu	1	3	22	甲子 Jia Zi	7
5	21	甲子 Jia Zi	4	4	22	乙未 Yi Wei	2	3	23	乙丑 Yi Chou	8
5	22	乙丑 Yi Chou	5	4	23	丙申 Bing Shen	3	3	24	丙寅 Bing Yin	9
5	23	丙寅 Bing Yin	6	4	24	丁酉 Ding You	4	3	25	丁卯 Ding Mao	1
5	24	丁卯 Ding Mao	7	4	25	戊戌 Wu Xu	5	3	26	戊辰 Wu Chen	2
5	25	戊辰 Wu Chen	8	4	26	己亥 Ji Hai	6	3	27	己巳 Ji Si	3
5	26	己巳 Ji Si	9	4	27	庚子 Geng Zi	7	3	28	庚午 Geng Wu	4
5	27	庚午 Geng Wu	1	4	28	辛丑 Xin Chou	8	3	29	辛未 Xin Wei	5
5	28	辛未 Xin Wei	2	4	29	壬寅 Ren Yin	9	3	30	壬申 Ren Shen	6
5	29	壬申 Ren Shen	3	4	30	癸卯 Gui Mao	1	3	31	癸酉 Gui You	7
5	30	癸酉 Gui You	4	5	1	甲辰 Jia Chen	2	4	1	甲戌 Jia Xu	8
5	31	甲戌 Jia Xu	5	5	2	乙巳 Yi Si	3	4	2	乙亥 Yi Hai	9

Write Xin You 辛酉 in the Day Pillar.

Hour 時	Day 日	Month 月	Year 年
	辛 *Xin* Yin Metal	辛 *Xin* Yin Metal	庚 *Geng* Yang Metal
	酉 *You* **Rooster**	巳 *Si* **Snake**	辰 *Chen* **Dragon**

Step 6: Identify the Hour Pillar

Lastly we need to find the Hour Pillar. This person was born at 11.58pm which we can see is the Rat Hour. Now, the Rat Hour, which is 11pm to 1am, requires a little bit of care and attention when plotting because there are actually TWO Rat Hours – a late Rat Hour (11pm-11.59pm) and a early Rat Hour (12am-12.59am)

戊 *Wu* **Yang Earth** 癸 *Gui* **Yin Water**	丁 *Ding* **Yin Fire** 壬 *Ren* **Yang Water**	丙 *Bing* **Yang Fire** 辛 *Xin* **Yin Metal**	乙 *Yi* **Yin Wood** 庚 *Geng* **Yang Metal**	甲 *Jia* **Yang Wood** 己 *Ji* **Yin Earth**	日 **Day** / 時 **Hour**	
甲子 *Jia Zi*	壬子 *Ren Zi*	庚子 *Geng Zi*	戊子 *Wu Zi*	丙子 *Bing Zi*	夜子 *Ye Zi* **Late Rat**	11 pm - 11.59 pm
壬子 *Ren Zi*	庚子 *Geng Zi*	戊子 *Wu Zi*	丙子 *Bing Zi*	甲子 *Jia Zi*	子 *Zi* **Early Rat**	12 am - 12.59 am

Only the Rat hour splits into Early and Late Rat Hour because half of the Rat hour belongs to the same day while the other belongs to the 'next' day. Remember a day transits at 12am!

11.58pm is called the Late Rate Hour (夜子).

This person's Day Master is Xin 辛. To find out the Stem of the Hour Pillar, run your finger vertically across the columns till you get to Xin 辛 – you will see it is Geng Zi 庚子. Write Geng Zi 庚子 in your diagram.

Fill in Geng Zi 庚子 into your Diagram.

Hour 時	Day 日	Month 月	Year 年
庚 *Geng* Yang Metal	辛 *Xin* Yin Metal	辛 *Xin* Yin Metal	庚 *Geng* Yang Metal
子 *Zi* **Rat**	酉 *You* **Rooster**	巳 *Si* **Snake**	辰 *Chen* **Dragon**

This is the BaZi chart for someone born on May 18, 1940 at 11.58pm.

It is very important that you try to plot as many charts as possible manually using the Ten Thousand Year Calendar. Practice after all makes perfect and although I've developed a computerised calculator on my website, the machine sometimes makes mistakes that a human would never make. So, even if you do use the computerised program on my website, remember to check it by plotting the chart manually.

Finding the Day Master

In BaZi, the Heavenly Stem found in the Day Pillar is the element that is known as your Self Element. In BaZi terminology, we call it the Day Master.

The Day Master is of great significance – it is the point of reference for all your BaZi readings and analysis. In other words, without the Day Master, it is not possible to read a person's BaZi. Conversely, an experienced BaZi practitioner can tell a lot about a person, just by looking at his or her Day Master.

Day Master

Hour 時	Day 日	Month 月	Year 年
甲 *Jia* Yang Wood	壬 *Ren* Yang Water	辛 *Xin* Yin Metal	丙 *Bing* Yang Fire
辰 *Chen* **Dragon**	辰 *Chen* **Dragon**	卯 *Mao* **Rabbit**	申 *Shen* **Monkey**

For example in the above chart, the Day Master is Ren 壬 (Yang Water). We can say that this person belongs to the Yang Water element or that he is a Ren 壬 Water person.

This is a good point to start putting into practice the BaZi language you have learnt in the last few chapters. Try not to say "Yang Water" person – refer to a person by their Day Master, ie: "Ren Water" man or woman.

If you are a guy and your Day Master is a Bing 丙, then address yourself as a Bing Fire Man or if you are lady and your Day Master is Xin 辛 Metal, you are a Xin Metal Lady.

Take a look at your own BaZi chart now and find out WHAT is your Day Master.

Keeping Things Straight.

If you are a student of Feng Shui, you may have heard about the Personal Gua or Life Gua or Ming Gua. This Gua is also represented by an Element (ie: Fire, Water)

Remember that BaZi and Feng Shui are two independent subjects. Your BaZi Day Master may not be the same as your Life Gua element. Feng Shui and BaZi, while inter-related, are systems used to analyse different things. Accordingly, it is best not to confuse the two. Remember, your Life Gua is your Life Gua and relates to your Feng Shui calculations and assessments. Your BaZi Day Master's element is used as a reference point for Destiny Analysis. Do not attempt to merge the two studies. They are not interchangeable.

Quick Practice:

Before you turn to the next chapter, find Five sets of date of births, complete with time of birth and manually plot out the BaZi charts. If you can do more, this is better. The more charts you do, the more fun you're going to have in the next few chapters especially in the chapters that cover BaZi analysis!

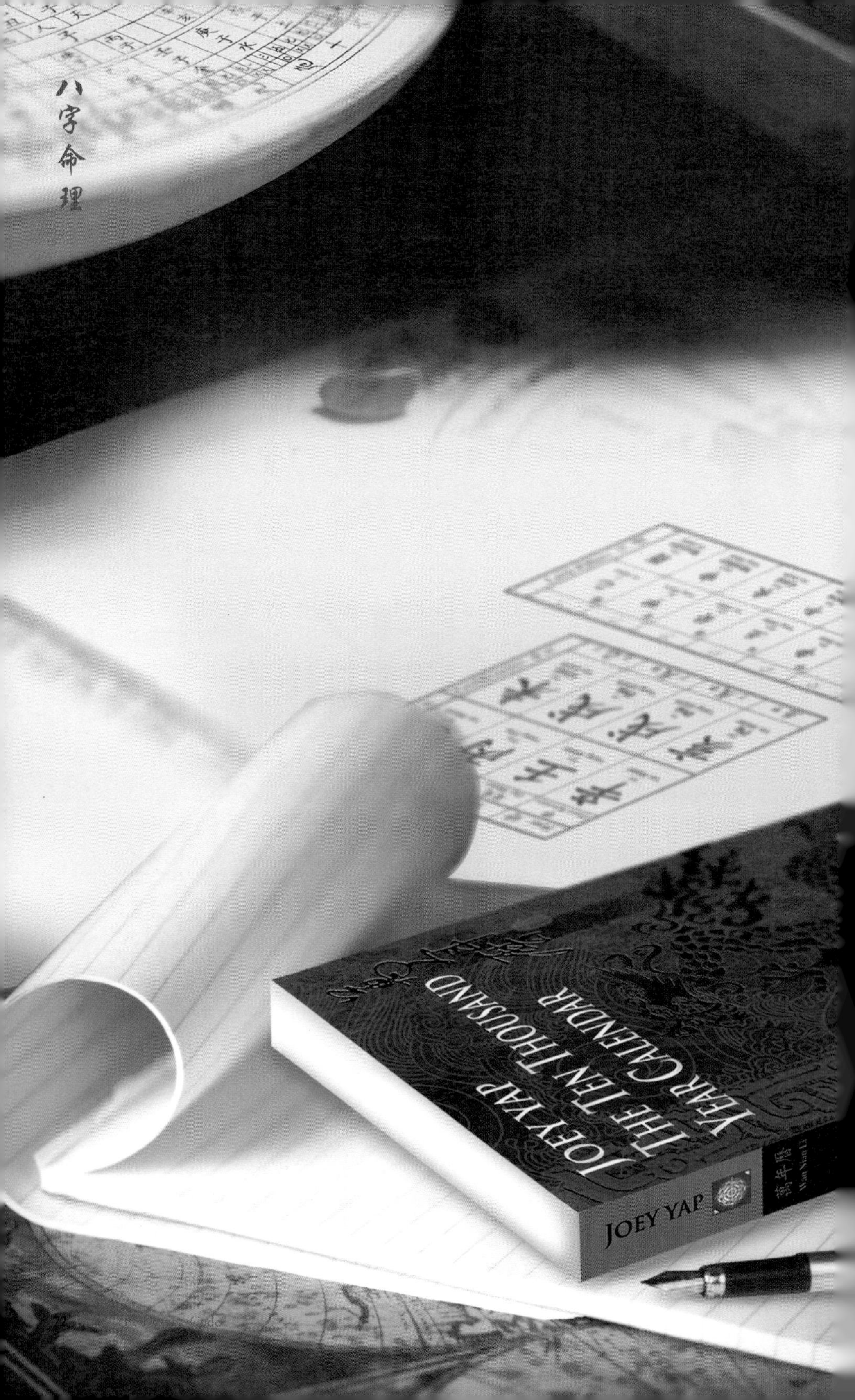
八字命理
JOEY YAP
THE TEN THOUSAND YEAR CALENDAR
JOEY YAP
萬年曆
Wan Nian Li

Chapter Four:
Have you got the Luck?

"Destiny might be difficult to Change, but Luck can Change".

The last three chapters have been about introducing the concept of Destiny to you and also, getting hands on with BaZi by learning how to plot a BaZi chart. I know you are impatient to get to the analysis bit but there's just one more step before we start analysing charts.

Let's get back to the big picture for a minute here. I want to explain the concepts of Destiny and Luck. The reason is that in this chapter, we will be learning how to plot a person's Luck Cycle and Luck Pillars. But before we get to the calculations and interpretations, we need to know what all this luck business is about.

Now, I realise that most people will be thinking - I know what luck means or is! Does it really need explanation?

For most people, luck is something random, something chance-like, a kind of if-it-happens-it-happens. Like striking a lottery.

In the study of BaZi, luck does not have such a random value to it. Instead, luck is something that can be calculated and evaluated, beyond merely good or bad. BaZi enables us to know what KIND of luck a person is going to go through or is going through and whether that luck is beneficial or not.

3 Levels of Luck: The Cosmic Trinity

The Chinese Sages believed that in the universe, three kinds of luck enter into play in our lives: Heaven Luck, Earth Luck and Man Luck.

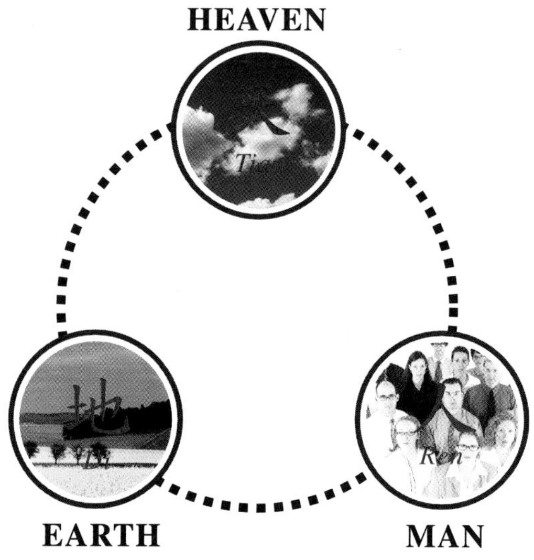

Heaven Luck refers to what is God given or bestowed by Heaven. It is fixed at birth and cannot be controlled or changed by man. Heaven's will is what decides when we are born, where we are born, who is our family, what race we are and what background and upbringing we will have. Sounds a bit like Destiny right?

Absolutely - Heaven Luck is in essence, Destiny.

Earth Luck is referenced to where a person lives and the Feng Shui of the place that he or she resides or works in. Like Destiny, the playing field is not level either when it comes to Qi (Living Force) distribution on the Earth. Some parts of a city, state or country are better than others, just as how sometimes slums and prime real estate can't be in the same postcode. Some areas have superior landform and mountains, producing wealthy individuals (here's a clue: the Hollywood Hills have a lot to do with why Hollywood is THE place for entertainment, movies and superstars!)

Finally, there is Man Luck. This refers to choices that people make, their morals, their virtues, their beliefs and life decisions. Man Luck is what makes individuals strive to better themselves, it is what positive thinking and motivational coaching is all about. If a persons has good Man Luck, they will strive hard to improve and advance themselves - by contrast, if their Man Luck is not so good, they are likely to be individuals who do not see the value in self-improvement or even reading the newspapers!

These three forces are inter-related and what we are essentially left with is a metaphysical Chicken-and-Egg scenario. Each of these types of Luck do not operate in a vacuum - they are inter-dependant. I call this interplay of inter-related forces of the Cosmic Trinity.

Let's Get a Bit Philosophical...

Understanding this interdependence or the concept is not difficult - I have found that most people have difficulty accepting the concept of the Cosmic Trinity (Heaven-Earth-Man). Allow me to illustrate how in fact the concept of the Cosmic Trinity is virtually infallible! (yes, this is one theory that has no flaw!)

Many people think that they can control their Destiny by being highly motivated, controlling their vices, constantly improving themselves by reading books or attending 'life-changing' self improvement seminars.

However, we must acknowledge that no amount of positive thinking, no amount of determination, drive or willpower can turn a person into 'Bill Gates' or 'Donald Trump'. Your average How To Get Rich 'Life Coach' is at best a millionaire or multi-millionaire. Now, if all that was required to overcome an unfavourable Destiny is the power of Mind over Destiny as it were, many motivational gurus would be 'positive thinking' themselves into billionaire-dom. Of course, wealth should not be the only measurement of success. There are many life or relationship coaches who also suffer from relationship problems, health or family issues. It is a fact that there are things beyond human control that affect our lives. Who you are born to, where you are born, who your parents are, who your relatives and close friends are from early life - all these factors are not controlled by mere 'motivation' or positive thinking.

From this, we can obviously and logically rationalise that there is an X factor that makes a difference. That would be Heaven Luck. You can't achieve something which you're not destined to achieve, no matter how much you want it or work for it or motivate yourself to achieve it.

I also like to use the example of the Feng Shui master as an illustration of the Cosmic Trinity concept. Now, the Feng Shui master is supposed to know 'the secrets of Heaven and Earth'. He is able to not only select the most suitable, most favourable location for his home or office, but he can also 'fix' a less suitable location to optimise it for wealth creation.

So how come there are hardly any billionaire Feng Shui masters? Again, it is Heaven Luck. They may have the Heaven Luck to be able to learn and practice Feng Shui well, they may have the skills to locate an excellent piece of land but they may not have the money to buy that piece of land or it may simply not be for sale at that particular point in time.

There is no lack of Man Luck. No lack of Earth Luck either (the Feng Shui Master naturally would have improved his own home or office to the maximum). But the missing piece in the puzzle is the Heaven Luck - it is not meant to be. There are factors that are beyond our Man or Earth Luck's control. This is called Heaven Luck, your Destiny.

Do the right thing, at the right time, at the right place. Heaven - Earth - Man. Thus, when each of these three factors CONNECT at their optimum points, that is when Kings, Emperors and Billionaires are made!

The X Factor: Luck

There are instances of individuals born with an excellent Destiny (a good BaZi chart) but who do not live up to their potential until late in life. Alternatively, promising individuals are cut down in the prime of their life - hit as it were, by a serious spate of bad luck.

It is said that sometimes, all a person needs is 'a little luck'. This could not be more true. Even in an optimum situation of highly favourable Man Luck, Earth Luck and Heaven Luck (in other words, a person who exerts effort, has good Feng Shui and is born to be great) will not succeed without LUCK! Consider these examples: Colonel Sanders of KFC fame did not truly become a household name until he was in his 60s. Abraham Lincoln failed 3 times to be President of the United States, died in office but yet is often considered the greatest American President.

JFK, John Lennon and Bruce Lee are examples of individuals who probably had a superb Destiny but didn't have the Luck to carry out what Destiny had in store for them.

The Chinese often talk of 'Ming Yun' (命運) or Destiny-Luck to indicate that these two are in fact ONE. It's not enough to be destined to succeed, you need a bit of luck too to enjoy that success!

Wriggle Room in Heaven

Destiny is not the be-all-and-end-all in the game of life. Each person's Destiny may be set at birth, but there's still 'wriggle room' as it were. If Heaven is not fair in not giving each and every person an equally stellar Destiny, then Heaven evens the odds by ensuring that no person has perpetual everlasting good luck or perpetual everlasting bad luck.

A person's Earth Luck and Man Luck have a role to play in his or her life. But there is also the Luck Cycle, a dynamic changing factor that is drawn from the BaZi chart.

You see, a person's BaZi chart, which is supposed to contain information about a person's Destiny (that is fixed and static), has a DYNAMIC feature which is the Luck Cycle. So, a superior Destiny chart, that also has a good Luck Cycle, enables a person to truly benefit and make use of what Heaven has bestowed upon him. A person with a superior Destiny chart but a less ideal Luck Cycle, may find that he only enjoys luck later in life!

Plotting the Luck Cycle

In Chapter three of this book, you would have plotted with the assistance of the Ten Thousand Year Calendar, your personal BaZi chart. Now remember that a BaZi chart only contains the static aspect of your BaZi. To unlock the dynamic aspect of your BaZi, to discover whether or not you have the luck (or when you WILL have the luck), you need to plot your Luck Cycle.

To plot your Luck Cycle, you first need your BaZi chart. The dynamic aspect of the BaZi is always drawn from the static aspect.

The order of Luck

Before we start, you need to familiarise yourself with two very important concepts: the Forward Cycle and the Reverse Cycle. The Forward Cycle and Reverse Cycle refer to the sequential order of the Heavenly Stems and Earthly Branches in a person's Luck Cycle.

Take a look at the diagram below:

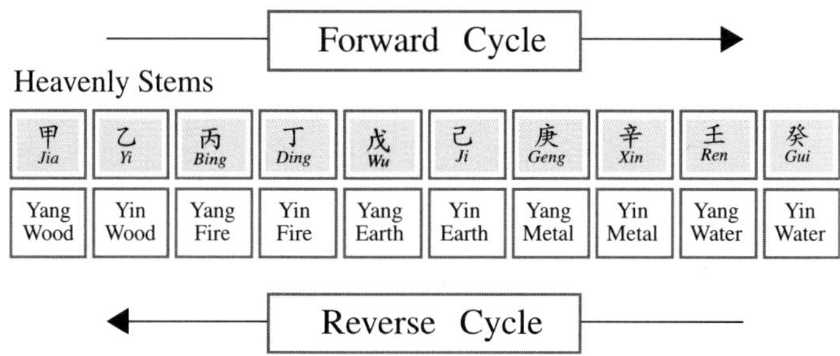

A few things to remember about the cycle of Heavenly Stems:

a) A Yang Stem is always followed by a Yin Stem, and a Yin Stem followed by a Yang Stem. This is the case no matter which direction the Cycle is in, be it Forward or Reverse.

b) The cycle does not skip - for instance Bing 丙 (Yang Fire) is always followed by Ding 丁 (Yin Fire) in a Forward Cycle, whilst Yi 乙 (Yin Wood) always follows Jia 甲 (Yang Wood) if it is a Reverse Cycle.

c) When you reach either end of the cycle (ie: Gui 癸 (Yin Water) or Jia 甲 (Yang Wood)), the cycle just continues. Therefore, Gui 癸 (Yin Water) is followed by Jia 甲 (Yang Wood) if it is a Forward Cycle and Jia 甲 (Yang Wood) is always followed by Gui 癸 (Yin Water) if it is a Reverse Cycle.

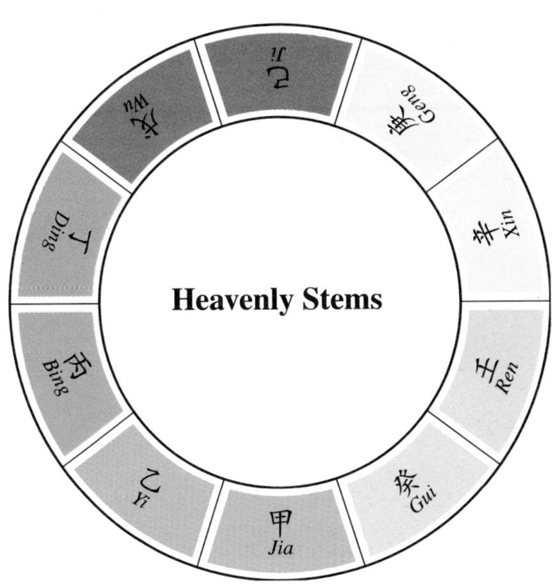

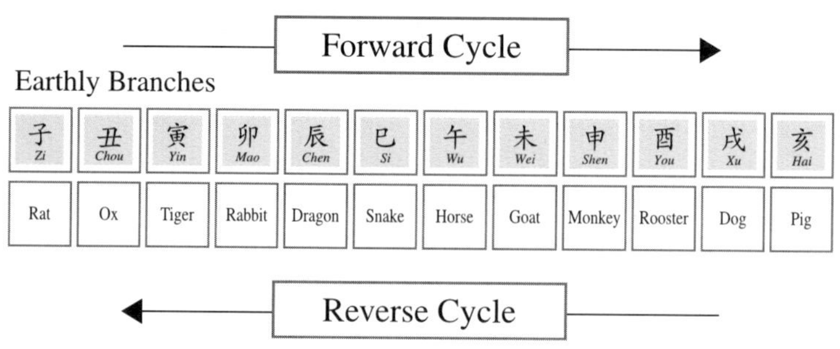

Now, a few things that you need to remember about the cycle of Earthly Branches:

a) The cycle does not skip, only the direction of movement changes. In other words, Wei 未 (Goat) will always proceed to Wu 午 (Horse) if in a Reverse Cycle or proceed to Shen 申 (Monkey) if in a Forward Cycle. It does not skip animals.

b) When you reach either end of the Cycle ie: Hai 亥 (Pig) or Zi 子 (Rat), the cycle simply continues. In other words, if you are in a Reverse Cycle at Zi 子 (Rat), the next animal is Hai 亥 (Pig). If you are in a Forward cycle at Hai 亥 (Pig), it goes to Zi 子 (Rat).

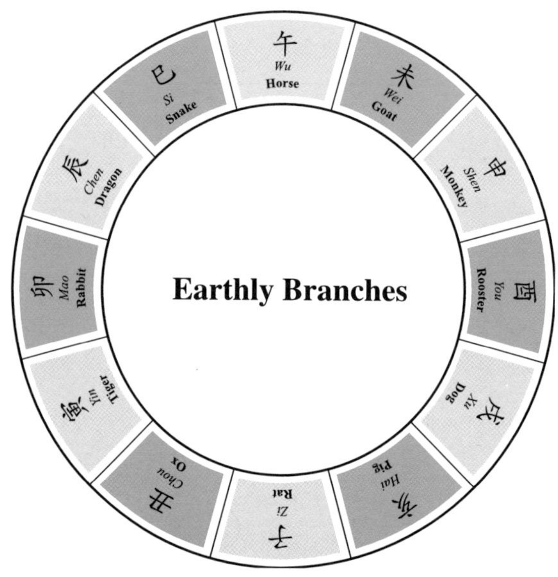

Forward or Reverse?
Finding out the Luck Cycle direction

Whether the Luck Cycle moves Forward or Reverse is determined by two factors:

a) Gender of the individual (Male or Female)

b) Polarity of the birth Year (Yang or Yin)

To determine if a Year is Yin or Yang, you simply look at the Heavenly Stem in the person's Year Pillar in his/her BaZi. If the Heavenly Stem is a Yang Element, it is a Yang Year. If it is a Yin Heavenly Stem, then it is a Yin Year. Refer to page 28 if you have forgotten the polarity of the Heavenly Stems.

Example: Year 2004

二月大 2nd Mth Big				正月小 1st Mth Small				月別 Month
丁 卯 Ding Mao				丙 寅 Bing Yin				干支 Branches and Stems
一白 One White				二黑 Two Black				九星 Nine Star
春分 Spring Equinox		驚蟄 Awakening of Worms		雨水 Rain Water		立春 Coming of Spring		節氣 Season
三十 30th day		十五 15th day		二十九 29th day		十四 14th day		
14時 50 分 14hr 50min		13時 57 分 13hr 57min		15時 51 分 15hr 51min		19時 58 分 19hr 58min		朔 Constellation
未 Wei		未 Wei		申 Shen		戌 Xu		
國曆 Gregorian		干支 Branches and stems	星 Star	國曆 Gregorian		干支 Branches and stems	星 Star	農曆 Solar Calender
2	20	己 巳 Ji Si	6	1	22	庚 子 Geng Zi	4	初一 1st day
2	21	庚 午 Geng Wu	7	1	23	辛 丑 Xin Chou	5	初二 2nd day
2	22	辛 未 Xin Wei	8	1	24	壬 寅 Ren Yin	6	初三 3rd day
2	23	壬 申 Ren Shen	9	1	25	癸 卯 Gui Mao	7	初四 4th day
2	24	癸 酉 Gui You	1	1	26	甲 辰 Jia Chen	8	初五 5th day
2	25	甲 戌 Jia Xu	2	1	27	乙 巳 Yi Si	9	初六 6th day
2	26	乙 亥 Yi Hai	3	1	28	丙 午 Bing Wu	1	初七 7th day
2	27	丙 子 Bing Zi	4	1	29	丁 未 Ding Wei	2	初八 8th day
2	28	丁 丑 Ding Chou	5	1	30	戊 申 Wu Shen	3	初九 9th day
2	29	戊 寅	6	1	31	己 酉	4	初十

2 0 0 4 甲 申 Jia Shen

Wood Monl

By referring to the Ten Thousand Year Calendar, we can see that the year pillar for 2004 is Jia Shen 甲申. Jia 甲 is a Yang Stem. So 2004 is a Yang Year.

Example: Year 2005

二月大 2nd Mth Big				正月小 1st Mth Small				月別 Month
己卯 Ji Mao				戊寅 Wu Yin				干支 Branches and Stems
七赤 Seven Red				八白 Eight White				九星 Nine Star
清明 Clear and Bright		春分 Spring Equinox		驚蟄 Awakening of Worms		雨水 Rain Water		節氣 Season
二十七 27th day		十一 11th day		二十五 25th day		初十 10th day		
0時 36 分 0hr 36min		20時 35 分 20hr 35min		19時 47 分 19hr 47min		21時 33 分 21hr 33min		宿 Constellation
子 Zi		戌 Xu		戌 Xu		戌 Xu		
國曆 Gregorian		干支 Branches and stems	星 Star	國曆 Gregorian		干支 Branches and stems	星 Star	農曆 Solar Calender
3	10	癸巳 Gui Si	3	2	9	甲子 Jia Zi	1	初一 1st day
3	11	甲午 Jia Wu	4	2	10	乙丑 Yi Chou	2	初二 2nd day
3	12	乙未 Yi Wei	5	2	11	丙寅 Bing Yin	3	初三 3rd day
3	13	丙申 Bing Shen	6	2	12	丁卯 Ding Mao	4	初四 4th day
3	14	丁酉 Ding You	7	2	13	戊辰 Wu Chen	5	初五 5th day
3	15	戊戌 Wu Xu	8	2	14	己巳 Ji Si	6	初六 6th day
3	16	己亥 Ji Hai	9	2	15	庚午 Geng Wu	7	初七 7th day
3	17	庚子 Geng Zi	1	2	16	辛未 Xin Wei	8	初八 8th day
3	18	辛丑 Xin Chou	2	2	17	壬申 Ren Shen	9	初九 9th day

2005 乙酉 Yi You

Wooc

By referring to the Ten Thousand Year Calendar, we can see that the year pillar for 2005 is Yi You乙酉. Yi 乙is a Yin Stem. So 2005 is a Yin Year.

A Male born in a Yang Year is called a Yang Male. A Female born in a Yang Year is called a Yang Female. Now this has nothing to do with the sexual orientation of the person - we are simply describing the polarity of the person born in a certain year.

The Table below tells us when to use the Reverse Cycle and when to use the Forward Cycle.

Forward Cycle	Yang Male, Yin Female
Reverse Cycle	Yin Male, Yang Female

命運密碼

Accordingly, a person born in a Yang Year who is Male will have a luck cycle that moves in a Forward Cycle. A person born in a Yin Year who is a Male will have a luck cycle that moves in a Reverse Cycle.

A Female born in a Yang Year will have a Reverse Cycle while a Female born in a Yin Year will have a Forward Cycle.

A Forward or Reverse Luck Cycles DO NOT indicate good or bad luck. It is just the way the luck cycle is plotted - nothing to do with the quality or type of luck the person would experience in his or her life time.

Plotting the Luck Pillars

Once the direction of the Luck Cycle has been determined, we can now plot the Luck Pillars. What are Luck Pillars?

Just like it is not possible to read a person's BaZi without the Day Master, so it is not possible to gain a complete picture of a person's Destiny without looking at his/her Luck Pillars.

Luck Pillars answer the two most important questions in BaZi: when and what. The Luck Pillars reveal when a person is going through what kind of luck.

In life, it is not just a case of being able to take the right action, but being able to take the right action at the right time. If your BaZi chart tells you what you can and cannot do, then your Luck Pillars tell you when you should and

should not take action and what kind of action you should or should not take.

Remember, nothing is permanently good and nothing is permanently bad. If you have a good Destiny, you need a good set of Luck Pillars to help bring out the best of your Destiny. Similarly, if your Destiny is not ideal, all you sometimes need is a run of good luck in your Luck Pillars to overcome your weak points and maybe even bring out the hidden potential of your BaZi. A good set of Luck Pillars can turn a bad Destiny chart around completely, making fortune smile on you, while a good Destiny chart can turn disastrous through untimely Luck Pillars. Your BaZi chart is akin to a ship that is given to you at the time of your birth and your Luck Pillars are like the winds and tide.

A good Destiny is like having a good ship from the start. If the wind and tides travel the same direction as your navigation, your life is as smooth as silk. If the winds and tide are blowing against your ship, your travels will be bumpy and at worst stormy.

In this respect, you could say Luck Pillars are like resources. When your resources are good and your Destiny is good, things proceed smoothly and according to plan. With good resources, even the tough times don't seem so tough and if things are not going that well, then a change of Luck is all it takes to bring those resources back to fore again.

The key reference point for plotting the Luck Pillars is the MONTH PILLAR in the person's main BaZi chart. Now, you will need to utilise what you have learnt from the preceding pages on the Forward and Reverse Cycles for the Heavenly Stems and Earthly Branches to plot the Luck Cycle.

Examples:

Male born on May 14, 1944 at 5.15am.

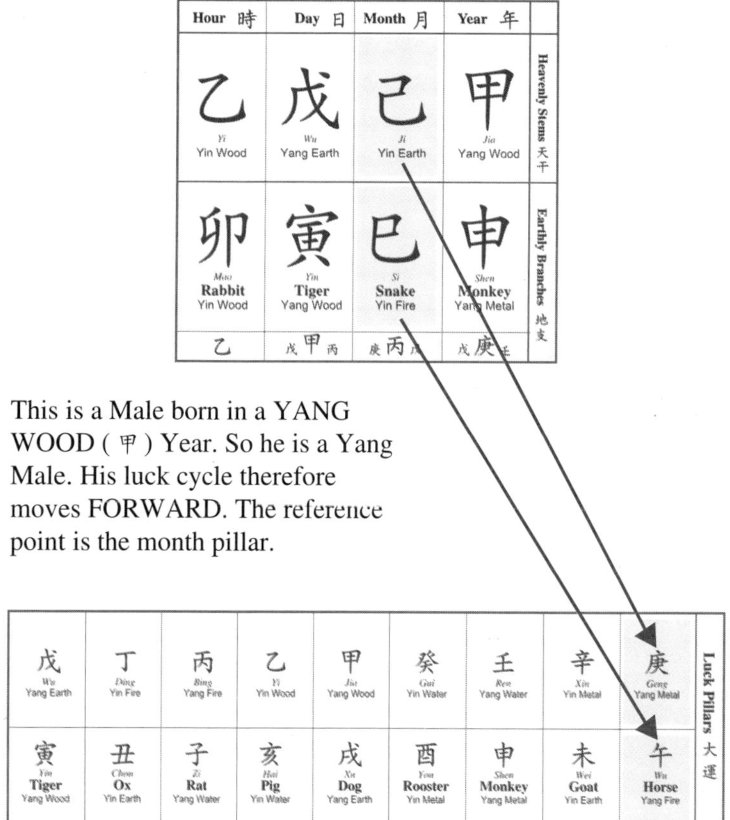

Hour 時	Day 日	Month 月	Year 年	
乙 Yi Yin Wood	戊 Wu Yang Earth	己 Ji Yin Earth	甲 Jia Yang Wood	Heavenly Stems 天干
卯 Mao **Rabbit** Yin Wood	寅 Yin **Tiger** Yang Wood	巳 Si **Snake** Yin Fire	申 Shen **Monkey** Yang Metal	Earthly Branches 地支
乙	戊 甲 丙	庚 丙 戊	戊 庚 壬	

This is a Male born in a YANG WOOD (甲) Year. So he is a Yang Male. His luck cycle therefore moves FORWARD. The reference point is the month pillar.

戊 Wu Yang Earth	丁 Ding Yin Fire	丙 Bing Yang Fire	乙 Yi Yin Wood	甲 Jia Yang Wood	癸 Gui Yin Water	壬 Ren Yang Water	辛 Xin Yin Metal	庚 Geng Yang Metal	Luck Pillars 大運
寅 Yin **Tiger** Yang Wood	丑 Chou **Ox** Yin Earth	子 Zi **Rat** Yang Water	亥 Hai **Pig** Yin Water	戌 Xu **Dog** Yang Earth	酉 You **Rooster** Yin Metal	申 Shen **Monkey** Yang Metal	未 Wei **Goat** Yin Earth	午 Wu **Horse** Yang Fire	

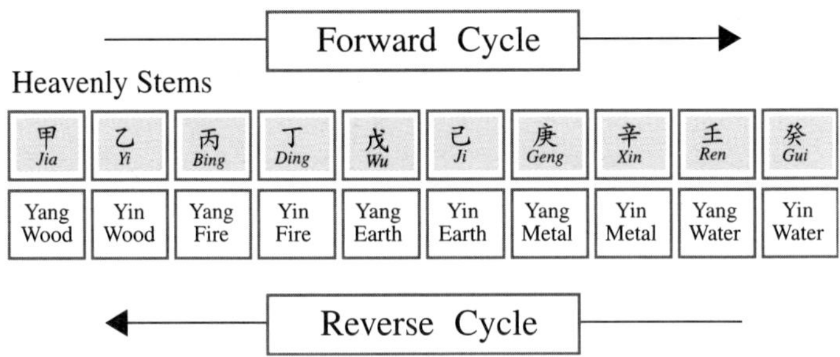

This person's Luck Cycle is a Forward Luck Cycle. The Heavenly Stem in the Month Pillar of his BaZi is Ji 己. Therefore, the Heavenly Stems for the Luck Cycle starts at Geng 庚 (the Heavenly Stem after Ji 己) and moves FORWARD. After Geng 庚 is Xin 辛, after Xin 辛 is Ren 壬 and so on.

What about the Earthly Branches then? Remember this table?

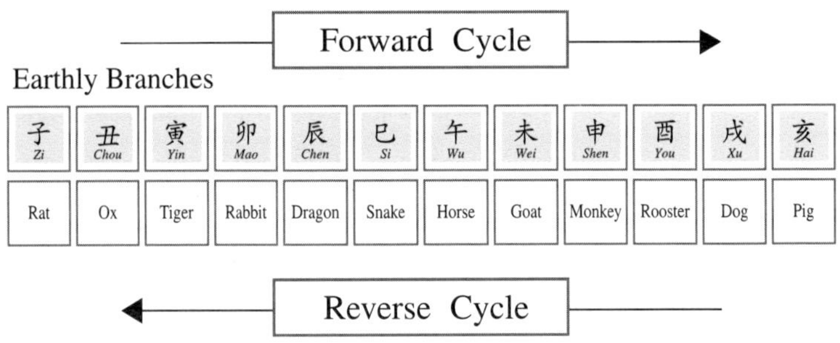

The Earthly Branch in the Month Pillar of his BaZi is Si 巳 (Snake). Therefore, the Earthly Branch of the Luck Cycle starts at Wu 午 (Horse), which is the animal after Si 巳 (Snake). Wu 午 (Horse) is followed by Wei 未 (Goat), and Wei 未 (Goat) is followed by Shen 申 (Monkey) and so on.

Accordingly, this person's First Luck Pillar is Geng Wu 庚午. His second Luck Pillar is Xin Wei 辛未.

Remember, the Luck Pillars are always plotted from RIGHT to LEFT and not from left to right. This is the standard universal BaZi chart plotting method and should be adhered to at all times when plotting a BaZi chart. Never plot the BaZi Luck Pillars from left to right.

Let's take a look at another example:

Female born August 14, 1971 at 7.18am.

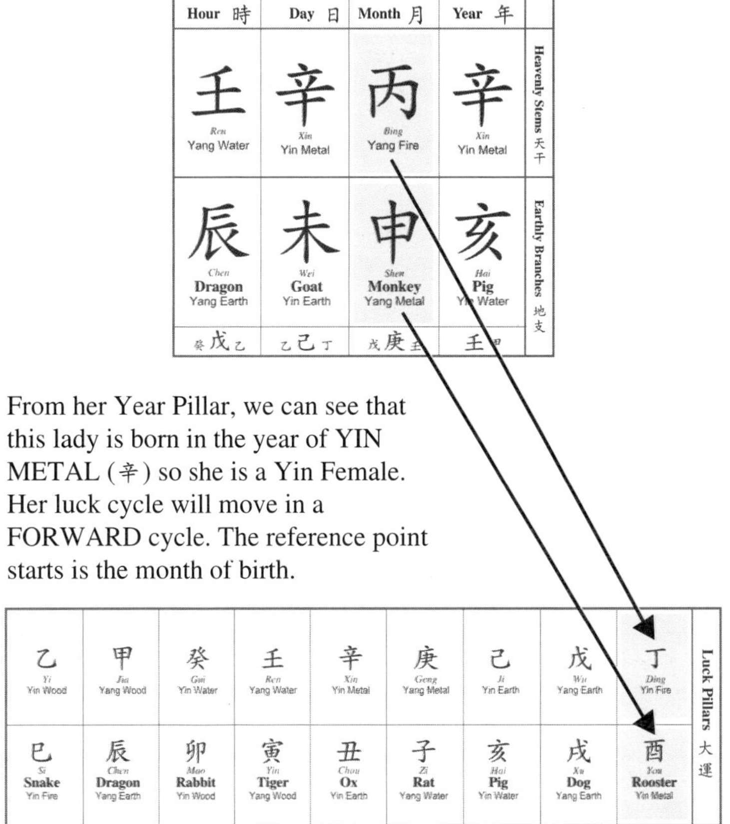

Hour 時	Day 日	Month 月	Year 年	
壬 *Ren* Yang Water	辛 *Xin* Yin Metal	丙 *Bing* Yang Fire	辛 *Xin* Yin Metal	Heavenly Stems 天干
辰 *Chen* **Dragon** Yang Earth	未 *Wei* **Goat** Yin Earth	申 *Shen* **Monkey** Yang Metal	亥 *Hai* **Pig** Yin Water	Earthly Branches 地支
癸戊乙	乙己丁	戊庚壬	壬甲	

From her Year Pillar, we can see that this lady is born in the year of YIN METAL (辛) so she is a Yin Female. Her luck cycle will move in a FORWARD cycle. The reference point starts is the month of birth.

乙 *Yi* Yin Wood	甲 *Jia* Yang Wood	癸 *Gui* Yin Water	壬 *Ren* Yang Water	辛 *Xin* Yin Metal	庚 *Geng* Yang Metal	己 *Ji* Yin Earth	戊 *Wu* Yang Earth	丁 *Ding* Yin Fire	Luck Pillars 大運
巳 *Si* **Snake** Yin Fire	辰 *Chen* **Dragon** Yang Earth	卯 *Mao* **Rabbit** Yin Wood	寅 *Yin* **Tiger** Yang Wood	丑 *Chou* **Ox** Yin Earth	子 *Zi* **Rat** Yang Water	亥 *Hai* **Pig** Yin Water	戌 *Xu* **Dog** Yang Earth	酉 *You* **Rooster** Yin Metal	

Here's another example:

Male born March 11, 1931 at 11.30pm.

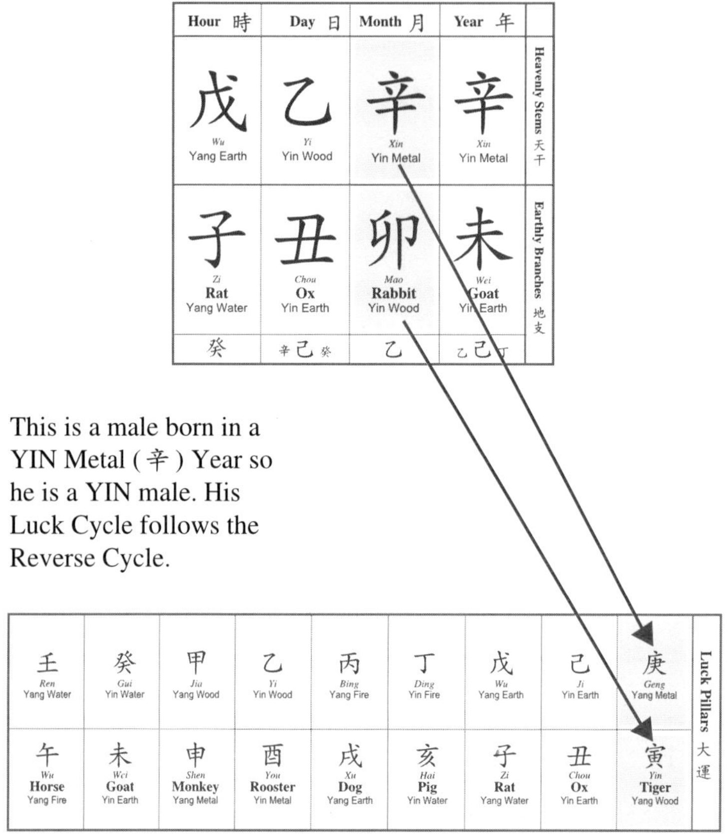

Hour 時	Day 日	Month 月	Year 年	
戊 Wu Yang Earth	乙 Yi Yin Wood	辛 Xin Yin Metal	辛 Xin Yin Metal	Heavenly Stems 天干
子 Zi **Rat** Yang Water	丑 Chou **Ox** Yin Earth	卯 Mao **Rabbit** Yin Wood	未 Wei **Goat** Yin Earth	Earthly Branches 地支
癸	辛 己 癸	乙	乙 己 丁	

This is a male born in a YIN Metal (辛) Year so he is a YIN male. His Luck Cycle follows the Reverse Cycle.

壬 Ren Yang Water	癸 Gui Yin Water	甲 Jia Yang Wood	乙 Yi Yin Wood	丙 Bing Yang Fire	丁 Ding Yin Fire	戊 Wu Yang Earth	己 Ji Yin Earth	庚 Geng Yang Metal	Luck Pillars 大運
午 Wu **Horse** Yang Fire	未 Wei **Goat** Yin Earth	申 Shen **Monkey** Yang Metal	酉 You **Rooster** Yin Metal	戌 Xu **Dog** Yang Earth	亥 Hai **Pig** Yin Water	子 Zi **Rat** Yang Water	丑 Chou **Ox** Yin Earth	寅 Yin **Tiger** Yang Wood	

Reverse Cycle means from Xin 辛 (the Heavenly Stem for the month of birth), the next in the cycle is Geng 庚, and following Geng 庚 is Ji 己 and after Ji 己 is Wu 戊 and so forth in reverse order. In the Earthly Branches, after Mao 卯 (Rabbit) will be Yin 寅 (Tiger) and after Yin 寅 (Tiger) will be Chou 丑 (Ox) and so forth in reverse order. This is the Reverse Cycle.

One final example:

Female born on January 6, 1969 at 4.16pm

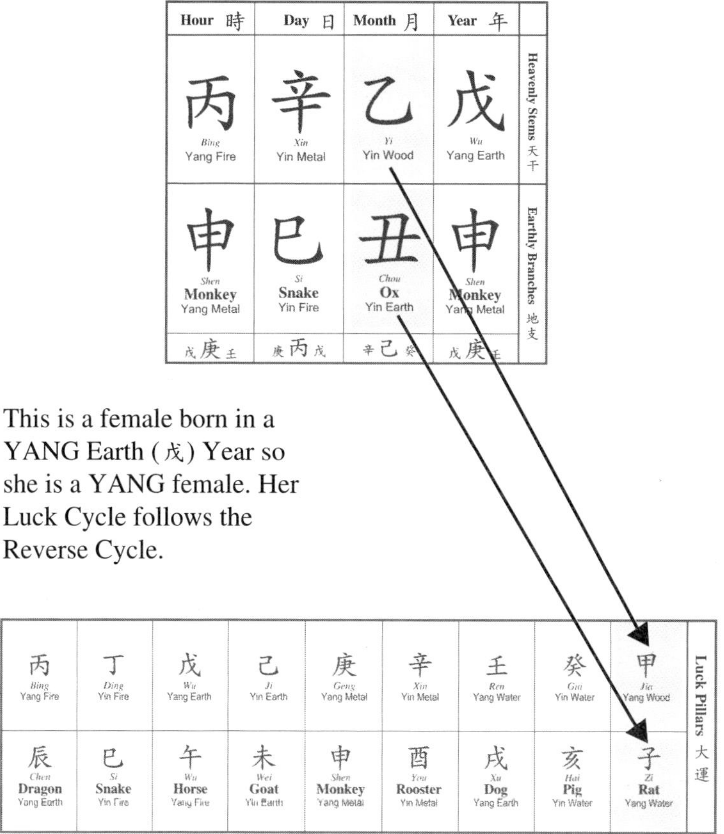

From the month pillar Yi Chou 乙丑, the luck pillar will be plotted in reverse order. From Yi 乙 Stem, the next stem, in reverse order will be Jia 甲, and then followed by Gui 癸 and then by Ren 壬 and so fourth. From month of Chou 丑, the luck pillar's month branches will be plotted in the reverse order. So the luck pillars branches will start with Zi 子 (Rat), and then followed by Hai 亥 (Pig), and then Xu 戌 (Dog) and so fourth.

Practice Time

It is time now to plot your own BaZi chart and your Luck Pillars. If you have a spouse or a partner, do theirs too. Practice makes perfect. Then proceed to the next step.

Calculating the age limits

Now, the Luck Pillars, which tell us WHAT kind of luck a person is undergoing, are not much use unless we know WHEN the years are good and when they are less favourable.

Therefore, the final step in plotting the dynamic aspect of a BaZi chart is to calculate the Age Limit.

The Age Limit marks of the blocks of Luck Pillars. Each Luck Pillar is a block of 10 years but what we need to know is WHEN that block of 10 years starts and ends, which is the Age Limit.

Age Limits vary from person to person - they can range from 0-10 for each block. The most important piece of information for calculating the Age Limit is the Day of Birth and whether the Luck Cycle is a Forward or Reverse Cycle.

Remember how you determine if it is a Forward or Reverse Cycle? Here is the Table for your reference again, just in case.

Forward Cycle	Yang Male, Yin Female
Reverse Cycle	Yin Male, Yang Female

Transition Date	Earthly Branch of the month		Seasons
February 4th	寅 Yin	Tiger	Spring
March 6th	卯 Mao	Rabbit	
April 5th	辰 Chen	Dragon	
May 6th	巳 Si	Snake	Summer
June 6th	午 Wu	Horse	
July 7th	未 Wei	Goat	
August 8th	申 Shen	Monkey	Autumn
September 8th	酉 You	Rooster	
October 8th	戌 Xu	Dog	
November 7th	亥 Hai	Pig	Winter
December 7th	子 Zi	Rat	
January 6th	丑 Chou	Ox	

The above chart is a quick reference for the Monthly Transition Dates. You should always double check the Monthly Transition Date using the Ten Thousand Year Calendar. (Sometimes the transition date varies by a day, so to be sure, check it up.)

Now, here's how we calculate the Age Limits

Step 1:
Determine if it is a Forward or Reverse Cycle.

Step 2:
Calculate the number of days between the Date of Birth and the nearest Forward or Reverse Monthly Transition Date. Exclude from your calculation the day of birth.

Step 3:
Divide the number of days between the Date of Birth and the nearest Monthly Transition Date by 3.

Let's look at a couple of examples so you can get an idea of how the calculation works:

Male born May 14, 2004 at 5.14am.

Hour 時	Day 日	Month 月	Year 年	
乙 *Yi* Yin Wood	癸 *Gui* Yin Water	己 *Ji* Yin Earth	甲 *Jia* Yang Wood	Heavenly Stems 天干
卯 *Mao* **Rabbit** Yin Wood	巳 *Si* **Snake** Yin Fire	巳 *Si* **Snake** Yin Fire	申 *Shen* **Monkey** Yang Metal	Earthly Branches 地支
乙	庚 丙 戊	庚 丙 戊	戊 庚 壬	

戊 *Wu* Yang Earth	丁 *Ding* Yin Fire	丙 *Bing* Yang Fire	乙 *Yi* Yin Wood	甲 *Jia* Yang Wood	癸 *Gui* Yin Water	壬 *Ren* Yang Water	辛 *Xin* Yin Metal	庚 *Geng* Yang Metal	Luck Pillars 大運
寅 *Yin* **Tiger** Yang Wood	丑 *Chou* **Ox** Yin Earth	子 *Zi* **Rat** Yang Water	亥 *Hai* **Pig** Yin Water	戌 *Xu* **Dog** Yang Earth	酉 *You* **Rooster** Yin Metal	申 *Shen* **Monkey** Yang Metal	未 *Wei* **Goat** Yin Earth	午 *Wu* **Horse** Yang Fire	

Step 1:
Determine if it is a Forward or Reverse Cycle.

This person is born on a Wood Monkey (Jia Shen 甲申) Year. He is a Yang Male. Accordingly, his Luck Cycle is a Forward Luck Cycle.

Step 2:
Calculate the number of days between the Date of Birth and the nearest Forward or Reverse Monthly Transition Date.

The number of days from May 15 and June 5, the nearest Monthly Transition Date going through the FORWARD cycle is 22 days, counting from May 15th onwards.

Step 3:
Divide the number of days between their Date of Birth and the nearest Monthly Transition Date by 3.

22 divided by 3, which is 7.3. Round up 7.3 to the nearest number, which is 7. His Age Limit starts from the age of 7. He will enter his first luck pillar at 7 years old. His next Luck Pillar is 17 since Luck Pillars are in blocks of 10 years.

The Age Limits for the Luck Pillars

87	77	67	57	47	37	27	17	7	
戊 *Wu* Yang Earth	丁 *Ding* Yin Fire	丙 *Bing* Yang Fire	乙 *Yi* Yin Wood	甲 *Jia* Yang Wood	癸 *Gui* Yin Water	壬 *Ren* Yang Water	辛 *Xin* Yin Metal	庚 *Geng* Yang Metal	**Luck Pillars** 大運
寅 *Yin* **Tiger** Yang Wood	丑 *Chou* **Ox** Yin Earth	子 *Zi* **Rat** Yang Water	亥 *Hai* **Pig** Yin Water	戌 *Xu* **Dog** Yang Earth	酉 *You* **Rooster** Yin Metal	申 *Shen* **Monkey** Yang Metal	未 *Wei* **Goat** Yin Earth	午 *Wu* **Horse** Yang Fire	

Here's another example, but this time, a Female born August 14, 1971 at 7.18am.

Hour 時	Day 日	Month 月	Year 年	
壬 *Ren* Yang Water	辛 *Xin* Yin Metal	丙 *Bing* Yang Fire	辛 *Xin* Yin Metal	Heavenly Stems 天干
辰 *Chen* **Dragon** Yang Earth	未 *Wei* **Goat** Yin Earth	申 *Shen* **Monkey** Yang Metal	亥 *Hai* **Pig** Yin Water	Earthly Branches 地支
癸戊乙	乙己丁	戊庚壬	壬甲	

乙 *Yi* Yin Wood	甲 *Jia* Yang Wood	癸 *Gui* Yin Water	壬 *Ren* Yang Water	辛 *Xin* Yin Metal	庚 *Geng* Yang Metal	己 *Ji* Yin Earth	戊 *Wu* Yang Earth	丁 *Ding* Yin Fire	Luck Pillars 大運
巳 *Si* **Snake** Yin Fire	辰 *Chen* **Dragon** Yang Earth	卯 *Mao* **Rabbit** Yin Wood	寅 *Yin* **Tiger** Yang Wood	丑 *Chou* **Ox** Yin Earth	子 *Zi* **Rat** Yang Water	亥 *Hai* **Pig** Yin Water	戌 *Xu* **Dog** Yang Earth	酉 *You* **Rooster** Yin Metal	

Step 1:
This is a lady born in a Yin Year so she is a Yin Female and her Luck Cycle is a Forward Cycle.

Step 2:
We count the number of days from August 15th until September 8, the nearest Monthly Transition Date going through the FORWARD cycle. The difference is 25 Days.

Step 3:
25 divide by 3 is 8.3, rounded off to the nearest number is 8. Accordingly, her age limit starts with 8 and she enters her first luck pillar at 8 years old.

Another example to make sure you understand.
Male born on March 11, 1931 at 11.30pm.

Hour 時	Day 日	Month 月	Year 年	
戊 *Wu* Yang Earth	乙 *Yi* Yin Wood	辛 *Xin* Yin Metal	辛 *Xin* Yin Metal	Heavenly Stems 天干
子 *Zi* **Rat** Yang Water	丑 *Chou* **Ox** Yin Earth	卯 *Mao* **Rabbit** Yin Wood	未 *Wei* **Goat** Yin Earth	Earthly Branches 地支
癸	辛 己 癸	乙	乙 己 丁	

82	72	62	52	42	32	22	12	2	
壬 *Ren* Yang Water	癸 *Gui* Yin Water	甲 *Jia* Yang Wood	乙 *Yi* Yin Wood	丙 *Bing* Yang Fire	丁 *Ding* Yin Fire	戊 *Wu* Yang Earth	己 *Ji* Yin Earth	庚 *Geng* Yang Metal	Luck Pillars 大運
午 *Wu* **Horse** Yang Fire	未 *Wei* **Goat** Yin Earth	申 *Shen* **Monkey** Yang Metal	酉 *You* **Rooster** Yin Metal	戌 *Xu* **Dog** Yang Earth	亥 *Hai* **Pig** Yin Water	子 *Zi* **Rat** Yang Water	丑 *Chou* **Ox** Yin Earth	寅 *Yin* **Tiger** Yang Wood	

Step 1:
He is born in a Yin Year so he is a Yin Male. His Luck Cycle is a Reverse Cycle.

Step 2:
We count the number of days between his Date of Birth and the nearest Monthly Transition Date going BACKWARDS, which is March 6. The difference is 5 days. (We count backwards here because he follows a Reverse Cycle)

Step 3:
5 divide by 3 is 1.6, which is rounded off to 2. So his age limit starts at 2 and he enters his first luck pillar at 2 years old.

Another example: Female born on January 6, 1969 at 4.16pm

Hour 時	Day 日	Month 月	Year 年	
丙 *Bing* Yang Fire	辛 *Xin* Yin Metal	乙 *Yi* Yin Wood	戊 *Wu* Yang Earth	Heavenly Stems 天干
申 *Shen* **Monkey** Yang Metal	巳 *Si* **Snake** Yin Fire	丑 *Chou* **Ox** Yin Earth	申 *Shen* **Monkey** Yang Metal	Earthly Branches 地支
戊 庚 壬	庚 丙 戊	辛 己 癸	戊 庚 壬	

80	70	60	50	40	30	20	10	0	
丙 *Bing* Yang Fire	丁 *Ding* Yin Fire	戊 *Wu* Yang Earth	己 *Ji* Yin Earth	庚 *Geng* Yang Metal	辛 *Xin* Yin Metal	壬 *Ren* Yang Water	癸 *Gui* Yin Water	甲 *Jia* Yang Wood	Luck Pillars 大運
辰 *Chen* **Dragon** Yang Earth	巳 *Si* **Snake** Yin Fire	午 *Wu* **Horse** Yang Fire	未 *Wei* **Goat** Yin Earth	申 *Shen* **Monkey** Yang Metal	酉 *You* **Rooster** Yin Metal	戌 *Xu* **Dog** Yang Earth	亥 *Hai* **Pig** Yin Water	子 *Zi* **Rat** Yang Water	

This is a Yang Female so we need to follow the Reverse Cycle. Her date of birth is January 6. The nearest transition date counting 'reverse' or backwards is January 5, which is only 1 day. Divide 1 by 3 is 0.3. Her age limit starts at 0 and she enters her first Luck Pillar at age 0.

BaZi Shortcut: Watch the Transition Years

The Luck Pillars are a very quick and immediate way to check your BaZi. The Luck Pillars usually represent years of capital transformation or change in your life. Things look up, proceed more smoothly, hidden talents appear, and opportunities that weren't there before suddenly appear.

Remember that the reference years in the Luck Pillars are your Chinese Age. What is this Chinese age? The Chinese count the 9 months spent in the womb of the mother as one year so everyone is born as one year old. Accordingly, a person's Chinese Age is his/her Western age, plus one year. Thus if you are 42 by the Western calendar this year, you are considered 43 in the Chinese age.

The Big Picture

This is a snapshot of a computer-generated BaZi, from the Joey Yap BaZi Ming Pan calculator at www.masteryacademy.com
It is best if you practice manually plotting the charts before resorting to using the calculator. I have explained here, each aspect of information that is derived from the Joey Yap BaZi Ming Pan calculator.

- The Ten Gods will be examined as you progress to higher levels of BaZi. They are basically manifestation of the basic Five Factors that we will discuss in Chapter 7. Each Ten God is actually a "Star Name" and nothing to do with the spiritual deities. They are just verbatim translations of special BaZi terms.

- Noble Man Star is not your "Secret Helper". This star is derived based on your Day Master and indicates the presence of helpful people in your life.

Why Learn about Luck and Destiny?

You have now learnt how to plot a full BaZi chart and in the chapters to follow, we'll be looking at how to analyse and 'de-code' a BaZi chart to establish a person's Destiny Code. This code holds the story of your life, your character, your talents, your future possibilities.

For the Feng Shui practitioner, BaZi is an indispensable tool, providing the diagnosis that forms the foundation for the prescription in Feng Shui. This is because Feng Shui only helps if a person has a good Destiny and suitable Luck in the first place. By studying a person's Destiny and Luck, we can then find out what is the 'real' problem and proceed to take the correct Man Luck (human actions) or Feng Shui (for those who practice this art) to help find a solution or resolution. BaZi is perhaps one of the most important diagnosis tools to understand a person.

Contrary to popular misconception, Feng Shui is not a one-cure-for-all art - what works for one person, will not always produce the same results for another (the moral of the story: don't copy someone else's Feng Shui!)

A little story on BaZi

A wealthy client called me to carry out a Feng Shui audit for his home. He was having money problems, but not a lack of it. Rather, his children were busy jostling and fighting over their inheritance, despite the fact that their father was still hale and healthy with plenty of good years ahead.

His home had been Feng Shui-ed - a so called "Water Dragon Formula" had been applied to increase his wealth. Unfortunately, this was a bad idea. Why?

My client's BaZi chart revealed that he was going through strong Wealth Luck. The powerful Water Formula that enhanced his wealth even further ended up throwing everything out of balance in his life. He had too much wealth and it was the root cause of his family problems!

Now you might be thinking: why is Joey against his client having more money luck?

This is a good point to go back to the introduction of the book and read it again! But let me save you the time and say it again:

Feng Shui is not about Wealth Creation
It's all about BALANCE.

In BaZi there is a saying, too much wealth deteriorates the health.(財多身子弱)

Remember the early section about how Feng Shui, BaZi and personal actions are all inter-dependent? Accordingly, a good Feng Shui practitioner will use BaZi to look at what should and should not be done with the Feng Shui to ensure that it produces a harmonious outcome and strengthens the weak areas (ie: family life, personal relationships), rather than one that throws the person's life into turmoil, all in the name of 'wealth enhancement'.

A Feng Shui practitioner also must work within the ambits of what Heaven has given a person in his or her Destiny. So wealth enhancement for someone who cannot take it is like giving penicillin to someone who is allergic to penicillin - the outcome is never pretty!

Understanding your Luck and Destiny will enable you to find out what's in store for you and help you plan ahead.

Remember the old saying: Failing to Plan is Planning to Fail. BaZi is all about making the best use of your life, avoiding the pitfalls and maximising your gains in favourable times.

Your Luck Pillars reveal to you where and what you should focus on to make the best out of your life and which areas will be causing you much heartache and setbacks. BaZi is about making Informed Decisions in life.

Same Time, Same Day, Same Month, Same Year - Why am I not a millionaire?

One question that I often get when it comes to BaZi is this: if two people are born on the same year, month, day and hour, does this mean that they all have the same Destiny?

If you happen to have the exact birth data, down to time, as say Bill Gates or Donald Trump, or Warren Buffett and you are reading this book, then you have your answer.

There are additional XX Factors in play that impact on the level of greatness a person can achieve assuming they have a superior BaZi chart to begin with.

Feng Shui's Influence

Yang and Yin House Feng Shui play a great role in determining how much of the potential contained in your Destiny Code can be unleashed.

You might have the same date and time of birth as Bill Gates, but if you aren't living in the same place he is living, knowing the same group of people he knows, meeting the same people he has met, you don't get to maximise your 'potential' as much as he does. Nevertheless, since you still share the same BaZi, you might enjoy similar greatness, just on a different level!

For example, a person sharing the same BaZi chart as Mr. Bill Clinton or Mr. George Bush but living in another country may not rise to become President of the United States but he or she may well achieve political success in his or her own country. This person is still a President of a country - he or she is just not the President of the United States. It is all a case of the playing field that you are in and where you get to unleash the potential of your BaZi.

Then there is the Yin House Factor. Yes, you have the exact same birth data, even time of birth, as Bill Gates, but are your ancestors buried in the same place as his? Yin House Feng Shui is the most powerful form of Feng Shui and plays an extremely important role in determining the quality of a family's fortune.

Qian Long Emperor's Tomb in Beijing

Emperors of the past from various Chinese Dynasties have painstakingly sought superior burial grounds solely to ensure a lasting dynasty. It is for this reason that the Ming Dynasty lasted for more than 300 years and the Qing Dynasty for 260 years. How many 'dynasties' of the business world today survive past the 3rd generation? Not too many unfortunately. This is the Yin House factor.

Ultimately, all things being equal, why does one person rise up and tower above the others - the answer probably lies in the graves of his/her ancestors. Ancestors who are buried in good locations with powerful Feng Shui give their descendants an added edge, icing on the cake that enables their descendants to enjoy good luck or power or wealth or all if the location is truly superb.

This is a book about BaZi so I will not dwell too much on the issue of the Yin House Feng Shui. Suffice to say that when the question arises as to how two people born on the exact same day, in the exact same time, may have different levels of greatness - the ancestral grave may hold the key!

If you wish to know a little bit more about Yin and Yang House Feng Shui - my book "Stories and Lessons on Feng Shui" has some of these fascinating stories about Yin House Feng Shui.

Besides the Feng Shui, look at the Face

Every year, I conduct an annual forecast talk for over a thousand Chinese Astrology and Feng Shui enthusiasts who wish to know more about the Feng Shui and Astrology for the year.

Once, during a Question and Answer session, a lady stood and asked a very pertinent and relevant question. She said: "There are thousands of people born in the same animal year and probably using the same Feng Shui door, how can they all suffer the same 'bad' luck?"

My answer was this: the thousands of people born in the same year using the same Feng Shui sector in their respective houses don't share the same face!

The Chinese Art of Face Reading or Mian Xiang explains how different features from the face reveal different fortunes and outcomes. By reading a person's Eyes, Nose, Ear, Mouth, Eyebrows, Forehead and other facial features, the fortunes of a person can also be ascertained.

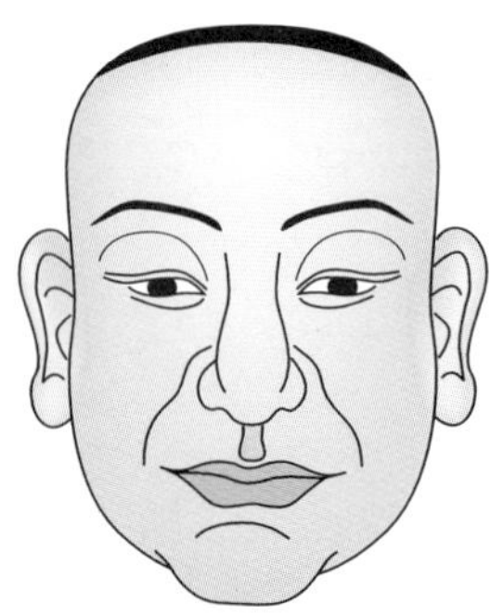

So much so, individuals can have the same BaZi, but since they all have different faces, they will all have different outcomes in life. Even twins, who share the same BaZi, do not share the same destiny.

The Things That You Do (or Don't)

Ultimately, making the right choice is what helps to swing your life one way or another. Remember Man Luck? Having the same BaZi as Bill Gates is no use if you don't utilise the potential - there is no shortcut to greatness, even with a superb BaZi. Actions set individuals with the same BaZi apart. Two people may share the same BaZi, but they may not take the same action when faced with a similar fork in the road.

A good BaZi chart is the basis of a good life and good luck. A good ancestral burial spot, and a good fortune face are icing on the cake. To have a good BaZi chart (such as being born on the same date and time as Bill Gates!) is already a tremendous advantage in life.

You may not play in the same field as he does, or be as rich as he is, but you arguably will not be a slouch either. (And remember, you will only have half of his problems!)

A good BaZi is like owning a Ferrari. You must know how to drive it and know what it is capable of doing. If you do nothing with it or drive it on bumpy roads all the time, it would be a waste of an excellent vehicle.
The best tool in the world must still be wielded by a master!

Now that you have better understood the potential of BaZi, let's get on with some analysis!

Chapter Five:
BaZi Fundamentals

An analyst is only as good as his tools. Now that you have learnt how to plot a BaZi chart and the Luck Pillars, you have two-thirds of the tools needed to analyse a BaZi chart and decode your own Destiny Code.

The most critical component to BaZi analysis is a mastery of the Five Elements and an understanding of the basic principles of Yin and Yang and Qi.

At any point in your BaZi studies, even as you advance past this book to more advanced materials, always try to co-relate everything you learn with these three key concepts: Yin and Yang, Qi and the Five Elements.

Yin and Yang 陰陽

There exist two opposing, inter-dependant and inter-related forces in our Universe. Yin and Yang are natural forms of energy that are in a constant state of change, movement and interaction. This dynamic relationship creates and governs all life. From Birth, Growth, Sickness and Death 生老病死, the stages of existence are in constant evolution.

The interaction of Yin and Yang is reflected by Night and Day, Positive and Negative, Active and Passive, Hard and Soft, Fast and Slow, Male and Female, Hot and Cold, Anger and Happiness, and so forth. We can see this interplay in nature in the form of the Four Seasons where Yang is reflected as the peak of summer and Yin in the coldness of winter.

Yin and Yang are therefore the two primordial forms of Qi. The interaction between Yin and Yang subsequently relates to the Five Phases of Qi, known as the Five Elements.

Let's relate this concept to BaZi. The BaZi chart has a Static and Dynamic quality – Yin and Yang. Luck, as I have said earlier, can never be always good or always bad. Again, this goes back to the principle of Yin and Yang.

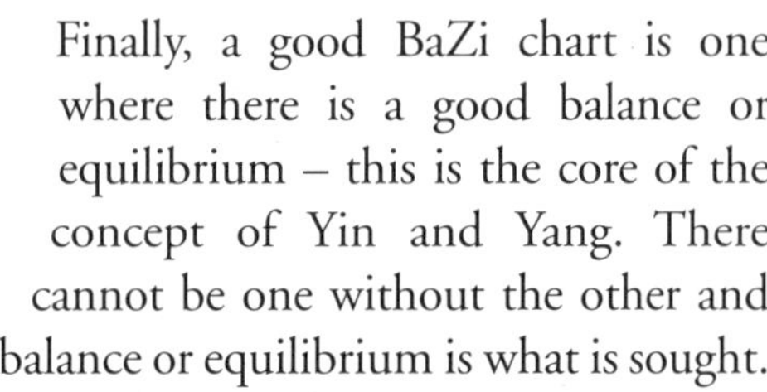

Finally, a good BaZi chart is one where there is a good balance or equilibrium – this is the core of the concept of Yin and Yang. There cannot be one without the other and balance or equilibrium is what is sought.

Now, with this very elementary knowledge of Qi and Yin and Yang, what can we deduce from a BaZi chart? Well, if the chart is predominantly Yin elements or Yang elements, we can automatically deduce that the particular BaZi chart is not very good because there is no balance of Yin and Yang. Why? Because anything that is too Yang or too Yin indicates a disharmony between the elements. Individuals with such charts may be lonely, or unable to express their emotions effectively.

A person's chart is completely Yang or completely Yin when ALL the Heavenly Stems and Earthly Branches in the BaZi are of the same polarity.

Every Heavenly Stem and Earthly Branch has its unique Yin or Yang polarity. Refer to the table on the next page for reference on their polarity.

The 10 Heavenly Stems 天干

Heavenly Stems	Element and Polarity
甲 *Jia*	Yang Wood
乙 *Yi*	Yin Wood
丙 *Bing*	Yang Fire
丁 *Ding*	Yin Fire
戊 *Wu*	Yang Earth
己 *Ji*	Yin Earth
庚 *Geng*	Yang Metal
辛 *Xin*	Yin Metal
壬 *Ren*	Yang Water
癸 *Gui*	Yin Water

The 12 Earthly Branches 地支

Earthly Branches	Animal Sign	Element
子 *Zi*	Rat	Yang Water
丑 *Chou*	Ox	Yin Earth
寅 *Yin*	Tiger	Yang Wood
卯 *Mao*	Rabbit	Yin Wood
辰 *Chen*	Dragon	Yang Earth
巳 *Si*	Snake	Yin Fire
午 *Wu*	Horse	Yang Fire
未 *Wei*	Goat	Yin Earth
申 *Shen*	Monkey	Yang Metal
酉 *You*	Rooster	Yin Metal
戌 *Xu*	Dog	Yang Earth
亥 *Hai*	Pig	Yin Water

Qi 氣 – The Essence of Life

Qi (pronounced as 'chee') is life force energy - it cannot be seen or heard. However, its influence can be felt around us and in all places. It is the invisible force that shapes, nurtures and governs all living beings.

From the peaks of the highest mountains to the depths of the deepest oceans, the flow of the rivers to the undulating ridges of the land, and from busy malls to the quaint little corners of the street – Qi permeates our world. Qi is the force that brings life to all beings.

What does Qi have to do with BaZi? In BaZi, we are studying the Qi that makes up and influences a person's life at the time of his/her birth: the Year Qi, the Month Qi, the Day Qi and the Hour Qi.

The Eight Characters, the Destiny Code that forms the BaZi chart, represents the type of Qi that is infused in us at the time of our birth. The Luck Pillars represent the changing or moving Qi that will influence us along the path of life. In a good BaZi chart, the Qi flows naturally through the chart and is not disrupted by too many clashes. The interaction and interrelations between the Qi of your BaZi chart and its corresponding Luck Pillars are your Destiny.

The Five Elements (Wu Xing 五行)

The theory of the Five Elements is the backbone of all Chinese Metaphysical studies – Feng Shui, Astrology, Chinese Medicine and even Martial Arts. I cannot overstate the importance of grasping the Five Elements when it comes to BaZi. The principle of the Five Elements is the core science of decoding a person's Destiny Code.

In the olden days, students of Chinese Metaphysics, especially in the professional field of Feng Shui, had to undertake BaZi studies as well. This is because BaZi gives the individual an extremely firm grasp and understanding of the Five Elements, which enables him/her to understand Feng Shui formulas better and apply them correctly. It is also because BaZi works hand in hand with Feng Shui in many aspects that a thorough understanding of BaZi is important in order to be able to effectively practice Feng Shui.

BaZi is akin to the diagnosis of a doctor. It probes the person's life to enable the practitioner to assess the past, present and future life-path. BaZi enables the Feng Shui practitioner to understand what the inherent problems are and where the potential dangers lie. When practitioners then apply Feng Shui, it is akin to a prescription to help smoothen the life path or perhaps to rectify certain problems or potential pitfalls. Hence, without proper diagnosis (BaZi), it is difficult to prescribe a remedy (Feng Shui).

Strictly speaking, the English term 'Five Elements' is not very accurate and perhaps even a little deceptive. It is supposed to be a translation of the Chinese term Wu Xing, which means the five transformations or five phases. The Five Elements – Wood, Water, Fire, Earth, Metal – are in fact the result of the interaction between Yin and Yang Qi during the five different phases – they are transformations of Qi.

The Five Elements represent certain key attributes in a person's chart. For example, Water represents a person's wisdom. A good quality Water element indicates a person is wise and intelligent and is capable of thinking clearly and acting astutely in appropriate instances. Conversely, a poor quality Water element indicates a person who is slow-witted, foolish, misguided or irrational in his/her thinking.

The element of Wood relates to the person's benevolence and gratitude. People who have a good heart, a positive outlook in life and those who are progressive in nature, have good quality Wood elements in their chart. Those who lack kindness or compassion, and who are unable to make progress in life, invariably have poor quality Wood elements.

The element of Fire is extremely important because it governs a person's elegance and mannerisms. A good Fire element in the chart denotes that the person behaves appropriately, elegantly and graciously. Fire also represents passion – a poor quality Fire element belongs to an individual who gets depressed easily and often feels inadequate.

How do you know if a person can be trusted? Look at his or her Earth element because Earth represents trustworthiness. Excessive or a lack of Earth elements causes problems with the person's stability.

Finally, the element of Metal – Metal is what gives a person decisiveness, a sense of justice and righteousness. A good quality Metal element in a person's chart means a person has good leadership and decision-making ability.

The Five Elements in Interaction

The Five Elements each have three distinctive reactive relationships with each other: a Productive relationship, a Controlling relationship and a Weakening relationship. We refer to these as the Productive Cycle, the Controlling Cycle and the Weakening Cycle.

The Productive Cycle 生

The productive cycle is a phase where the Elements support and strengthen each other. In this phase, the relationship is supportive, giving, attractive, pleasing and generous. This cycle is in harmony and in constant movement. In the productive cycle, the elements feed and support each other. The Qi flows smoothly.

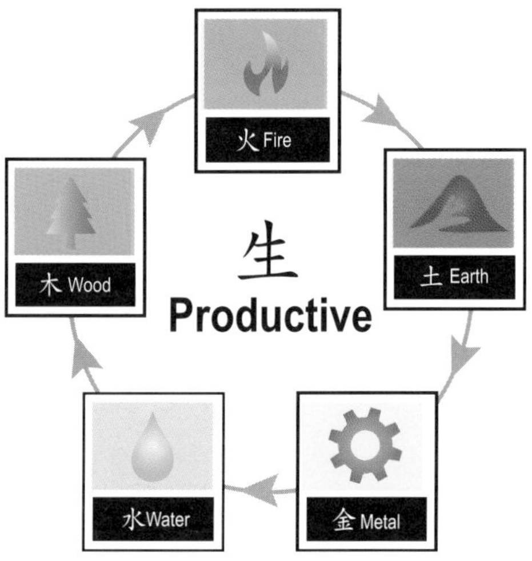

The Cycle can be easily remembered if we rationalise the cycle and see it in a logical manner.

Water nourishes plants: thus Water produces Wood. Wood is used to make Fire; so Wood produces Fire. Fire in turn burns material into ashes and forms Earth. Fire produces Earth. Earth is where we can find minerals. So Earth produces Metal. Metal through condensation produces Water, thus Metal produces water.

The Controlling Cycle 剋

At first glance, the word 'controlling' sounds negative. Many newcomers to the subject of Five Elements tend to see 'controlling' as something unfavourable or despotic. This is far from the truth. In the context of the Five Elements, 'controlling' merely means to guide and to keep in order.

In the area of Chinese Metaphysics, the translation of the term from Chinese to English sometimes results in some confusion because it is not possible to exactly translate the words. The Chinese word is "Ke 剋". There is no actual and accurate translation for this word. The closest words are to Control, to Counter or to Destroy.

It's not correct to classify the Controlling Cycle as 'good' or 'bad'. Remember Yin and Yang? There are always two sides of a coin. A world without control is a world without law and order and chaos reigns. So control is good if it brings order. Proper control denotes responsibility, stability and peace. On the other hand, too much control becomes a dictatorship and a stifling situation - so too much control is not desirable either.

Good Control is akin to the control of a mother over her child. The mother exercises restriction and concern over her child's actions and behaviour so that her child would not be endangered or grow up to become a bad person. Bad Control is analogous to an abusive parent, beating up his child, causing emotional torment and physical pain.

So remember, it is fine to 'control'. Control brings order and direction to an element. Thus it is always desirable to have appropriate controlling element in your BaZi.

However, to 'over-control', now that is different because 'over-control' involves excessive restriction or stifling. Over-control brings hatred, anger and frustration.

The Controlling Cycle is how the Five Elements interact to manage, manipulate, restrain or influence each other.

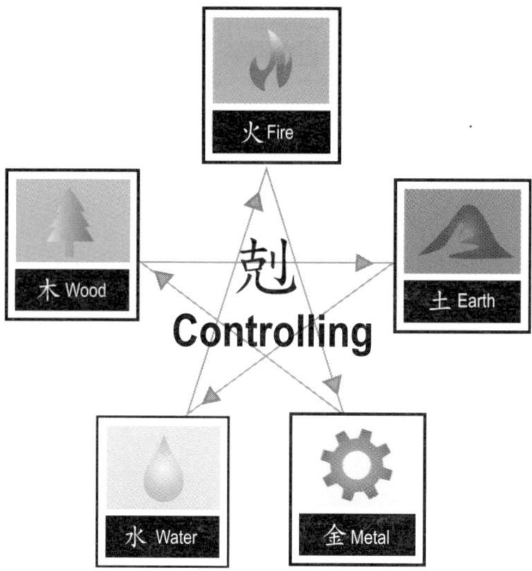

Learning the Controlling Cycle is relatively easy as long as you focus on thinking pictorially and using logical deduction. In the Controlling sequence, Water controls Fire because Water puts out fire. When the weather is hot, you drink more water to cool down your body temperature or jump into a pool.

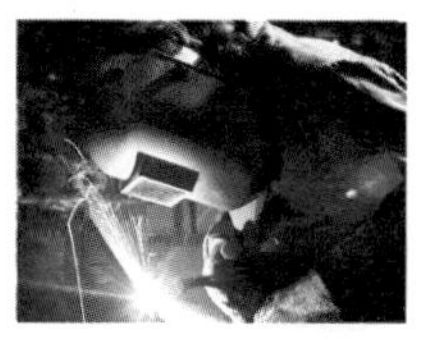

Fire controls Metal because the heat of Fire melts and molds Metal. This is how raw iron is molded into useful tools or machinery.

Metal controls Wood – why? Because a large tree or a small bush is cut and trimmed using objects made from Metal, such as an axe or a saw, scissors and blades.

Wood controls Earth. How do you prevent a landslide? You plant trees, shrubs and bushes to hold the Earth together.

Earth controls Water because no matter how large the lake or ocean is, it is still bordered by Earth. A large river can be blocked off by a dam. Earth holds water.

The Weakening Cycle 洩

The third cycle is called the Weakening Cycle. Once again, do not jump to conclusions about 'Weakening' being negative just because it weakens. Remember, in BaZi we are striving for balance.

When an element in the chart is excessively strong, it should be weakened to a certain extent so that there is balance among the elements.

Weakening actually means an element has "produced" another element. It is like a product or an invention. Energy is consumed to generate something.

Why do we have a Weakening Cycle? Any object that is produced weakens what produced it. For example, if a mother gives birth or delivers a baby, her energy and stamina is weakened. The Weakening Cycle exemplifies this within the context of the Five Elements.

Thus, when an element produces another, it is weakened by its product. For example, when Earth produces Metal, Metal become stronger while Earth depletes in strength. Now, think pictorially: if you mine for minerals (Metal) inside the Earth, don't you have to dig and penetrate the Earth, weakening the Earth?

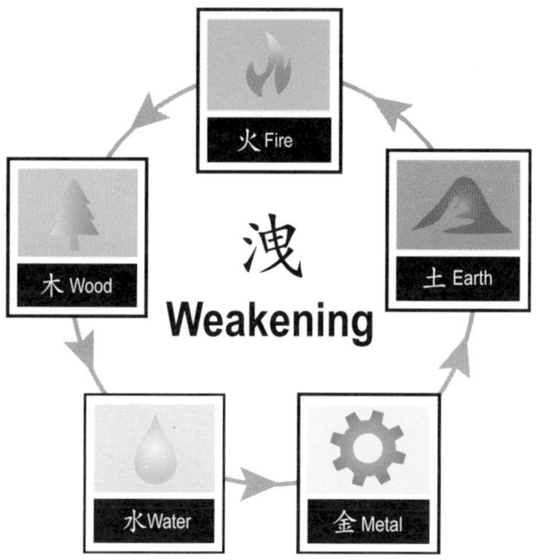

Metal needs to liquefy to produce Water; hence, Water weakens Metal. Water is used to nourish plants. When the plants absorb the water, Water's energy is consumed. Hence, Wood weakens Water.

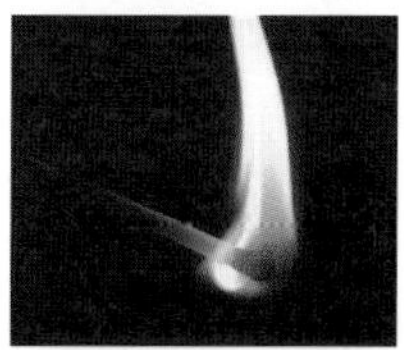

When we want to make Fire, we burn Wood. Fire consumes the Wood and produces heat. So Wood is weakened by Fire Element.

Fire burns and produces ashes, dust and earth. After combusting everything into ashes, Fire will extinguish naturally. Thus, Earth weakens Fire.

Connecting the Elements

By understanding the nature and order of the Five Elements, we are able to understand the Qi balance in a BaZi and in turn, see the strengths and flaws of a person. In a BaZi chart where the Five Elements are balanced, the Qi flows smoothly and this denotes a good life.

Now, once you have mastered the Five Elements and the three Cycles, you need to place the Five Elements within the context of the 10 Heavenly Stems and the 12 Earthly Branches.

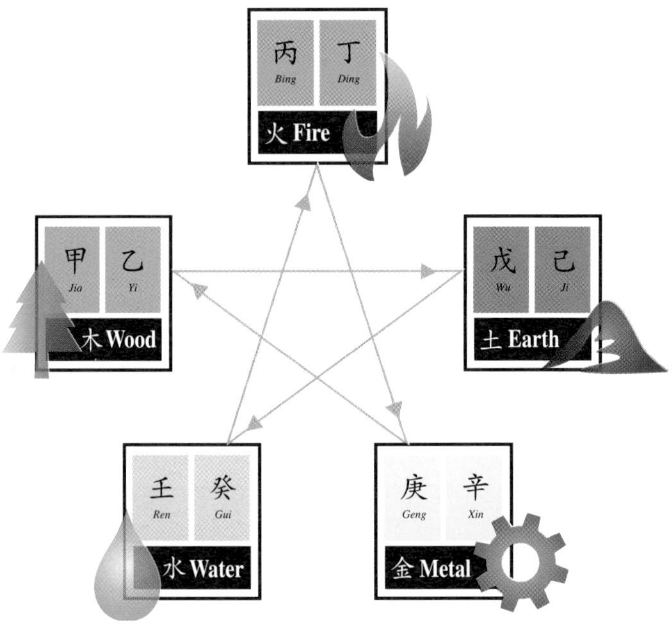

The Heavenly Stems Five Element Cycle Relationship

The Earthly Branches Five Element Relationships

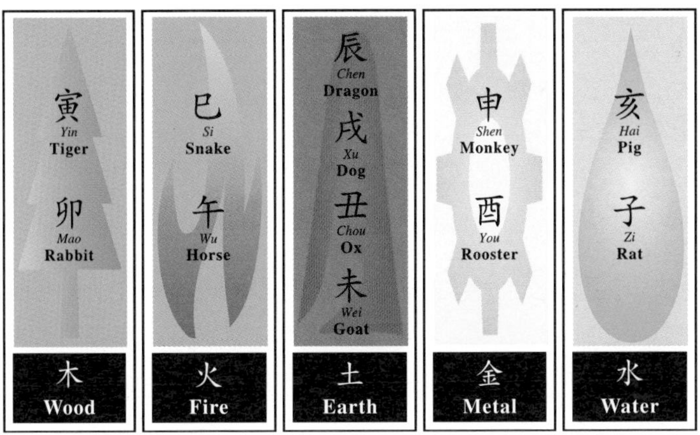

A BaZi chart consists entirely of the Five Elements, as represented by the Heavenly Stem and Earthly Branches. When we are examining the inter-relationship and interaction between the Heavenly Stems and Earthly Branches, we use the Five Elements to understand and appreciate the relationship. Accordingly, it is good to try to commit to memory the Five Element cycles – this will help you a lot as you progress through this book. Alternatively, bookmark this section so that you can keep referring back to the Five Element cycles.

A little teaser: the Five Elements in your BaZi chart will subsequently transform to five main key aspects in a person's life – I call them the Five Factors: Wealth, Influence, Companion, Resource and Output. These Five Factors will help you decode your Destiny Code.

It is essential to convert your understanding of the Five Elements into Heavenly Stems or Earthly Branches. For instance, Jia 甲 and Yi 乙 Wood will produce Bing 丙 /Ding 丁 Fire, control Wu 戊 / Ji 己 Earth and weakens Ren 壬 /Gui 癸 water. Follow the diagram below to familiarise yourself with the Five Element cycle using the Heavenly Stems format.

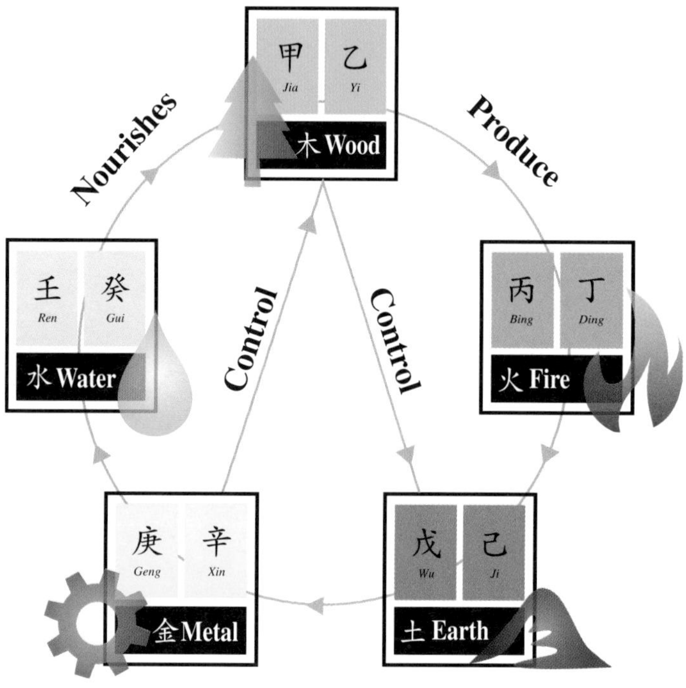

After you've achieved a firm grasp on the Five Elements, proceed to the next chapter. We are going to do some analysis!

Chapter Six:

Finding the Favourable Element

Despite its over-use in this world, the concept of Yin and Yang is the core and an essential part of Chinese Metaphysical subjects such as Feng Shui and BaZi. At the center of the concept of Yin and Yang is the idea of equilibrium.

Hence, when evaluating a BaZi chart, we are really looking to see if the chart has a good balance of elements. We don't want in a BaZi too few or too many of certain elements, or certain elements being too weak or too strong either. Balance is the key.

Balance carries a different meaning in each chart. Sometimes, charts are in themselves fairly well-balanced, comprised mainly of Favourable Elements – these are considered superior charts. Other times, a chart is strongly dependant on a single element to bring balance. If this 'balancing' element is not only in the chart, but is of 'good' quality, then the chart is still considered a superior chart.

B-Grade charts, or less superior charts, are usually charts where the chart is not balanced intrinsically, and the element that is needed to balance the chart is of poor quality. In C or D-Grade charts, the balancing element is not the best choice for the particular Day Master.

Hence, an important part of evaluating a BaZi chart is the process of weighing the strengths and weaknesses of the Five Elements in the chart and determining which are the crucial elements that either bring balance to the chart or maintain the balance in the chart.

Now, since there are only Five Elements, the process of elimination is a relatively easy process. The difficulty lies in determining WHICH of the Five Elements it is and in the case of certain charts, where 2 or 3 of the elements appear to hold the key to the balance of the chart, which is the BEST element to chose.

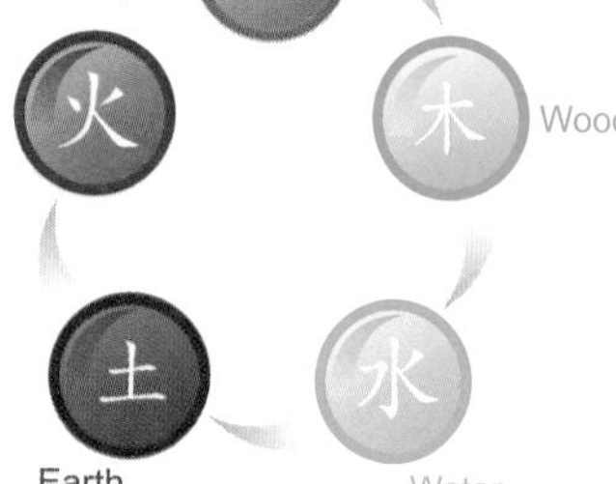

Now of course, you might be asking yourself: is there such a thing as a perfectly balanced chart?

Remember, the quantity of the elements is not the indicator of balance. In BaZi, we must not ever be fixated on quantity when it comes to finding the chart's balance or conducting a BaZi analysis. We must always be looking at quality. Having an equal number of all the elements is by no means the definitive means of judging whether or not a BaZi chart is balanced. The quality of the elements is also an important consideration.

What do we mean when we talk about the quality of the elements? We are evaluating whether these elements are sentimental or antagonistic and whether or not there is a smooth inter-dependant relationship between the elements. Does the Qi flow smoothly in the chart? Is each element interdependent on one another?

Begin with the Day Master

The reference point for ANY BaZi chart is always the Day Master. Quick reminder: the Day Master is the Heavenly Stem found in the Day Pillar. The Day Master is also known as the *Self Element.*

Day Master

Hour 時	Day 日	Month 月	Year 年

The first step in evaluating a BaZi is to determine the strength of the Day Master. To do this, we look at the Earthly Branch found in the Month Pillar. This is known as identifying the SEASON of your birth.

Hour 時	Day 日	Month 月	Year 年

Month of Birth's Earthly Branch

You do not need to be concerned with the entire Month Pillar, just look at the month of birth's Earthly Branch. This is the first and most important step in analysing a BaZi chart.

The Earthly Branch of the Month Pillar is known as the Yue Ling 月令 or Season Master. The Strength of the Day Master is almost always evaluated with reference to the SEASON.

At this point, you might be wondering – what is all this talk about the seasons? What if I live in New Foundland where it's cold 9 months of the year? Or in Malaysia where there is no winter? Or in Australia, where Christmas is probably the hottest time of the year?

The concept of the Seasons in BaZi is simply a form of descriptive terminology. It is not based on the real climates or the real seasons changing.

Remember how the ancient sages used household domestic animals to describe the Earthly Branches? Similarly, the use of the seasons is just a code to describe the Strength of the Qi of a particular element.

子 *Zi* Rat	丑 *Chou* Ox	寅 *Yin* Tiger	卯 *Mao* Rabbit	辰 *Chen* Dragon	巳 *Si* Snake
午 *Wu* Horse	未 *Wei* Goat	申 *Shen* Monkey	酉 *You* Rooster	戌 *Xu* Dog	亥 *Hai* Pig

So how do you know which Season you are born in? Look at the chart below:

寅 *Yin* Tiger	卯 *Mao* Rabbit	辰 *Chen* Dragon
Feb	Mar	Apr
春 Spring		
巳 *Si* Snake	午 *Wu* Horse	未 *Wei* Goat
May	Jun	July
夏 Summer		
申 *Shen* Monkey	酉 *You* Rooster	戌 *Xu* Dog
Aug	Sept	Oct
秋 Autumn		
亥 *Hai* Pig	子 *Zi* Rat	丑 *Chou* Ox
Nov	Dec	Jan
冬 Winter		

The table on the page before explains which animal sign of the Earthly Branches belongs to which season. It is useful to commit to memory the information in the table on the previous page. For example, it's helpful to be able to remember that Yin 寅 (Tiger), Mao 卯 (Rabbit) and Chen 辰 (Dragon) as 'Spring' and Si 巳 (Snake), Wu 午 (Horse) and Wei 未 (Goat) are 'Summer'.

So what does the season have to do with the strength of the Day Master or Self Element? You see, in each season, certain elements are stronger or weaker. Wood, for example, is very strong in Spring while Fire is prosperous in Summer.

It's not difficult to remember which element is strongest in which season if you utilise the pictorial method. What flourishes blooms and grows during Spring? The trees, the flowers, the grass – all which are represented by Wood. At the height of summer, naturally, Fire is strong because Summer is when it is hottest.

You might be thinking – there are Five Elements, but only Four Seasons – so what is the season of Earth? Earth is read rather uniqucly, and determining how to read Earth lies in the 'ending' month of each season. For example, the Chen 辰 (Dragon) month is the last month of Spring, so people born in the Chen 辰 (Dragon) month are considered to have Spring Earth. The Wei 未 (Goat) month is regarded as the last month of Summer and is regarded as Summer Earth. The Xu 戌 (Dog) month is the Autumn Earth while the Chou 丑 (Ox) month is the Winter Earth.

Earth Months	Season
辰 **Dragon**	Spring Earth
未 **Goat**	Summer Earth
戌 **Dog**	Autumn Earth
丑 **Ox**	Winter Earth

Strength Of The Elements

死 Dead	囚 Trap	休 Weak	相 Strong	旺 Prosperous	Strength / Season
土 Earth	金 Metal	水 Water	火 Fire	木 Wood	春 Spring
金 Metal	水 Water	木 Wood	土 Earth	火 Fire	夏 Summer
木 Wood	火 Fire	土 Earth	水 Water	金 Metal	秋 Autumn
火 Fire	土 Earth	金 Metal	木 Wood	水 Water	冬 Winter

The above chart describes the Five stages of strength for each of the Five Elements, with reference to the Four Seasons. This chart provides a very simple and quick means to evaluate the strength of a Day Master based on the season of birth.

The Four Seasons

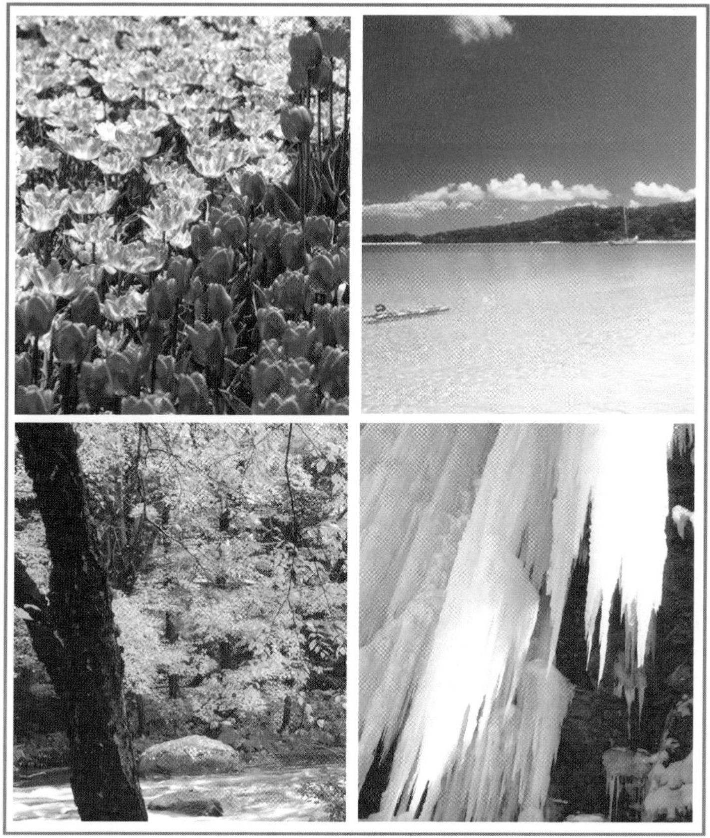

In this section, I delve a little more deeply into how the seasons are used to evaluate the strength of the Day Master or Self Element. Remember at all times while you are reading through this book to think pictorially. Finally, look out for key words like PROSPEROUS, WEAK, TRAP, STRONG and DEAD – these are the keys to appreciating the importance of the seasons in evaluating a person's BaZi. Also, remember to think about the Five Element cycle pictorially and not just the Production Cycle, but the Controlling and the Countering Cycle.

Spring Season

Spring is the season of Wood, hence Wood is the most prosperous element. Thus, a Wood Day Master (meaning Jia 甲 or Yi 乙 Wood) born in any of the Spring season's Earthly Branches, namely Yin 寅 (Tiger), Mao 卯 (Rabbit) or Chen 辰 (Dragon), it is considered to be a Day Master born in a timely, prosperous season. This means the Wood is vibrant and thriving.

Hour 時	Day 日	Month 月	Year 年
	甲 / 乙 Jia Yi		
		寅/卯/辰 Yin Mao Chen Tiger Rabbit Dragon	

In the Five Elements, Wood produces Fire, so Fire in the month of Spring is also considered strong, with long lasting flames of the fire. Thus, Fire element is strong in Spring.

Hour 時	Day 日	Month 月	Year 年
	丙 / 丁 Bing Ding		
		寅/卯/辰 Yin Mao Chen Tiger Rabbit Dragon	

In Spring, Wood is strong, thus Water is weak. Why? Remember the Five Elements? Think now of the Weakening Cycle. When Wood is so prosperous and strong, it naturally 'consumes' a lot of Water. But Water is not completely drained of Qi either because the Spring season comes just after Winter and Winter is the season of Water. Hence, Water is weak in Spring.

Hour 時	Day 日	Month 月	Year 年
	壬/癸 Ren Gui		
		寅/卯/辰 Yin Mao Chen Tiger Rabbit Dragon	

In Spring, Metal is considered to be trapped – this means the Qi is frail and fragile. Furthermore, in Spring, Wood is strong, vibrant and thriving. Metal, which in the Five Elements Controlling Cycle, controls Wood, cannot do so and will be blunted from all the chopping of wood.

Hour 時	Day 日	Month 月	Year 年
	庚/辛 Geng Xin		
		寅/卯/辰 Yin Mao Chen Tiger Rabbit Dragon	

In the season of Spring where Wood rules supreme, Earth would be dead. Why? Because in the cycle of the Five Elements, Wood controls Earth. As Wood is very strong, it will over-control Earth, therefore making Earth very weak.

Hour 時	Day 日	Month 月	Year 年
	戊/己 Wu Ji		
		寅/卯/辰 Yin Mao Chen Tiger Rabbit Dragon	

Although the Chen 辰 (Dragon) element is Earth, it is still the Spring season where Wood Qi is strong. Thus this type of Wu 戊 /Ji 己 Earth in this month looks hard and thick, but is actually weak inside. This concept of analysing Earth is slightly sophisticated and I will elaborate on it in later books – right now, treat this as just a taster and don't worry if you don't understand the concept right away.

Summer Season

In Summer season, because it is the season of Fire , clearly Fire is the most prosperous element. So a Fire Day Master (meaning Bing丙 or Ding丁) born in any of the Summer season Earthly Branches - Si巳(Snake), Wu午(Horse), Wei未(Goat) it is considered to be born in a timely, prosperous season. This means the Fire is very vibrant, shining and bright.

Hour 時	Day 日	Month 月	Year 年
	丙/丁 Bing Ding		
		巳/午/未 Si Snake, Wu Horse, Wei Goat	

As Fire produces Earth in the Five Element cycle, so an Earth Day Master (meaning Wu戊 or Ji己) born in the month of Summer is considered strong.

Hour 時	Day 日	Month 月	Year 年
	戊/己 Wu Ji		
		巳/午/未 Si Snake, Wu Horse, Wei Goat	

In the season of Fire, Wood will be weak. Why? Wood is weak because when Fire is so prosperous, a lot of Wood will be 'consumed' for it to burn brightly. But Wood cannot be regarded as totally and extremely weak because Summer is just one season away from Spring (which is the season of Wood) so Wood Qi is weak in Summer.

Hour 時	Day 日	Month 月	Year 年
	甲 / 乙 *Jia* *Yi*		
		巳/午/未 *Si* Snake *Wu* Horse *Wei* Goat	

Water is very weak in Summer. As the heat of Summer is strong, Water will evaporate. Water is in the trap stage of Qi during summer months, meaning Qi at this stage is frail and fragile.

Although in the Controlling Cycle, Water controls Fire, in Summer, Fire is very strong so Water, which is already weak, cannot control Fire adequately.

Hour 時	Day 日	Month 月	Year 年
	壬 / 癸 *Ren* *Gui*		
		巳/午/未 *Si* Snake *Wu* Horse *Wei* Goat	

In the season of Summer when Fire rules supreme, Metal is dead. Why? Because in the cycle of the Five Elements, Fire will control Metal. As Fire is extremely powerful and strong, it will over-control the Metal element, thus Metal will be very weak.

Hour 時	Day 日	Month 月	Year 年
	庚/辛 *Geng* *Xin*		
		巳/午/未 *Si* *Wu* *Wei* **Snake Horse Goat**	

Autumn Season

Autumn is the season of Metal, so we say that Metal is the most prosperous element. So a Metal Day Master (meaning Geng 庚 or Xin 辛) born in any of the Autumn season Earthly Branches - Shen 申 (Monkey), You 酉 (Rooster) and Xu 戌 (Dog) is considered to be born in a timely, prosperous season. This means the Metal is very shiny, strong and beautiful.

Hour 時	Day 日	Month 月	Year 年
	庚 / 辛 Geng Xin		
		申 / 酉 / 戌 Shen You Xu Monkey Rooster Dog	

Metal produces Water, so Water in the month of Autumn is also considered strong.

Hour 時	Day 日	Month 月	Year 年
	壬 / 癸 Ren Gui		
		申 / 酉 / 戌 Shen You Xu Monkey Rooster Dog	

In the season of Metal, Earth will be weak. Why? Because for Metal to be so prosperous, a lot of Earth will be dug up to produce Metal. However, the Earth element cannot be regarded as completely weak because Autumn is just one season away from Summer (which is the season of Fire) so there's plenty left over of Earth (remember, Earth is also strong in Summer). So we say Earth Qi is only weak (but not that weak) in Autumn.

Hour 時	Day 日	Month 月	Year 年
	戊/己 Wu Ji		
		申/酉/戌 Shen You Xu Monkey Rooster Dog	

Fire is very weak in Autumn – it is in the trap stage of Qi, meaning Qi at this stage is frail and fragile. Now, in the Controlling Cycle of the Five Elements, Fire controls Metal. But in Autumn, Metal is so strong - Fire cannot heat, mold or melt the excess metal. Fire is outnumbered and weak.

Hour 時	Day 日	Month 月	Year 年
	丙/丁 Bing Ding		
		申/酉/戌 Shen You Xu Monkey Rooster Dog	

In the Metal season of autumn where Metal Qi rules supreme, Wood would be dead. Again, let's refer to the Five Elements, Metal controls Wood but since this is over-control of an element, Wood will be very weak.

Hour 時	Day 日	Month 月	Year 年
	甲/乙 Jia Yi		
		申/酉/戌 Shen You Xu Monkey Rooster Dog	

Winter Season

Winter is the season of Water so Water is the most prosperous element. A Water Day Master (meaning Ren 壬 or Gui 癸) born in any of the Winter season's Earthly Branches Hai 亥 (Pig), Zi 子 (Rat) and Chou 丑 (Ox) is considered to be born in a timely, prosperous season. This means the Water is very strong, radiant and flowing.

Hour 時	Day 日	Month 月	Year 年
	壬/癸 Ren Gui		
		亥/子/丑 Hai Zi Chou Pig Rat Ox	

Water produces Wood, so Wood in the month of Winter is also considered strong.

Hour 時	Day 日	Month 月	Year 年
	甲/乙 Jia Yi		
		亥/子/丑 Hai Zi Chou Pig Rat Ox	

In the season of Water, Metal will be weak. Why? Because for Water to be so prosperous, Metal will be exhausted by the task of condensing water. However, the Metal element cannot be regarded as completely weak because Winter is just one season away from Autumn (which was the season of Metal) so there's plenty left over of Metal Qi. So we say Metal Qi is weak in Winter.

Hour 時	Day 日	Month 月	Year 年
	庚/辛 *Geng* *Xin*		
		亥/子/丑 *Hai* *Zi* *Chou* **Pig** **Rat** **Ox**	

Earth Qi is very weak in Winter – it is in the trap stage of Qi, meaning Qi at this stage is frozen and hardened. Now, in the Controlling Cycle of the Five Elements, Earth is supposed to control Water. But in Winter, Water is so strong and Earth is frozen - it cannot control the excess Water. Earth is flooded and weak.

Hour 時	Day 日	Month 月	Year 年
	戊/己 *Wu* *Ji*		
		亥/子/丑 *Hai* *Zi* *Chou* **Pig** **Rat** **Ox**	

In the season of Winter where Water Qi rules supreme, Fire would be dead. Again, let's refer to the Five Elements, Water controls Fire but since this is over-control of an element, Fire will be completely extinguished.

Hour 時	Day 日	Month 月	Year 年
	丙/丁 *Bing* *Ding*		
		亥/子/丑 *Hai* *Zi* *Chou* **Pig** **Rat** **Ox**	

The Season Says It All

You might be wondering, hey what about the other Heavenly Stems and Earthly Branches in the BaZi chart? Don't they count towards something? **Yes of course they do**, and as your understanding of BaZi develops, the other Heavenly Stems and Earthly Branches will come into play. Even then, they are of 'secondary' importance. The primary indicator of the strength of every chart is significantly dependent on the month of birth as this dictates the seasonal Qi strength.

The above method of determining the strength of the Day Master based on the Season is just the first step in the study of BaZi. There are always exceptions to the general principles and other more sophisticated techniques of evaluating Day Masters, as well as exceptions that relate to the 'condition' of the Day Masters - this will be discussed in my more advanced books. This is a beginners' book so I have begun with simple ideas, concepts and techniques designed to enable you to be able to engage in analysis by the end of this book.

Having said that, basing the judgment of the Day Master's strength on the month of birth is by and large still the most accurate means of quickly and simply evaluating the strength of a BaZi. As you progress through this book and the other books in this series, you will be exposed to more sophisticated techniques for evaluating the Day Master's strength. But for now, stick to the month of birth.

In later books, I will share with you more sophisticated concepts, methods and techniques on determining the Day Master's strengths.

Finding the Favourable Element

After you've determined the strength of the Day Master through the season of your birth month, you need to determine which is the most Favourable Element that the BaZi chart needs to achieve balance.

The concept of balance is not an easy one. If only it were as simple as making the number of elements add up! In essence, in the study and practice of BaZi, what we are looking for is a Day Master that is not too weak, not too strong, but just right.

Take a look at this example:

Hour 時	Day 日	Month 月	Year 年
	甲 *Jia*		
		午 *Wu* Horse	

This is a Wood Day Master born in the month of Wu 午 (Horse). Which season does the Horse month belong to? Summer. This Wood is born at the height of Summer, when Fire is the strongest.

Now, remember, think pictorially. If Fire is strong, it will consume Wood. Wood Qi in Summer month is considered weak. So what then is the Favourable Element? Whatever strengthens and supports the Wood, which in this case is Water.

How do we arrive at this conclusion? Let's think about the Five Element cycle and use it to eliminate the possibilities.

Weak Wood does not need to be weakened any further, but strengthened. Fire, as we already know, consumes wood, therefore weakening it. So Fire cannot be the Favourable Element. Weak Wood does not want to be chopped by Metal either, so Metal is not the Favourable Element. So what grows Wood then? Water, hence Water is the Favourable Element.

What does this mean now that we've found the Favourable Element?

After pinpointing the Favourable Element, let's evaluate the person's luck based on his or her Luck Cycle. If this person is to go through the Water element in the Luck Pillars or Annual Pillars, then this person will experience good fortune and his life path is likely to be smooth and generally not too difficult during these years.

Example:

By contrast, if he were to go through the Fire element in his Luck pillars, he will suffer bad fortune or bad luck. What is this bad luck? It may mean obstacles in life, difficulties with relationships with those around him – generally, a less than smooth situation.

Hour 時	Day 日	Month 月	Year 年
	甲 Jia		
		午 Wu Horse	

									Luck Pillars 大運
			未 Wei Goat	午 Wu Horse	巳 Si Snake				

Fire luck (未 Goat, 午 Horse, 巳 Snake)

Useful God vs Favourable Element

If you've had some exposure to BaZi, you may have heard of this concept called the Useful God or Yong Shen 用神 in Chinese. This is an advanced BaZi concept that will be covered in my next book. Remember, the journey of a thousand miles begins with the first step. Practice familiarising yourself with the Five Elements and finding the Favourable Element first.

Don't be misled into thinking beginner's material is not useful. Sometimes, like all wisdom in life, the most profound things are often the simplest ones. Complicated techniques do not always necessarily ensure accuracy or the right answer and in Chinese Metaphysical studies, we must always remember to go back to the basics and key principles.

Your goal at this point (and by the end of this book) is to be able to tell whether a person is currently undergoing good or bad luck and when they will experience good or bad luck. Focus on answering this question first – the rest will come as you progress through this book and this BaZi series (I promise!)

命運密碼

The HAVE and The HAVE NOTS

Let's look at the same BaZi chart but change a few elements a little bit and you'll see how the situation is very different.

Example A:

Hour 時	Day 日	Month 月	Year 年
	甲 *Jia*		癸 *Gui*
		午 *Wu* **Horse**	

Example B:

Hour 時	Day 日	Month 月	Year 年
	甲 *Jia*	丙 *Bing*	
		午 *Wu* **Horse**	

Now, both A and B are born in the SAME MONTH – based on our earlier analysis, we concluded that a Jia 甲 person born in a Horse 午 month would have Water as his Favourable Element and Fire as his Unfavourable Element.

In example A above, there is a Gui 癸 Water in the Year Stem and in example B, there is Bing 丙 Fire in the Month Stem. Which is the better BaZi chart?

A's chart is better because there is a Favourable Element present in the chart. In B's chart, not only there is NO Favourable Element, but there is an additional Unfavourable Element Bing 丙 Fire right in the month pillar. So, the person

in example B must wait until he goes through Water Element years in his Luck or Annual Pillars to have the benefit of his Favourable Element. The person in example A by contrast already has the Water Element in his BaZi to help him out.

What do these two examples, coupled with the earlier example show us? How we separate the wheat from the chaff – what is a good chart and a not-so-good chart.

Remember, the chart WITH the Favourable Element actually present is always better than the one without the Favorable Element in it.

What if both charts also have the Favourable Element? Then your comparison would be which one is in a better 'position' in the chart than the other.

Let's try another example:

Hour 時	Day 日	Month 月	Year 年
	庚 *Geng*		
		申 *Shen* **Monkey**	

This Day Master is Geng 庚 Metal born in the Shen 申 (Monkey) Metal month. Shen 申 (Monkey) is the season of Autumn. In Autumn, Metal is prosperous so clearly, this is a strong, prosperous Metal Day Master.

Since it is strong Metal, what element do you think is this chart's Favourable Element and Unfavourable Element?

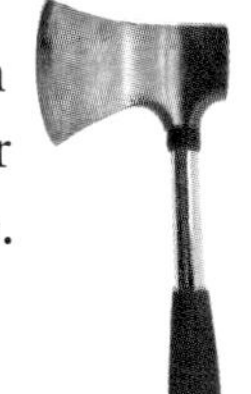

Geng 庚 is raw metal or iron ore. Metal that has been dug out from the Earth is useless unless it is forged or molded into something useful, like a sword or an axe. So strong Metal needs Fire to make it useful.

So you might be thinking – easy, obviously the Favourable Element for this chart is Fire right?

Flip back to the section on the Four Seasons which explains the strength of each of the Five Elements in the individual seasons. Remember, that in Autumn, Fire is in the trap stage. It is weak and fragile. Imagine weak Fire trying to mold and melt a huge boulder of raw metal ore – this would be extremely difficult.

So, what is the solution? We need to feed the Fire a little to make it strong. So some Wood would be helpful. So the Favourable Element in this chart would be BOTH Fire and Wood. Which means, if this chart encounters Fire and Wood in the Luck Pillars, this person will enjoy good luck.

Hour 時	Day 日	Month 月	Year 年
	庚 Geng		
		申 Shen Monkey	

									Luck Pillars 大運
					丁 Ding				
					卯 Mao Rabbit				

Ding 丁 Mao 卯 (Fire and wood) Luck Pillar brings good fortune to this chart

Does this chart need more Metal element? Definitely not. Why not? It is already strong Metal, so more Metal would not balance out the Qi. Remember what I said earlier about how a chart had to be balanced? The Day Master should neither be too strong nor too weak. Too strong an element is a flaw in the BaZi chart and means that when the person goes through Metal element pillars in the Luck Cycle, he will not enjoy good fortune.

Hour 時	Day 日	Month 月	Year 年
	庚 *Geng*		
		申 *Shen* **Monkey**	

				庚 *Geng*	辛 *Xin*				**Luck Pillars** 大運
				申 *Shen* **Monkey**	酉 *You* **Rooster**				

Metal (Rooster and Monkey) Luck Pillar brings bad fortune to this chart

The chart reading will of course be a little more complicated than this because there are Eight Characters instead of just a few we've chosen as examples. Sometimes, in BaZi, people get confused because they try to look at a BaZi and derive everything from it all at one go. The trick with BaZi is to always focus on looking for one thing at a time. At this stage, concentrate on evaluating the BaZi based on the Strength of the Day Master.

Joey Yap's Quick Guide to Assessing the Favourable Element

These are very simplified guidelines that will enable a QUICK evaluation of the Favourable Element. BaZi is a layered and deep subject so to keep things simple, I have come up with these general guidelines. As your knowledge of BaZi grows and deepens, the exceptions to these guidelines are easier to understand. But for now, you may utilise these guidelines to help you analyse your own chart.

The key to utilising these guidelines is to first determine if your Day Master is **Strong** or **Weak**.

The Strong Day Master

Strong Day Master Favours	Controlling another element
	Being Controlled by another element
	Producing another element

If your Day Master is STRONG, your choices of Favourable Elements are

- the Element the Day Master controls
- the Element that controls the Day Master
- the Element that the Day Master produces.

Now, you might be curious as to why?

Remember again what I said earlier about *Balance*. We want a Day Master that is not too strong, not too weak.

If your Day Master is strong, you should make it less strong to achieve balance. How do we reduce the strength? Now, let's think Five Elements again.

By 'controlling' another element, the Day Master has to exert strength. So a strong Day Master will usually favour the element it controls. A strong Day Master can also keep its excessive strength in control by being controlled by another element.

For example, very strong Geng 庚 Metal needs to be kept in shape by the Fire element. Since Fire controls Metal in the Five Element cycle, Fire is needed to mold the excessive Metal.

A strong Day Master can also achieve balance by producing an element. Remember the Five Elements Cycle? To produce something, the Day Master's strength will be reduced. So, using the example of Strong Wood (i.e Wood born in Spring or in Winter season), we can say that Fire is a Favourable Element because Fire will consume some of the excessive Wood Qi, thus, weakening the Wood slightly.

Remember, if your Day Master is strong, it should either Control, Be Controlled or Produce.

Now, what is *Unfavourable* then for a Strong Day Master? Clearly, that which is already strong does not need to be strengthened even more as this will lead to imbalance. So, any element that adds to the strength of the Day Master will be considered Unfavourable.

Strong Day Master Dislikes	The same element
	The element that produces the Day Master

If for example your Day Master is a Strong Gui 癸 Water, your chart will not favour any additional Water obviously. Your Day Master would also not favour Metal because Metal produces Water, thus adding to its strength and making the BaZi imbalanced.

Remember, if your Day Master is strong, it does not need the same element or the element that produces it. Why? Because the same element and the element that produces the Day Master only serves to make it even stronger!

The Weak Day Master

Weak Day Master Favours	The same element
	The element that produces the Day Master

Things are a bit easier if the Day Master is Weak. If your Day Master is weak, then your choices for Favourable Elements can only be the element that produces your Day Master or the element that is the same with the Day Master. Why?

A Weak Day Master needs more of the same element to be stronger (imagine a puddle of water that has more water added to it – doesn't it get stronger?) or the element that produces it, which has the effect of creating more of the Element.

So if you are a weak Ren 壬 Water for example, Water and Metal would be your Favourable Elements.

Weak Day Master Dislikes	Controlling another element
	Being Controlled by another element
	Producing another element

What are the elements that a weak Day Master dislikes? A weak Day Master does not like to be further 'controlled' by an opposing element since it is already weak and more control will be 'over-control! (Remember what we said earlier about how over-control is not desirable?).

A weak Day Master also does not like to have to produce more because this weakens it even further by depleting its strength. A weak Day Master also does not like to Control another element as this saps its strength as well.

Analyse This

Now that you have established your Favourable and Unfavourable Element, you can begin to determine not just your own Luck Cycle (whether you are currently going through Good or Bad Luck) but also utilise this knowledge to unlock your Destiny Code and the meaning behind the elements in your BaZi.

Chapter Seven:
The Five Factors

命裡有時終須有，命裡無時莫強求

If it is destined to be in your life, you will eventually get it, but if you are not destined to have such a thing, don't force it, let it be. - Chinese Saying

At this stage, you should already be familiar with your own BaZi chart and the various elements in your chart. You would also have identified your Day Master and determined your Favourable and Unfavourable Elements.

In this chapter, we look at the question of just what all those different elements really mean.

Your BaZi is your Destiny Code. Each of the elements holds within it a meaning. The elements can represent people (such as a superior, an employee or a family member) or actions or personality traits or abilities. At later stages of your studies, you will learn that these elements also represent events and outcomes.

In this chapter, I will explain to you what the elements mean for each of the ten types of Day Masters. Yes, each element means something different to each one of the 10 different Day Masters. Why are there 10 different types of Day Masters? Because there are 10 types of Heavenly Stems and each can be an individual's Day Master.

In case you've forgotten, here are the Ten Heavenly Stems again:

Heavenly Stems	Element and Polarity
甲 *Jia*	Yang Wood
乙 *Yi*	Yin Wood
丙 *Bing*	Yang Fire
丁 *Ding*	Yin Fire
戊 *Wu*	Yang Earth
己 *Ji*	Yin Earth
庚 *Geng*	Yang Metal
辛 *Xin*	Yin Metal
壬 *Ren*	Yang Water
癸 *Gui*	Yin Water

As there are Five Elements, so each element represents one of what I call the Five Factors.

What are the Five Factors then? They are:

- Wealth 財星
- Output 食傷
- Influence 官殺
- Resource 印星
- Companion 比劫

Now, the names may not make sense to you at this point in time. The important thing is not to try to put 'dictionary' type meanings to these phrases but to remember that the meaning becomes specific once the context has been ascertained. For now, view them as part of the language of BaZi. You are now starting to learn the language of BaZi. If you want to learn this art, you must learn to speak its language.

Remember also that the elements that represent these Five Factors change, depending on what is your Day Master. So for example, the element of Fire may be the Companion Element for a Fire Day Master, but it will be the Output Element for a Wood Day Master. I must emphasise that at all times, the Day Master is the reference point when evaluating a BaZi chart.

In the following section, I will explain the meaning of each of the Five Factors. Just remember that each factor is neither 'good' nor 'bad'. Whether they are 'good' or 'bad' will depend on whether these are Favourable or Unfavourable Elements.

Throughout this book and this chapter, you must always keep in mind the Five Elements and the various Five Element Cycles – whenever you are not sure, do try to refer back to the Five Elements Cycle, which is reproduced below for your reference.

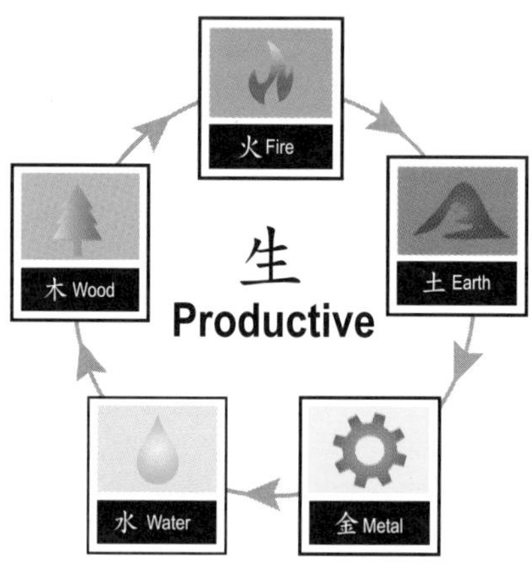

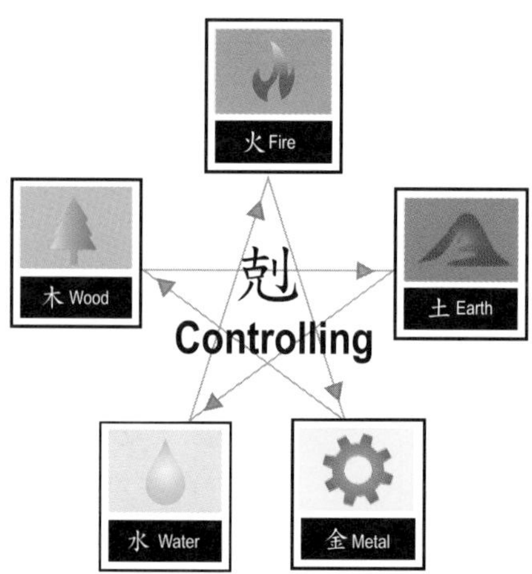

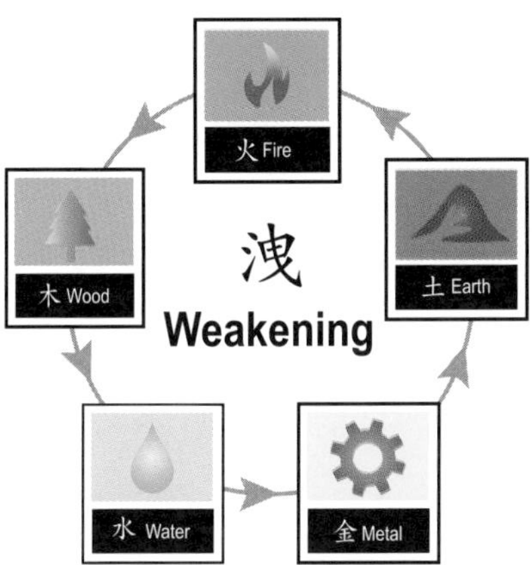

Remember that in BaZi, our goal is about the BALANCE of these elements in the chart!

Wealth 財星

'Money may not help you achieve everything in life, but without money there is a whole lot more you cannot achieve" – Chinese Saying

In this world, whether we like it or not, an individual's financial condition does shape his or her destiny tremendously. There are a lot of things money can't buy, but without money there would be a lot of inconvenience and lack of opportunities.

The Wealth Element in a person's BaZi chart represents direct income and indirect income. Direct income refers to salary or earned and residual income. Indirect income refers to revenue from businesses, your investment portfolio, income from real estate sales, royalties and other investment-related revenue.

The Wealth Element is the element that is controlled by the Day Master in the Five Elements cycle. The rationale for this is quite simple – a person controls his/her assets or property, which is how his/her wealth is established or tabulated. Accordingly, in BaZi, what your Day Master (which represents you) controls therefore represents your wealth.

Sometimes the Wealth Element is referred to as the "Wealth Star". In BaZi terminology, 'Star' and 'Element' are used synonymously and sometimes inter-changeably.

Remember what I said earlier about how BaZi is like an onion with many layers? Well, the Wealth Star, to a Male, also represents his Wife star.

This concept harks back to the old days, when a man's wealth was measured by the number of wives he had and the fact that in the old days, a man's wife was considered his 'chattel'. Thus if a man has a good quality 'Wealth Star' in his Destiny Code, he will also have a very good 'wife'. Vice versa, a poor quality Wealth star denotes a less than desirable wife.

I must emphasise that this principle applies ONLY TO MEN. For Women, the Wealth Element does not represent the husband. For a lady, her husband is represented by what is called the Influence Element. A little patience – we will get there!

A little personal note: in the course of teaching BaZi over the years, I have noticed that some women do not like to be viewed as an 'asset'. I think ladies shouldn't take this concept

too personally. Remember, this is just the way we classify the 'attributes' of the Elements and their relationships in the study of BaZi. This is the way it has been since the inception of BaZi and we should not change this approach just because we 'don't like the idea' of a woman being an asset. I often tell the female students in my class that being viewed as an 'asset' is infinitely better than being classified as a 'liability' surely?

I must emphasise that the Wealth Element need not be 'many' to make a chart of a rich person. It is always the QUALITY and not the QUANTITY that we are concerned with when analysing a person's Destiny Code.

How do you find out what your Wealth Element is? For quick reference, check the chart below to find out what your Wealth Element is. So for example, if you are a Wood Day Master, then your Wealth Element is Earth.

Day Master		Wealth Element
木 Wood	甲, 乙	Earth
金 Metal	庚, 辛	Wood
水 Water	壬, 癸	Fire
土 Earth	戊, 己	Water
火 Fire	丙, 丁	Metal

You will need to know the elements of the Heavenly Stems and Earthly Branches in order to fully appreciate the little table above. In case you have forgotten these elements, here is a quick reference for you:

Heavenly Stems	Element and Polarity
甲 *Jia*	Yang Wood
乙 *Yi*	Yin Wood
丙 *Bing*	Yang Fire
丁 *Ding*	Yin Fire
戊 *Wu*	Yang Earth
己 *Ji*	Yin Earth
庚 *Geng*	Yang Metal
辛 *Xin*	Yin Metal
壬 *Ren*	Yang Water
癸 *Gui*	Yin Water

Earthly Branches		Animal Sign	Element
子 *Zi*	Pronounced as 'Zh-er'	Rat	Yang Water
丑 *Chou*	Pronounced as 'Ch-o' as in the word 'go'	Ox	Yin Earth
寅 *Yin*	Pronounced as 'Yeen' as in the word 'seen'	Tiger	Yang Wood
卯 *Mao*	Pronounced as 'Mow' as in the word 'how'	Rabbit	Yin Wood
辰 *Chen*	Pronounced as 'Ch-earn' with a silent 'r'	Dragon	Yang Earth
巳 *Si*	Pronounced as 'Sir' with a silent 'r'	Snake	Yin Fire
午 *Wu*	Pronounced as Woo	Horse	Yang Fire
未 *Wei*	Pronounced as Way	Goat	Yin Earth
申 *Shen*	Pronounced as 'Sh-earn' with a silent 'r'	Monkey	Yang Metal
酉 *You*	Pronounced as YOU	Rooster	Yin Metal
戌 *Xu*	Pronounced as 'Shoot' with a silent 't'	Dog	Yang Earth
亥 *Hai*	Pronounced as 'Hi' as in hi !	Pig	Yin Water

Keep in mind that each Wealth Element has a Yin and Yang manifestation. In my later books, I will introduce this concept called the Ten Gods (十神), which provides more depth for BaZi analysis and further analyses the Wealth Star as Direct Wealth and Indirect Wealth. In a man's BaZi, the wife is usually represented by the Direct Wealth Star specifically. But to keep things simple for now, we will keep the analysis collectively to just the term Wealth Star.

How do we analyse the Wealth Element? Sometimes in a BaZi chart, you may see the Wealth Element being clashed away. This means that the man may face the possibility of losing wealth at that particular period of time., or may face separation from his wife or the loss of his wife.

For example, a BaZi chart with a Xin 辛 (Yin Metal) Day Master, its Wealth Element is Wood. In this chart, the Wealth Element is the Mao 卯 (Rabbit) Earthly Branch.

Hour 時	Day 日	Month 月	Year 年
	辛 Xin Yin Metal		
		卯 Mao Rabbit	

Now, remember what I keep saying about the NUMBER of elements. It's not about how many you have. A chart that is surrounded by Wealth Elements is not necessarily the chart of a rich person. It could be the chart of the teller who works at the bank! They are after all surrounded by money – it just isn't theirs!

Keep reminding yourself - Quality, not Quantity. In BaZi, there is a saying, 'Too Much Wealth deteriorates the Health' 財多身子弱. Remember that too many Wealth Elements weaken the Day Master.

Let's take a look at this example.

Hour 時	Day 日	Month 月	Year 年	
卩 Indirect Resource	日元 Day Master	財 Direct Wealth	傷 Hurting Officer	Heavenly Stems 天干
己 *Ji* Yin Earth	辛 *Xin* Yin Metal	甲 *Jia* Yang Wood	壬 *Ren* Yang Water	
亥 *Hai* **Pig** Yin Water	巳 *Si* **Snake** Yin Fire	辰 *Chen* **Dragon** Yang Earth	寅 *Yin* **Tiger** Yang Wood	Earthly Branches 地支
壬 甲	庚 丙 戊	癸 戊 乙	戊 甲 丙	

87	77	67	57	47	37	27	17	7	Luck Pillars 大運
癸 *Gui* Yin Water	壬 *Ren* Yang Water	辛 *Xin* Yin Metal	庚 *Geng* Yang Metal	己 *Ji* Yin Earth	戊 *Wu* Yang Earth	丁 *Ding* Yin Fire	丙 *Bing* Yang Fire	乙 *Yi* Yin Wood	
丑 *Chou* **Ox** Yin Earth	子 *Zi* **Rat** Yang Water	亥 *Hai* **Pig** Yin Water	戌 *Xu* **Dog** Yang Earth	酉 *You* **Rooster** Yin Metal	申 *Shen* **Monkey** Yang Metal	未 *Wei* **Goat** Yin Earth	午 *Wu* **Horse** Yang Fire	巳 *Si* **Snake** Yin Fire	

This gentleman is Xin 辛 Metal born in Chen 辰 (Dragon) month. Chen 辰 (Dragon) is the season of Spring when Wood is the strongest.

Note that although the Chen 辰 (Dragon) Earthly Branch is an Earth element, Chen 辰 (Dragon) month is one of the months in the Season of Spring so we view it as Spring Earth. In Spring, naturally the strongest element is Wood. Inside this Spring Earth (Chen 辰), there is no Metal.

This chart is surrounded by Wealth Elements, which is Wood. Notice the Jia 甲 Wood in the Month stem is rooted in the Month and the Year Branches of Chen 辰 (Dragon) and Yin 寅 (Tiger).

Perhaps at this point you might be puzzled with the term "rooted". Rooted refers to an instance when the same element is found in the Hidden Stems underneath the Earthly Branches. Every Earthly Branch contains Hidden Stem(s). Don't worry about the technicalities of Hidden Stems at this stage – as you progress through this book and your knowledge of BaZi grows, you will be able to appreciate better their significance.

This Xin 辛 Metal Day Master is weak. The cause for this weakness? There are too many Wealth Elements. The Wealth Elements are his Unfavourable Elements! That is why this gentleman has trouble making ends meet and is constantly having 'money problems'. He is surrounded by money but it is not money that he can 'take' in the sense of putting it in his pocket. His Xin 辛 Metal Day Master is not strong enough to control the Wealth Element, which is Wood. This also means that Wood becomes a negative element.

Next, take a look at the Luck Pillars below. This chart first goes through 30 years of Fire luck – check the Earthly Branches between the ages of 7 – 27 – they are Si 巳 (Snake), Wu 午 (Horse) and Wei 未 (Goat). These are known as the Southern Fire direction.

This means that during the first 30 years of this gentleman's life, he is going through Fire luck. This Xin 辛 Metal is weak, it does not want to see the Fire element because Fire further weakens its strength. From our analysis, we can say that this person can expect the first 30 years of his life to be hard and difficult years.

Hour 時	Day 日	Month 月	Year 年	
卩 Indirect Resource	日元 Day Master	財 Direct Wealth	傷 Hurting Officer	
己 *Ji* Yin Earth	辛 *Xin* Yin Metal	甲 *Jia* Yang Wood	壬 *Ren* Yang Water	Heavenly Stems 天干
亥 *Hai* **Pig** Yin Water	巳 *Si* **Snake** Yin Fire	辰 *Chen* **Dragon** Yang Earth	寅 *Yin* **Tiger** Yang Wood	Earthly Branches 地支
壬 甲	庚 丙 戊	癸 戊 乙	戊 甲 丙	

87	77	67	57	47	37	27	17	7	
癸 *Gui* Yin Water	壬 *Ren* Yang Water	辛 *Xin* Yin Metal	庚 *Geng* Yang Metal	己 *Ji* Yin Earth	戊 *Wu* Yang Earth	丁 *Ding* Yin Fire	丙 *Bing* Yang Fire	乙 *Yi* Yin Wood	Luck Pillars 大運
丑 *Chou* **Ox** Yin Earth	子 *Zi* **Rat** Yang Water	亥 *Hai* **Pig** Yin Water	戌 *Xu* **Dog** Yang Earth	酉 *You* **Rooster** Yin Metal	申 *Shen* **Monkey** Yang Metal	未 *Wei* **Goat** Yin Earth	午 *Wu* **Horse** Yang Fire	巳 *Si* **Snake** Yin Fire	

Fire Luck

Output 食傷

Output is the term used to describe the element that is Produced by the Day Master. For example, if your Day Master is Wood, then your Output Element is Fire.

Why? Because Wood produces Fire in the Five Elements Production Cycle. Look at the quick reference table below to determine what your Day Master's Output Element is.

Day Master	Output Element
木 Wood 甲, 乙	Fire
金 Metal 庚, 辛	Water
水 Water 壬, 癸	Wood
土 Earth 戊, 己	Metal
火 Fire 丙, 丁	Earth

What does this concept of Output mean? The Output Element has many layers. It can represent a person's creativity, intelligence, ability to perform, ability to rise to the occasion, or it can represent a person's expressive abilities or quickness of mind. It also represents the ability to go against the norm, to achieve the extraordinary, to stand out in front of a crowd, to initiate a plan or to execute a strategy. The Output Element also represents the individual's products, things he or she has created or invented.

Output Element of course also represents a person's persuasive prowess. Whether you can get your message across clearly and effectively all depends on the quality of your BaZi's Output Element.

When you use your abilities or intelligence to produce outcomes or results at work, you are using your Output Element. Output enables the person to express his or her ideas effectively and productively, to get the message across, to communicate and to persuade others.

A chart where the Output Element is a Favourable Element normally belongs to people who have a strong personal drive and determination to succeed. A Favourable Output Element may also denote that the person will be creative and have talents relating to speaking, teaching, marketing or in performing arts like acting, singing and dancing. Authors, musicians, directors and scriptwriters are people who usually have beautiful Output Elements.

When we judge the Output Element, we are looking at its quality. Finding one is not good enough. It needs to be of good quality, to be beautiful, to be useful to a BaZi chart.

You might be wondering why I keep using the words 'beautiful' and 'quality' to describe the elements. This is because not every Day Master reacts the same way to their Output Elements, nor do all Day Masters use their Output Elements equally as well. As your study of BaZi advances, you will appreciate this concept better but for now, just remember that having a certain

Element, while it is a start, is not the be all and end all when it comes to BaZi analysis. This is a beginner's book you are holding, so I'll go slow and steady!

Without a good Output Element, an individual will be gullible and an easy mark for everything ranging from school children selling raffle tickets to con men. A person with a weak or Unfavorable Output Element may find themselves in possession of unwanted magazine subscriptions or tickets to the secretary's fundraiser ball. An Unfavorable Output Element normally is one of the big reasons why people who should say no, end up saying yes!

Charts where the Output Element is an Unfavorable Element usually belong to persons who have difficulties in expressing themselves. Alternatively, they will be timid individuals or people who despite their abilities, never quite seem to get noticed or recognition for their efforts or work.

An Output Element problem, such as a Clash or Combination usually indicates a problem with staff, such as your staff being headhunted or resigning.

Quick aside – don't be too concerned about what the Clash or Combination concepts are at this point. You will learn more about them as you advance through this book.

Now, let's take a look at an example of the Output Element

Hour 時	Day 日	Month 月	Year 年	
財 Direct Wealth	日元 Day Master	傷 Hurting Officer	才 Indirect Wealth	Heavenly Stems 天干
戊 *Wu* Yang Earth	乙 *Yi* Yin Wood	丙 *Bing* Yang Fire	己 *Ji* Yin Earth	
子 *Zi* **Rat** Yang Water	未 *Wei* **Goat** Yin Earth	寅 *Yin* **Tiger** Yang Wood	未 *Wei* **Goat** Yin Earth	Earthly Branches 地支
癸	乙 己 丁	戊 甲 丙	乙 己 丁	

This lady is Yi 乙 Wood, born in Yin 寅 (Tiger) month. Yin 寅 (Tiger) is the season of Spring, when the Wood element is the strongest. Notice also that the Wei 未 (Goat) Earthly Branch contains minor roots of Wood. Most importantly, look at the time of birth – it is Zi 子 (Rat) hour, which contains water to feed the Wood Day Master.

This Yi 乙 wood is strong and vibrant. What it needs is some Output Element, which is Fire. Fire helps bring warmth to the cold, early Spring month. Fire also brings balance to the chart as the Wood is strong and needs to be weakened a little. So the Favourable Element is Fire, which is right next to the Day Master!

Hour 時	Day 日	Month 月	Year 年	
財 Direct Wealth	日元 Day Master	傷 Hurting Officer	才 Indirect Wealth	Heavenly Stems 天干
戊 *Wu* Yang Earth	乙 *Yi* Yin Wood	丙 *Bing* Yang Fire	己 *Ji* Yin Earth	
子 *Zi* **Rat** Yang Water	未 *Wei* **Goat** Yin Earth	寅 *Yin* **Tiger** Yang Wood	未 *Wei* **Goat** Yin Earth	Earthly Branches 地支
癸	乙 己 丁	戊 甲 丙	乙 己 丁	

Fire in this chart is the Output Element. And it is a Favourable Element. This person's BaZi shows that she is talented, outspoken and has the ability to learn quickly. Her talents will bring her wealth as Fire produces Earth, her Wealth Element. This person also already has Wealth Elements in her chart – notice the Wu 戊 and Ji 己 Earth inside the Yin 寅 (Tiger) and two Wei 未 (Goat) Earthly Branches – she will eventually be very wealthy.

Influence 官殺

The Influence Element is sometimes described as the Power Element in some books on Four Pillars of Destiny. I think that the term 'Power' does not do justice to the concept, nor does it provide sufficient shading to the concept, which can be subtle and indirect. So, I prefer to use the word 'Influence'.

The Influence element in BaZi is the Element that controls the Day Master. Don't be misled by the word 'control'. It doesn't always carry a negative connotation. 'Control' here is more like the control a mother exerts over her child. When a mother tells her child what to do and what not to do to prevent the child from growing up to be a bad person, this is not 'negative' control. This is control in the form of guidance and supervision.

Look at the chart below to determine what is the Influence Element for your Day Master.

Day Master		Influence Element
木 Wood	甲, 乙	Metal
金 Metal	庚, 辛	Fire
水 Water	壬, 癸	Earth
土 Earth	戊, 己	Wood
火 Fire	丙, 丁	Water

What does the Influence Element refer to? Broadly, the Influence Element refers to nobility, authority and charisma. Ever been at a function or party where one person walks in to a room and suddenly, all the attention just moves towards this person? Or what about people who seem to bring the sunshine with them whenever they enter a room? This is the effect of the Influence Element in a person's chart.

The Influence Element also represents law and order, rules and regulation. It makes sense – after all, rules, regulations and laws exist to 'control' people, correct? Imagine a world without laws? A world without traffic laws would mean that people would be driving in different directions, no traffic lights and massive chaos. Control is the means to bring order to the world and therefore eliminate chaos.

Hence, the Influence Element, the element which enables control, is important in a person's chart as it enables them to exercise self-control and behave. A Favourable Influence Element normally denotes a person who is law abiding, conservative, respectful and honest.

Now, like all things, we don't want too much control. Too much Influence will cause the chart to become imbalanced and the Day Master will dislike being overly-controlled. What happens when a parent over-controls their child? The child rebels. The same thing with a BaZi. If the Influence Element is too strong, you are looking at the BaZi of a rebel, non-conformist, someone who defies authority or must always walk their own path in life. An Unfavorable Influence Element usually results in a person who is radical, restless and does not like to take orders and advice from others.

Ladies should take special note of the Influence Element as this is the Element that represents the Husband. The Influence Element is also called the Husband Star in a lady's BaZi.

Hour 時	Day 日	Month 月	Year 年	
丁 *Ding* Yin Fire	壬 *Ren* Yang Water	戊 *Wu* Yang Earth	乙 *Yi* Yin Wood	**Heavenly Stems** 天干
巳 *Si* **Snake** Yin Fire	戌 *Xu* **Dog** Yang Earth	子 *Zi* **Rat** Yang Water	酉 *You* **Rooster** Yin Metal	**Earthly Branches** 地支
庚 丙 戊	丁 戊 辛	癸	辛	

This Ren 壬 Water man is born in the month of Zi 子 (Rat). Zi 子 (Rat) month is the Winter season. In Winter, the strongest element is Water. So this person's Ren 壬 Water Day Master is classified as strong. Perhaps a little too strong – Ren 壬 Water is the water of the river or the lake. Think pictorially now – this Ren 壬 Water is not the calm lake where the waves lap gently on the banks. It's more like a torrential gushing waterfall.

What is needed to balance it? A little Earth to help control and direct the Water by damming it up. Earth is the Influence Element in this chart and because it is needed by the Ren 壬 Water Day Master, it is a Favourable Element.

Having decoded this person's BaZi, we can determine that this individual is someone who respects the rules, is law abiding, is principled, righteous and disciplined, since the Influence Element also represents self control.

Now, remember the Influence Element also represents a person's status and position. A Favourable Influence Element denotes that the person will achieve certain ranking or certain positions in life and/or will command respect from others. Finally, the Influence Element also represents elegance, nobility and charisma.

Hour 時	Day 日	Month 月	Year 年	
癸 *Gui* Yin Water	己 *Ji* Yin Earth	甲 *Jia* Yang Wood	戊 *Wu* Yang Earth	Heavenly Stems 天干
酉 *You* **Rooster** Yin Metal	未 *Wei* **Goat** Yin Earth	寅 *Yin* **Tiger** Yang Wood	戌 *Xu* **Dog** Yang Earth	Earthly Branches 地支
辛	乙 己 丁	戊 甲 丙	丁 戊 辛	

Remember what I said earlier about the Influence Element being the Element that represents a woman's Husband Element? Take a look at the example above.

This lady is Ji 己 Earth born in Yin 寅 (Tiger) Month. It is the season of Spring, when Wood is the strongest element. Wood is the Influence Element to a Ji 己 Earth person. This means that this lady's Influence Element is born in the season in which it is strongest – her Influence Element (Wood) is very strong.

You will notice that I have read the chart slightly differently this time. You see, you can actually, using the Month's Earthly Branch, determine the strength of each and every one of the Elements, and not just that of the Day Master. Now, this is quite an advanced concept in BaZi analysis so if you don't quite understand how it works, don't worry. Remember, analysing your BaZi and unveiling the Destiny Code is like peeling an onion, go layer by layer.

Now, what about the Day Master? This Ji 己 Earth Day Master is not weak. It has roots in the Wei 未 (Goat) which contains Earth and also the Xu 戌 (Dog) in the Year Pillar, which also contains Earth.

In BaZi, if you're too weak, you don't like to be controlled. You need to be a little bit strong. This Ji 己 Earth is strong enough to be able to accept the control of the Influence Element. Since this Ji 己 Earth actually likes the control of the Influence Element and the Influence Element is of good quality, this denotes that this Ji 己 Earth lady has good Husband Luck and will enjoy a good marriage.

Resource 印星

The Resource Element is the Element that produces your Day Master. Since Resource is the element that 'feeds' the Day Master, it represents the person's thinking and knowledge, the person's learning ability, wisdom, thoughts and knowledge. This Element also represents a person's family background or the support from superiors. Resource also represents intuition or sixth sense. It represents help or assistance received.

Day Master	Resource Element
木 Wood 甲, 乙	Water
金 Metal 庚, 辛	Earth
水 Water 壬, 癸	Metal
土 Earth 戊, 己	Fire
火 Fire 丙, 丁	Wood

Individuals with good Resource Elements are individuals who are intelligent, who enjoy learning and are focused on self-improvement. Individuals with Resource as their Unfavourable Element however will have poor intellectual skills and probably will have many bad habits. If a person has too many Resource Elements, they are likely to be lazy and pessimistic. So, as I said earlier, balance is the key. You do not want too many or too little Resource.

As Resource represents the ability to learn, so an Unfavourable Resource Element indicates a person who doesn't like to learn. On the other hand, if a person's Resource Element is needed or is one of the Favourable Elements in the chart, this is likely to be an individual who likes to study or learn many new things.

The Resource Element is usually what BaZi practitioners evaluate when asked to determine if a child will excel in his or her examinations. If the Resource Element is in good condition, then the child will likely enjoy academic or scholastic success. What does good condition mean? This means it is supported or correctly utilised based on the entire BaZi chart.

In a chart where the Resource Element is clashed away or is hurt by opposing Heavenly Stems and Earthly Branches, this denotes bad fortune in examinations. It may also indicate that a person's mother will be ill during that period, since the Resource Element also represents a person's Mother in his or her chart. An Unfavourable Resource Element can also result in a person being a negative thinker.

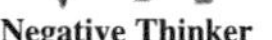

Negative Thinker

Hour 時	Day 日	Month 月	Year 年	
戊 *Wu* Yang Earth	丁 *Ding* Yin Fire	丁 *Ding* Yin Fire	乙 *Yi* Yin Wood	**Heavenly Stems** 天干
申 *Shen* **Monkey** Yang Metal	卯 *Mao* **Rabbit** Yin Wood	亥 *Hai* **Pig** Yin Water	丑 *Chou* **Ox** Yin Earth	**Earthly Branches** 地支
戊 庚 壬	乙	壬 甲	辛 己 癸	

This is Ding 丁 Fire born in Hai 亥 (Pig) month. Hai 亥 (Pig) is Winter season, where the Water element is the strongest. Water puts out Fire. Fire needs Wood to strengthen itself. So Wood is regarded as Favourable in this chart. Wood to a Fire Day Master is the Resource Element.

A person with Resource as a Favourable Element will naturally like to learn a lot and pursue many academic dreams as Resource represents input or knowledge. When a person 'needs' Resource, he or she will naturally tend to pursue intellectual pursuits. You can say that the person is also intelligent, as Resource Element represents intelligence. This person's chart indicates that he or she is also gentle and forgiving as such are the characteristics of the Resource Element.

Companion 比劫

The companion element is the 'same' element as the Day Master.

Look at the quick reference chart below to determine what is your Companion Element.

Day Master	Companion Element
木 Wood 甲,乙	Wood
金 Metal 庚,辛	Metal
水 Water 壬,癸	Water
土 Earth 戊,己	Earth
火 Fire 丙,丁	Fire

As the Companion Element is the same element as your Day Master, it represents a person's will-power, thoughts, sense of self-esteem, self-consciousness and self-confidence. It also represents his/her personal outlook in life, how a person perceives or feels about him/herself. Companion Elements also represent friends, siblings and rivals or competitors.

Companion Elements help a person have a healthy measure of personal ambition and drive to succeed. A person whose chart has good Companion Elements will never be lonely in life. This person will always be surrounded by friends and supporters. By contrast, a person without any Companion Elements or too many Companion Elements is likely to be solitary or always feel lonely. Having no Companion Elements or having too many creates an imbalanced chart.

Now, you might be wondering: how can having 'many' Companion Elements result in a person being lonely? Remember, we are never concerned with about quantity, we are always talking about quality. And as the section on Wealth has demonstrated, many does not always denote 'better'.

In a BaZi chart, your Companion Elements also represent your siblings. If your Companion Element is Unfavourable to you, you will not have good affinity with your siblings. Conversely if your Companion Element is Favourable, you will enjoy good affinity with your siblings. A chart with Negative or Unfavourable Companions Elements belongs to a person with either an ego problem or low self-esteem.

Just a quick clarification: the word or term 'Companion' here does not refer to spouse or lover. Remember your spouse element is, if you are a man, your Wealth element and if you are a lady, your Influence Element. Don't let the word 'Companion' give you the wrong idea.

Hour 時	Day 日	Month 月	Year 年	
甲 *Jia* Yang Wood	乙 *Yi* Yin Wood	甲 *Jia* Yang Wood	癸 *Gui* Yin Water	**Heavenly Stems** 天干
申 *Shen* **Monkey** Yang Metal	卯 *Mao* **Rabbit** Yin Wood	寅 *Yin* **Tiger** Yang Wood	巳 *Si* **Snake** Yin Fire	**Earthly Branches** 地支
戊 庚 壬	乙	戊 甲 丙	庚 丙 戊	

This person is a Yi 乙 Wood born in the month of Yin 寅 (Tiger). Yin 寅 (Tiger) is the Spring season, when the Wood element is prosperous. What does prosperous mean? It's a notch up from strong – it means the Wood element is very strong.

You will notice that there are many Wood Elements or Companion Elements in this BaZi. Look at the Month and Hour Pillars – there are Jia 甲 Woods in both those Pillars. Notice that the Yi 乙 Wood Day Master is also 'seated' on top of a Mao 卯 (Rabbit) Earthly Branch. The Mao 卯 (Rabbit) is yet another Wood Element.

This person has too many Companion Elements, to the point that the Companion Element becomes an Unfavourable or Negative Element. Why? Because strong Wood doesn't need to be strengthened any more. More Wood here will cause the BaZi to become imbalanced. This person is likely to be selfish, opinionated, stubborn and self-destructive because these are the negative traits of the Companion Element.

Balancing your BaZi with the Five Factors

BaZi is a study of 'balancing' the elements. The name of the game is to look for the balancing element. Find it, name it and think about what it relates to.

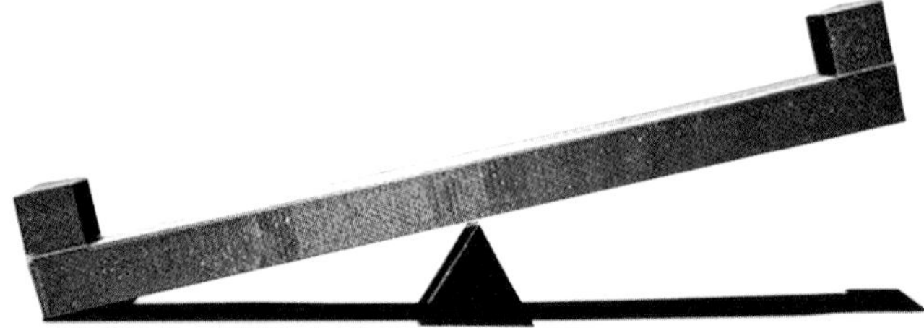

Remember in the previous chapter we talked about the Favourable and Unfavourable elements? You need to now relate those to your Five Factors. Here's a reminder for you, with the added layer of the Five Factors:

Strong Day Master Favours	財星 Wealth Elements
	官殺 Influence Elements
	食傷 Output Elements

A strong Day Master, meaning, a Day Master that is born in the right season and gets reasonably good support from its neighbouring branches, would normally favour meeting Wealth, Influence and Output Elements. What does meeting mean? This means that the BaZi 'sees' these Elements in either the Annual or 10 Year Luck Pillars.

So a strong Day Master meeting the Wealth Luck pillars will have good wealth luck – an excellent time to invest or go into business.

Strong Day Master Dislikes	印星 Resource Elements
	比劫 Companion Elements

By contrast, the Strong Day Master does not like meeting the Companion Element or Resource Element. Meeting more Companion Elements in the luck pillars denotes that there is possibility of 'losing wealth' or loss of income. Why? Because Companion Element represents 'rivals' to a Strong Day Master and throws the Strong Day Master off-balance by making it too strong. Companions to a Strong Day Master chart will fight for control over the Wealth Element - meaning there will be others coming in to rob your wealth!

Your analysis will be different when the Day Master of the chart is Weak. A weak Day Master responds and reacts differently to the other Five Elements. Weak Day Master favours Companion Elements Resource Elements.

Weak Day Master Favours	比劫 Companion Elements
	印星 Resource Elements

A Weak Day Master, meaning one that is not born in the right season or one that lacks surrounding elements that support or strengthen the Day Master, needs help from Companion and Resource Elements.

Why? The Companion Element is the 'same' element as the Day Master. A Weak Day Master needs to get help from a companion, who lends strength and helps establish balance.

The Resource Element feeds and nourishes the Weak Day Master. Thus Resource Element is a Weak Day Master's Favourable Element. In instances where the Resource Element is a Favourable Element, the person would favour studying, learning and self-improvement as these things are Favourable to the weak Day Master.

Weak Day Master Dislikes	財星 Wealth Elements
	官殺 Influence Elements
	食傷 Output Elements

A Weak Day Master does not favour meeting the Wealth Element. Why? Because it is not strong enough to control the Wealth Element and it also throws the entire BaZi chart off-balance by weakening an already weak Day Master. A Weak Day Master meeting the Wealth Element usually indicates problems involving money or in some instances, income tax problems!

A Weak Day Master also is not strong enough to withstand further 'control' from the Influence Element. The Influence Element pressures the Weak Day Master as it tries to exert control. A Weak Day Master meeting Influence Element usually indicates problems with the law or authority, job related obstacles such as problems getting promoted or advancing or being retrenched.

The Weak Day Master also does not like to meet Output Elements in the Luck Pillars. Why? It is already Weak – it does not have enough strength to produce even more. When a Weak Day Master meets an Output Element, it is forced to produce out, depleting its strength and again, causing an imbalance in the BaZi.

Situations like these normally indicate staffing problems. A Weak Day Master meeting an Output Element may also result in arguments or disputes that arise out of accidentally saying the wrong thing or offending someone.

Working out the Favourable and Unfavourable Elements

It is very important that you must first determine the strength of the Day Master. Then you will be able to determine what elements the chart favours and what it does not favour. From this, you can derive what 'type' of luck is the person going through in which particular point in time or what kind of obstacles the person is likely to face during certain luck pillars.

Determining the strength of the Day Master is a very complex form of analysis with many layers and subtleties. However, it is always the month branch that gives you the bulk of the information. In later books I will discuss concepts such as about the 'roots' and 'formation' when it comes to the strength of the pillars but at the beginner level, focus your attention on determining the strength of the Day Master, determining your Favourable and Unfavourable Elements and corresponding these to your Five Factors.

Chapter Eight:
Will I Be Rich?

My e-mail box is constantly inundated with e-mails from many individuals who are often desperate to know, when they will be rich (and not just rich, but millionaires!). Now of course, money and wealth are not everything in this world, but it is an important consideration for many people today.

One of the reasons why the 'When Will I Be Rich' question is difficult to answer in BaZi is because the meaning of 'rich' or 'wealthy' is difficult to define. How much money is enough? Or how much is a lot? Indeed, how much is too much?

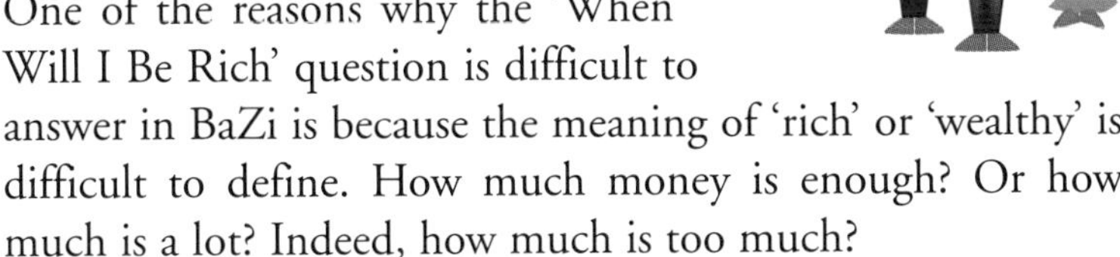

Donald Trump once remarked that when he owed hundreds of millions of dollars in debt to the banks at one point in his life, he considered the beggar who had 2 dollars in his begging bowl richer than him. It's all about context.

Unfortunately, and I must disappoint some readers with this statement: your BaZi is not read like a bank statement. It does not tell you 'how much' money you will have in exact figures or net worth. Instead, what a BaZi chart tells you is whether or not you have the 'capacity' to amass great wealth and whether or not this wealth will last or will simply be a flash in a pan.

How do you judge your Wealth capacity? Usually, a BaZi practitioner will first look at the BaZi and determine if the Wealth Element is present. If the Wealth Element is not present, you already start out with a disadvantage, money-wise, in life.

Assuming that the Wealth Element is present, the next thing we have to evaluate is whether the Wealth Element is strong or weak.

Even if the Wealth Element is strong, we still want to check your Luck Cycle to determine if you are going through Good Luck (thus allowing you to capitalise on your wealth potential) or even better, going through Wealth Luck.

Now, it's not enough to just be able to make it. The famous rap artist, MC Hammer, managed to make over 30 million dollars a year and lose it all in that same year. So, we must also look at whether a person will be able to hang on to his wealth or will he make it and lose it just as quickly?

Finally, we need to look at issues of personality and career. You have to enter the right career in order to maximise your wealth potential but you also need the right personality and attitude to amass the wealth. You can have all the wealth potential in the world but being a lazy bum isn't going to help you get rich!

Let's take each of these issues one at a time.

Evaluating the Wealth Element

The Wealth Element in your BaZi chart is the element that your Day Master controls. For example, for a Metal person, his Wealth is Wood. For a Water person, his Wealth is Fire. So first and foremost, identify what is the Wealth Element in your chart.

Day Master	Wealth Element					
火 Fire 丙, 丁	庚 *Geng* Yang Metal	辛 *Xin* Yin Metal	申 *Shen* Yang Metal	酉 *You* Yin Metal		
土 Earth 戊, 己	壬 *Ren* Yang Water	癸 *Gui* Yin Water	子 *Zi* Yang Water	亥 *Hai* Yin Water		
金 Metal 庚, 辛	甲 *Jia* Yang Wood	乙 *Yi* Yin Wood	寅 *Yin* Yang Wood	卯 *Mao* Yin Wood		
水 Water 壬, 癸	丙 *Bing* Yang Fire	丁 *Ding* Yin Fire	巳 *Si* Yin Fire	午 *Wu* Yang Fire		
木 Wood 甲, 乙	戊 *Wu* Yang Earth	己 *Ji* Yin Earth	辰 *Chen* Yang Earth	戌 *Xu* Yang Earth	丑 *Chou* Yin Earth	未 *Wei* Yin Earth

Now, after you have identified your Wealth Element, you need to determine if your Day Master can actually exert control over your Wealth Element or not. What do I mean by this? You see, the Day Master must be strong enough to exert control over the Wealth Element. If your Day Master is weak, then it cannot effectively control the Wealth Element.

This is the essence of understanding and interpreting the wealth capacity of a chart.

Take a look at the following two examples – one BaZi chart belongs to a rich man and the other BaZi chart belongs to a guy who can barely make ends meet.

Hour 時	Day 日	Month 月	Year 年	
丙 *Bing* Yang Fire	乙 *Yi* Yin Wood	己 *Ji* Yin Earth	庚 *Geng* Yang Metal	Heavenly Stems 天干
戌 *Xu* **Dog** Yang Earth	卯 *Mao* **Rabbit** Yin Wood	丑 *Chou* **Ox** Yin Earth	辰 *Chen* **Dragon** Yang Earth	Earthly Branches 地支
丁 戊 辛	乙	辛 己 癸	癸 戊 乙	

This man is Yi 乙 Wood born in Chou 丑 (Ox) month. Chou 丑 (Ox) month is considered Winter season. In this chart, Water is hidden inside Chou 丑 (Ox) and inside Chen 辰 (Dragon). This is an advanced concept called the "Hidden Stems".

While the Chou 丑 (Ox) is dominated by the Earth Element, when we are looking at the Month Pillar, we are interested in looking at the season of birth first.

We know that Chou 丑 (Ox) is the Winter season and in Winter, the Water element is strong. Now, as Water produces Wood, we can conclude that Wood is strong. So this Yi 乙 Wood Day Master is quite strong.

Now, I know you might be wondering – isn't Chou 丑 (Ox) the Earth element and since Wood controls Earth, this weakens Wood's Qi – so shouldn't this Wood be weak? The answer is because Chou 丑 (Ox) is (in this chart) the month of birth. That is why you need to consider the season and not just the Earth element. The Chou 丑 (Ox) belongs to the Winter season, that is why the Water element is considered strong.

The Earth in this chart, which is the Wealth Element for Yi 乙 Wood, is NOT weak either. Can you see that there are a number of Earth elements in the Earthly Branches? Look in the Chou 丑 (Ox), Chen 辰 (Dragon) and Xu 戌 (Dog). Do you see how the Earth element 'penetrates' to the Heavenly Stem?

Hour 時	Day 日	Month 月	Year 年	
丙 *Bing* Yang Fire	乙 *Yi* Yin Wood	己 *Ji* Yin Earth	庚 *Geng* Yang Metal	Heavenly Stems 天干
戌 *Xu* **Dog** Yang Earth	卯 *Mao* **Rabbit** Yin Wood	丑 *Chou* **Ox** Yin Earth	辰 *Chen* **Dragon** Yang Earth	Earthly Branches 地支
丁 戊 辛	乙	辛 己 癸	癸 戊 乙	

Earth Elements in the Earthly Branches

What does this concept of 'Penetrate to Heavenly Stem' mean? It means that the same element appears on both the Heavenly Stem and Earth Branch. In BaZi, this means the element is strong because from the Branch, it pierces all the way to Heaven. The Element is very dominant and strong.

Hour 時	Day 日	Month 月	Year 年	
丙 *Bing* Yang Fire	乙 *Yi* Yin Wood	己 Yin Earth	庚 *Geng* Yang Metal	Heavenly Stems 天干
戌 *Xu* **Dog** Yang Earth	卯 *Mao* **Rabbit** Yin Wood	丑 *Chou* **Ox** Yin Earth	辰 *Chen* **Dragon** Yang Earth	Earthly Branches 地支
丁 戊 辛	乙	辛 己 癸	癸 戊 乙	

Penetrating to Heaven

So, we can conclude that the Day Master and Wealth Element are strong. This means that this Yi 乙 Wood can control the Earth Element, its Wealth star. So we can conclude that this person has the potential to become rich.

What makes this BaZi chart stand out is the Bing 丙 Fire in the hour pillar. Bing 丙 Fire, as explained in previous chapters, is the fire of the sun. Now let me introduce yet another advance concept of BaZi called Tiao Hao 調候 (Regulating the Climate). The 'temperature' of this chart is cold – why do I say that? This person was born in the Chou 丑 (Ox) month, which is the Winter season. In Winter – it's COLD!

A BaZi chart should be warm and comfortable. Otherwise the elements will not foster growth and there will be no liveliness in the chart. So what this chart needs is a little bit of warmth to help the Yi 乙 Wood grow. That is exactly what the Bing 丙 Fire in his Hour Pillar supplies. Bing 丙 Fire, in case you have forgotten, is the fire of the Sun. (Go back to Chapter Two for a quick recap on the Heavenly Stems). Hence, this person is able to become wealthy because he is able to use both Fire and Earth well.

Hour 時	Day 日	Month 月	Year 年	
癸 *Gui* Yin Water	庚 *Geng* Yang Metal	癸 *Gui* Yin Water	戊 *Wu* Yang Earth	Heavenly Stems 天干
未 *Wei* **Goat** Yin Earth	子 *Zi* **Rat** Yang Water	亥 *Hai* **Pig** Yin Water	子 *Zi* **Rat** Yang Water	Earthly Branches 地支
乙 己 丁	癸	壬 甲	癸	

This person could hardly make ends meet most of his life. Let's find out why.

He is Geng 庚 Metal, born in the Hai 亥 (Pig) month. Hai 亥 (Pig) month is the Winter season, when Water Element is the strongest. Take a look at the other characters in his BaZi chart. Do you also see the two Zi 子 (Rat) characters? These are Water branches.

Observe the Heavenly Stems – notice the two Gui 癸 Water Heavenly Stems on the top? (One on the month and the other

on the hour pillar?) In this chart, we have Water penetrating to the Heavenly Stems from the branch. So we know that Water element is very strong in this chart. In fact, it's too strong and has the effect of weakening the Metal Day Master, as it has to produce too much water. In advanced BaZi, this is termed 'Metal Sinking in Water'.

So this person's Geng 庚 Day Master is in fact, weak.

What about his Wealth Element? Metal controls Wood so this person's Wealth Element is Wood. You will notice that there is only one Wood Element, hidden inside the Hai 亥 (Pig) and the Wei 未 (Goat).

Now, Wood cannot grow if Water is too strong because when the water is too strong, it floods the chart and flushes away the Wood. Remember my previous emphasis on the importance of balance in the BaZi? Too much of any element is not a good thing. In this chart, we can see how that is the case. Even though Water 'grows' Wood, too much of Water will only uproot and flush the Wood away!

So this person's Wealth Element is also considered weak.

If a person's Day Master is weak and the Wealth Element is also weak, it is very unlikely that the person can become a wealthy person.

Many beginners make the mistake of 'counting' how many Wealth Elements they have in their charts. This method of reading charts is wrong. It is always the *quality* of an element, never the quantity that matters. So when you evaluate the Wealth Element in your own chart, don't get carried away with 'counting' the number of Wealth Elements. The key is to find out the *quality* of the Wealth Element (ie: its strength, whether it penetrates to the Heavenly Stem) and not count the number of elements.

Choosing the Right Career

女人最怕嫁錯郎，男人最怕入錯行

Ladies are most afraid of marrying the wrong man, and Men are most afraid of choosing the wrong career – Chinese Saying

Imagine this. Bill Gates, instead of going into the software business, went into the business of selling watches. He would probably still have gotten rich but perhaps, not quite to the extent of having a global empire.

Choosing the right career is an extremely important factor when it comes to wealth. It's one thing to have a rich man's chart – this simply tells you that in your lifetime, you will have money. But HOW RICH you will be depends on how well you chose your career to match your life path. In other words, you need to go into the right field in order to make the money that you're destined to have. Entering the wrong field, even if you have the capacity to make money, is like asking Michael Jordan to play tennis – it just doesn't happen.

Chicken Rice

The Chinese have an old saying 'Every field comes with a Hero' meaning there's always someone that makes it in every field. However, remember the capacity in each field is different. A person selling lunch boxes or 'chicken rice' (a popular local Malaysian lunch meal) would probably need to sell a million meals to make a million dollars, something an expert bond or stock market trader can make in a few minutes.

In the course of my travels and consultations all over the world, I have encountered many instances of individuals who entered a field that did not suit them, but they persisted with it because 'it was the best choice' at that time. At the same time, I have also met individuals who had consciously made it a point to move into a field that was suitable to them. Despite some initial adjustments, they later found that their decisions (which sometimes were very difficult and painful at first) have led them to a bigger playing field and increased their sense of fulfillment and satisfaction in life.

However one can safely say that if you at least choose the right 'field', you have a major advantage over others who don't. It is always better to 'go with the flow' than to work against the odds. There are fields of work with elements that suit you while there are those that would make your work a permanent uphill climb all the time. So, a wise choice goes a long way!

Choosing Career Based on Your BaZi

Using BaZi to help someone select a suitable career could be a subject of an entire book in itself! The variations are infinite because every individual and his/her BaZi chart is unique. Hence, for the purposes of this section, we're going to keep it simple and just use the Five Elements to help guide you on the question of a suitable career.

Before we get started, remember: Your best career field may not necessarily refer to the element of your Day Master. That is just one method of looking at career choices.

A better technique is to examine your suitable career fields based on your Favourable Element or Elements. Remember how in earlier chapters, I showed you the ways to establish your Favourable and Unfavourable Elements?

Based on your Favourable Elements, you can establish the relevant industry that you will excel or do well in, or will invariably be drawn to. For example, if your Favorable Element is Fire, then you should select the fields that are related to the Fire element. If your Favourable Element is Water, then you would do better in the Water element related industry.

Conversely, it is inadvisable to enter the fields related to your Unfavourable Elements. Generally, in the study of BaZi, an individual's achievements and performance in life would be limited at best, fruitless at worst, if he chose to enter a career field that is 'unfavourable' to his BaZi.

Entering a field of work that is represented by your unfavourable or negative element can disadvantage you significantly, not to mention the fact that most of the time you will probably feel dissatisfied and unfulfilled with your life.

So, what careers relate to each of the Five Elements? Here is a general guide:

Fire Industry

Fire in the study of the Five Elements represents exuberance, beauty, mannerisms and politeness. It also represents advancement and illumination.

Fields in the service industry are usually Fire-related. If you are in the business of making others beautiful (ie: cosmetics, beauty products), you are in a Fire-related industry.

Pilots, air hosts and hostess are doing Fire-related jobs. Why? Fire Qi rises to the top, Water Qi flows to the bottom. A plane uses fuel and flies in the sky so it is of a Fire Element.

Computer and Electronics and all items that use electricity are related to fire. So if you sell computers and gadgets, you are in a Fire business.

If you are in an industry that relates to petrol, oil lamps, lighting, then these are all related to the Fire Element and thus, are Fire industry jobs.

Water Fields

All mobile/moving businesses are related to Water. So if you are in the transportation, courier or tourism business, you are involved in a Water-related field. Any business that involves or requires the use of Water, such as raring fishes, supplying mineral water, filtering mineral water, is also part of the Water business.

Water also relates to wisdom and intelligence, so if your work involves thinking, creativity or innovation, you are in a Water field. If you are involved in strategic planning and your job entails a lot of analysis, you are also in a Water field.

If you are working in a hygiene company, in a laundry shop or the cleaning industry – you are also in a Water-related field.

Earth Occupations

The most obvious example of an Earth occupation is real estate. If you buy and sell houses or if you sell land, you are in the Earth element business.

If you are involved in the building materials, minerals, stone craft industry, then you are involved in an Earth-related industry. If you sell tiles and marble or engage in a business which is involved in these items, you are also involved in an Earth element industry.

Antique dealers and art dealers are regarded as involved in Earth related industries since these involve objects that last through time.

Earth also relates to trustworthiness in the study of Five Elements. If your work relates to selling "trust" and "sense of security", such as healing and insurance, then you are in an Earth element related business.

Metal Jobs

Metal represents justice and righteousness in the study of the Five Elements. Thus people in the armed forces, in the police force and in the legal profession, usually belong to the Metal element industry.

Many people think that if they work with metal objects like televisions or computers they are in a 'Metal' element line. This is not correct. Television, computers and other electronic items that require 'electricity' and 'energy' to function belong to the Fire element.

Metal fields include goldsmith, coin collection, pewter industry, grills and aluminum, and selling automobiles. Metal also represents finance. If you have a lot of Metal in your chart, you will be attracted to the finance, banking or stock trading industry. If Metal is Favourable for you, then it means you will do well in this field. If Metal is Unfavourable for you, you will dread to be in the industry but you probably have no choice but to continue in this line!

Wood Work

In the study of the Five Elements, Wood relates to growth and progress. So jobs that involve teaching or helping others to succeed are jobs that involve the use of Wood.

Obvious examples of the Wood industry are timber, plantation, furniture or goods made from wood. Businesses that are seasonal in nature, such as fashion design or the clothing business, are also regarded as Wood. If your work involves creating, inventing or designing, you are also in the Wood business.

Defining your industry

Gone are the days when people were farmers or soldiers or fishermen or traders. Job descriptions have evolved, as have the types of jobs around. The Marketing Manager is a relatively recent incarnation, much like the Chief Information Officer (CIO). Most jobs nowadays involve more than one of the Five Elements, what BaZi practitioners call 'mix' elements industries. The trick is to identify the main element of the industry.

Take for example, the hair saloon business. What element is it? Hair, in the study of the Five Elements, relates to Wood. So it is a Wood industry. But the hair saloon offers haircuts, which involves the use of scissors, which are Metal. So, the hair saloon business involves Wood and Metal.

But what if you work as a marketing executive for a company that deals in hairstyling products, such as Vidal Sassoon? You don't cut hair, you don't even touch hair. Are you still in the Wood/Metal industry?

In advanced BaZi, a practitioner looks not just at the suitable field for a person to enter, but what 'role' they should play. This is done using a concept in BaZi known as the Ten Gods (十神). So, using our earlier example of the marketing executive for hairstyling products, this person is in a Wood field using his/her Hurting Officer star.

Luck Periods for Wealth

So you have Wealth Elements in your chart and you're in the right career to ensure you can maximise that wealth potential. Why then is the pot of gold at the end of the rainbow still not visible?

They say opportunity only knocks once and perhaps in BaZi, this is very true. People imagine that they need 20, maybe 30 years of good luck in order to amass wealth.

Not true.

Sometimes, all you need is one good 10 year block. And if you work hard and go all out during those 10 years, you may just be able to fulfill that wish of retiring to the Bahamas!

Having the potential and capacity for wealth in your BaZi is one thing, you still need to time your actions correctly. You have to know WHEN is your prime time and when is your down time and act appropriately. Knowing WHEN to take action is as important as knowing WHAT to do. The idea in BaZi is to go with the flow and not against the tides.

Of course there are those that say that we should live our life with a little sense of 'adventure'. True, life wouldn't be fun if everything was predictable or predicted, but knowing when is the best time to take advantage of opportunities doesn't take the fun out of life – it's just the wise thing to do. That is why there are so many 'forecasts' out there each year. There are financial specialists who forecast the performance of share market every year. Then there's the weatherman who tells us when to bring our rain coats and of course we have our geologists who are supposed to forecast for us the earthquakes and tsunamis. Are forecasts a bad thing? I think not. It helps us plan and prepare. BaZi is a similar 'forecast' tool to help us shape and run our lives better.

By knowing what to expect and then being able to make the best of the situation, you take advantage of your BaZi's potential and minimise any negative effects.

Hour 時	Day 日	Month 月	Year 年	
庚 *Geng* Yang Metal	丁 *Ding* Yin Fire	辛 *Xin* Yin Metal	癸 *Gui* Yin Water	**Heavenly Stems 天干**
子 *Zi* **Rat** Yang Water	丑 *Chou* **Ox** Yin Earth	酉 *You* **Rooster** Yin Metal	卯 *Mao* **Rabbit** Yin Wood	**Earthly Branches 地支**
癸	辛 己 癸	辛	乙	

This chart belongs to a gentleman with a Ding 丁 Fire Day Master. From the chart we can tell that he is a Weak Ding 丁 Fire because he is Ding 丁 Fire born in the You 酉 (Rooster) month. You 酉 (Rooster) month is Autumn season, when Fire is weak. (In case you have forgotten why Fire in the Autumn season is weak, go to page 145 for a quick recap).

Also, there are too many Metal elements in this chart. There are Geng 庚 and Xin 辛 Metals flanking the Day Master's left and right. In the Day and Hour branches, the Chou 丑 (Ox) which is Earth and the Zi 子 (Rat) which is Water both weaken the Ding 丁 Day Master.

What does this mean? It means that while this person's Day Master, which is Fire, is weak, the strength of his Wealth Element, which is Metal, is very strong.

So this gentleman is not super rich but clearly he has the potential to be wealthy. All he needs is, yes, the right type of luck. So, let's take a look at his Luck Pillars.

88	78	68	58	48	38	28	18	8	
壬 *Ren* Yang Water	癸 *Gui* Yin Water	甲 *Jia* Yang Wood	乙 *Yi* Yin Wood	丙 *Bing* Yang Fire	丁 *Ding* Yin Fire	戊 *Wu* Yang Earth	己 *Ji* Yin Earth	庚 *Geng* Yang Metal	Luck Pillars 大運
子 *Zi* **Rat** Yang Water	丑 *Chou* **Ox** Yin Earth	寅 *Yin* **Tiger** Yang Wood	卯 *Mao* **Rabbit** Yin Wood	辰 *Chen* **Dragon** Yang Earth	巳 *Si* **Snake** Yin Fire	午 *Wu* **Horse** Yang Fire	未 *Wei* **Goat** Yin Earth	申 *Shen* **Monkey** Yang Metal	

What does Ding 丁 Fire need to make itself stronger so that it can control the already strong Metal Wealth Element? Wood of course.

Between the ages of 58-77, this gentleman will go through 20 years of wood luck. Thus, he can expect to experience much Wealth later in life.

88	78	68	58	48	38	28	18	8	
壬 *Ren* Yang Water	癸 *Gui* Yin Water	甲 *Jia* Yang Wood	乙 *Yi* Yin Wood	丙 *Bing* Yang Fire	丁 *Ding* Yin Fire	戊 *Wu* Yang Earth	己 *Ji* Yin Earth	庚 *Geng* Yang Metal	Luck Pillars 大運
子 *Zi* **Rat** Yang Water	丑 *Chou* **Ox** Yin Earth	寅 *Yin* **Tiger** Yang Wood	卯 *Mao* **Rabbit** Yin Wood	辰 *Chen* **Dragon** Yang Earth	巳 *Si* **Snake** Yin Fire	午 *Wu* **Horse** Yang Fire	未 *Wei* **Goat** Yin Earth	申 *Shen* **Monkey** Yang Metal	
		Wood Luck	Wood Luck						

He can also seek to maximise his Wealth potential during the ages of 38-47, when he goes through strong Fire luck. During these years, he will enjoy wealth through partnerships, which will be successful.

88	78	68	58	48	38	28	18	8	
壬 *Ren* Yang Water	癸 *Gui* Yin Water	甲 *Jia* Yang Wood	乙 *Yi* Yin Wood	丙 *Bing* Yang Fire	丁 *Ding* Yin Fire	戊 *Wu* Yang Earth	己 *Ji* Yin Earth	庚 *Geng* Yang Metal	**Luck Pillars** 大運
子 *Zi* **Rat** Yang Water	丑 *Chou* **Ox** Yin Earth	寅 *Yin* **Tiger** Yang Wood	卯 *Mao* **Rabbit** Yin Wood	辰 *Chen* **Dragon** Yang Earth	巳 *Si* **Snake** Yin Fire	午 *Wu* **Horse** Yang Fire	未 *Wei* **Goat** Yin Earth	申 *Shen* **Monkey** Yang Metal	

Fire Luck

Why partnership? The Fire element to a Ding 丁 Fire person is the Companion Element. Since Fire is a Favourable Element to this chart, he can use Fire – meaning, he can have partners in business and create wealth through partnerships. This gentleman will most likely a mass his wealth through joint-ventures or working together in partnership with others during those 20 years.

But his real Wealth luck comes in during Wood luck years. This is because Wood directly strengthens his 'Ding 丁 Fire' and the wealth that he can acquire during these years will not have to be 'shared' with anyone!

Easy Come, Easy Go

One or two silly mistakes can in some instances literally cost a fortune. I've had clients who have lost their entire fortunes due to mishaps.

If making money is about making sure that you seize the opportunities when your luck is good, then keeping your money is recognising the times when you may experience a loss of wealth and staying away from anything too risky during those periods.

The key to guarding against mishaps related to wealth is to look for elements that will cause imbalance to the BaZi chart, in particular, imbalance which relates to your ability to control your Wealth Element or something which results in the removal of your Wealth Element.

I will introduce one of the easiest and certain method of recognising this scenario – it is one of the Earthly Branch Relationships called the Six Clashes (Liu Chong 六沖).

Six Clashes is a BaZi term for a type of relationship between the elements. There are SIX different types of Clashing relationships. Hence the term Six Clashes.

A Clash between the Earthly Branches denotes an 'opposing' force between one Earth Branch with another. It usually results in the removal of an element.

Table of Six Clashes (六沖)

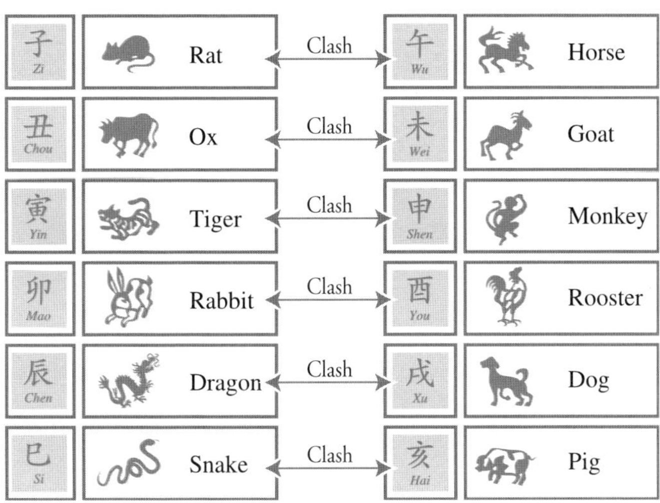

Branch	Animal		Branch	Animal
子 Zi	Rat	← Clash →	午 Wu	Horse
丑 Chou	Ox	← Clash →	未 Wei	Goat
寅 Yin	Tiger	← Clash →	申 Shen	Monkey
卯 Mao	Rabbit	← Clash →	酉 You	Rooster
辰 Chen	Dragon	← Clash →	戌 Xu	Dog
巳 Si	Snake	← Clash →	亥 Hai	Pig

It is useful to commit the above Six Clashes into memory because this principle can be used for other types of BaZi analysis besides Wealth analysis.

Now, let's see what the effect of a clash is when it comes to matters of money.

Hour 時	Day 日	Month 月	Year 年	
	日元 Day Master			Heavenly Stems 天干
	戊 Wu Yang Earth			
			子 Zi Rat Yang Water	Earthly Branches 地支
			癸	

						Luck Pillars 大運
		午 Wu Horse Yang Fire				
		丁 乙				

This Day Master is Wu 戊 Earth. Wu 戊 Earth's Wealth Element is Water. In this particular BaZi, the Wealth Element of Water can be found inside the Zi 子 (Rat)branch in the Year Pillar.

When this person enters the Wu 午 (Horse) luck pillar in his destiny, the Wu 午 (Horse) will clash with Zi 子 (Rat). This clash will 'clash away' his Wealth Element. This indicates loss of wealth since the Wealth Element is being clashed away. Which means that when this person enters the Wu 午 (Horse) luck pillar, he or she will encounter problems with money.

Should you advise him to make major investments in this period of his life? Or should you advise him to lay low and keep a low profile – perhaps save up for the rainy day? Remember, BaZi is all about taking the right action during the good or bad luck cycles with a view to improving your life.

If one of your Earthly Branches is your Wealth Element, and it is involved in a Clash in any particular Year or Luck Pillar, than this is likely that year will be a 'loss of wealth' year. Simple isn't it?

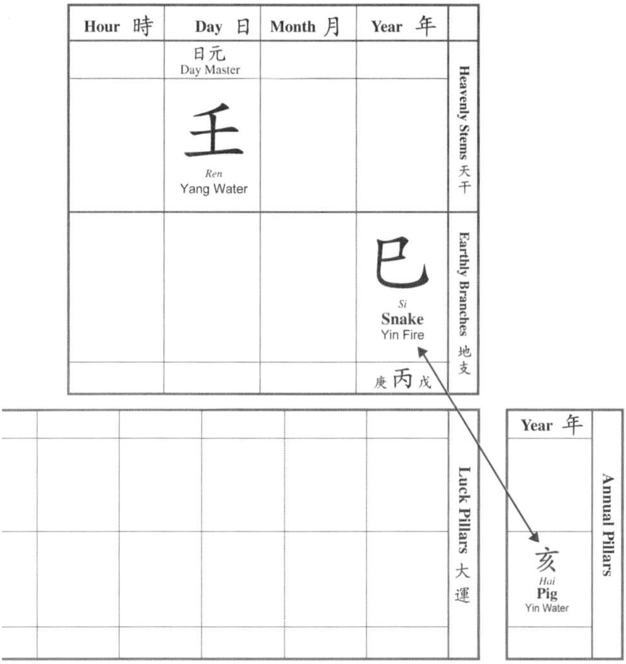

Hour 時	Day 日	Month 月	Year 年	
	日元 Day Master			
	壬 *Ren* Yang Water			Heavenly Stems 天干
			巳 *Si* **Snake** Yin Fire	Earthly Branches 地支
			庚 丙 戊	

Luck Pillars 大運

Year 年	
	Annual Pillars
亥 *Hai* **Pig** Yin Water	

Year of the Pig

Let's look at another example. Ren 壬 Day Master's Wealth Element is Fire. The Wealth Element of this Ren 壬 Day Master is located inside the Si 巳 (Snake) Earthly Branch in the year pillar. Now, refer to the Table of Six Clashes – you will notice that the Hai 亥 (Pig) clashes with the Si 巳 (Snake). This means that during the Hai 亥 (Pig) year, this person will experience a loss of wealth.

	Hour 時	Day 日	Month 月	Year 年
Heavenly Stems 天干	辛 *Xin* Yin Metal	丁 *Ding* Yin Fire	丙 *Bing* Yang Fire	丁 *Ding* Yin Fire
Earthly Branches 地支	丑 *Chou* **Ox** Yin Earth	卯 *Mao* **Rabbit** Yin Wood	午 *Wu* **Horse** Yang Fire	酉 *You* **Rooster** Yin Metal
	辛己癸	乙	丁己	辛

Luck Pillars 大運	86	76	66	56	46	36	26	16	6
Stem	丁 *Ding* Yin Fire	戊 *Wu* Yang Earth	己 *Ji* Yin Earth	庚 *Geng* Yang Metal	辛 *Xin* Yin Metal	壬 *Ren* Yang Water	癸 *Gui* Yin Water	甲 *Jia* Yang Wood	乙 *Yi* Yin Wood
Branch	酉 *You* **Rooster** Yin Metal	戌 *Xu* **Dog** Yang Earth	亥 *Hai* **Pig** Yin Water	子 *Zi* **Rat** Yang Water	丑 *Chou* **Ox** Yin Earth	寅 *Yin* **Tiger** Yang Wood	卯 *Mao* **Rabbit** Yin Wood	辰 *Chen* **Dragon** Yang Earth	巳 *Si* **Snake** Yin Fire
Hidden	辛	丁戊辛	壬甲	癸	辛己癸	戊甲丙	乙	癸戊乙	庚丙戊

Let's look at a more complete example.

This man lost a lot of money just before he reached the age of 36. Let's find out why.

He is Ding 丁 Fire born in Wu 午 (Horse) month. Now, Wu 午 (Horse) is the height of the Summer season when Fire is the strongest element. Clearly, his Ding 丁 Fire Day Master is strong.

Take a look at what is around him. There are two more Fire Elements on the Month and Year stems – a Bing 丙 and a Ding 丁. This man's chart has many Companion Elements. Now, remember, when a Day Master is Weak, then Companion elements help to strengthen it but when a Day Master is strong, it doesn't need more Companions!

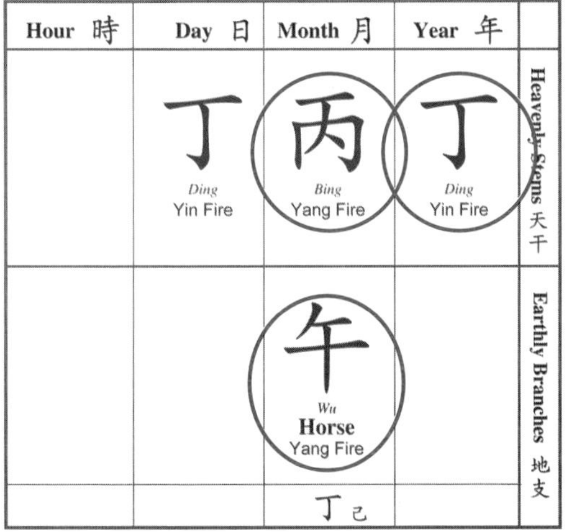

These Companions will end up competing with the Day Master to control the Wealth Element. Why? Because his Day Master is strong he does not need more Companion Elements to make him stronger. His Companion Elements are therefore negative elements.

When did he lose a substantial sum of money? During the ages of 26-35, when he was going through the Luck Pillar of Gui Mao 癸卯 (Water Rabbit). What happened?

86	76	66	56	46	36	26	16	6	
丁 *Ding* Yin Fire	戊 *Wu* Yang Earth	己 *Ji* Yin Earth	庚 *Geng* Yang Metal	辛 *Xin* Yin Metal	壬 *Ren* Yang Water	癸 *Gui* Yin Water	甲 *Jia* Yang Wood	乙 *Yi* Yin Wood	**Luck Pillars** 大運
酉 *You* **Rooster** Yin Metal	戌 *Xu* **Dog** Yang Earth	亥 *Hai* **Pig** Yin Water	子 *Zi* **Rat** Yang Water	丑 *Chou* **Ox** Yin Earth	寅 *Yin* **Tiger** Yang Wood	卯 *Mao* **Rabbit** Yin Wood	辰 *Chen* **Dragon** Yang Earth	巳 *Si* **Snake** Yin Fire	

Mao 卯 (Rabbit) and You 酉 (Rooster) are one of the Six Clashes in BaZi study. Remember the Six Clashes I mentioned earlier?

Now, the You 酉 (Rooster) is Metal, which is the Wealth element of Ding 丁 Fire. The Mao 卯 (Rabbit) branch of the Luck Pillar clashes away the You 酉 (Rooster) in the year pillar, thereby removing the Wealth Element from his chart.

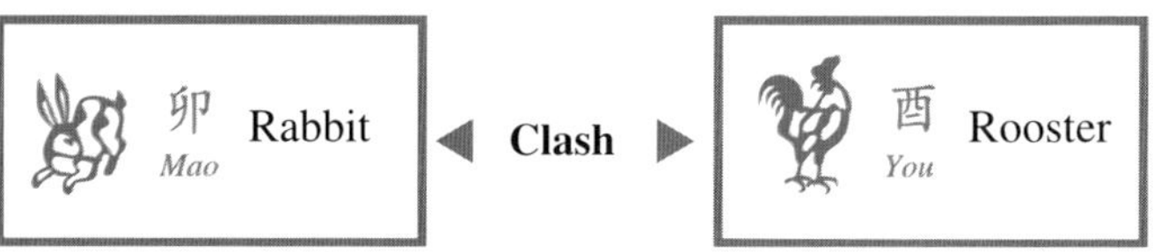

Furthermore, the Mao 卯 (Rabbit) is Wood and Wood in this man's chart is an Unfavourable Element. Why? Being a strong Fire element, he does not need to be strengthened any further by a Resource Element. Wood strengthens Fire, thus Wood is an Unfavourable Element to him.

Wood comes in and throws off the balance in the chart by making the already strong Fire too strong and at the same time, removing the Wealth Element in this chart. Hence, the loss of wealth!

Are there exceptions to rule? Yes of course there are. However, in general, whenever a clash involves a Wealth branch, there is a 65 – 75% chance it will be related to loss of money. Of course, there are exceptions and one has to qualify the Clash on the basis of its severity but these are advance methods of analysis that I will share in my later books. For now, look out for these clashes in your chart – they could literally, save you a fortune!

Who Wants To Be A Millionaire?

Much of our world today seems to revolve around making money in the fastest, shortest possible way. Have you seen that TV show 'Who wants to be a millionaire?' It is a good illustration of how today, we worship individuals who get rich overnight on a single stock market trade or IPO, who go from rags to riches on a TV show, who receive a windfall as it were, from the Heavens by winning the lottery.

I think the question when it comes to wealth, should never be if you can be a millionaire but if you can STAY a millionaire! Remember, easy come, easy go. There are people who may well be able to reap a great amount of money in a short span of time but in the same amount of time, manage to squander it all.

That is why in BaZi analysis of a person's Destiny Code, we look for Wealth and source of Wealth. Just wealth alone is not enough to ensure long lasting financial fortunes. You need to have continuous source of Wealth. So what do we look for in a BaZi that indicates a continuous source of Wealth?

Essentially, you also need the Output Element to support your Wealth Element.

Remember the Five Elements? Well, you will notice that your Output Element is what creates your Wealth Element. If you have Output, then your Wealth Element has support and can continue to grow.

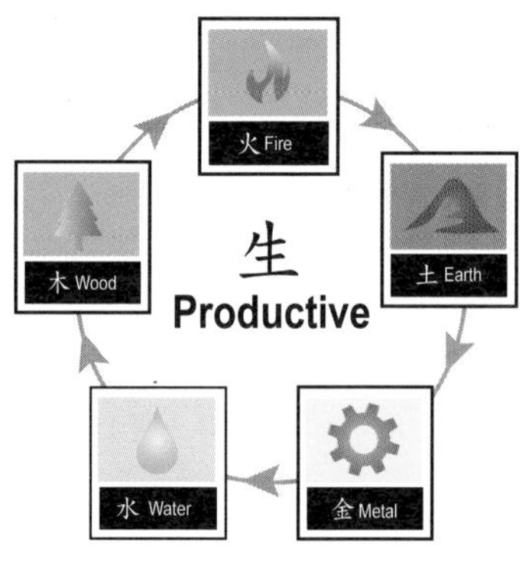

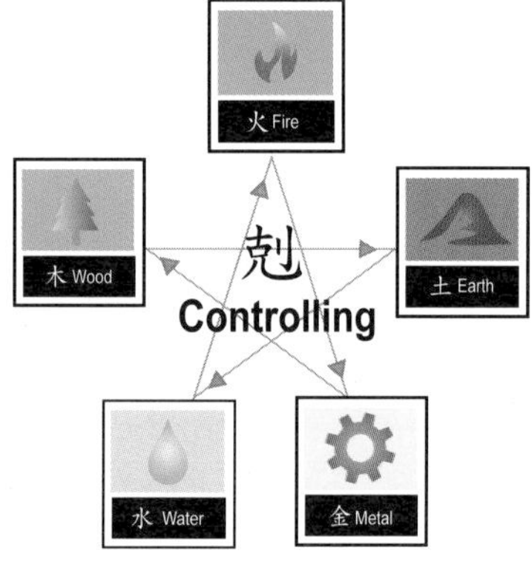

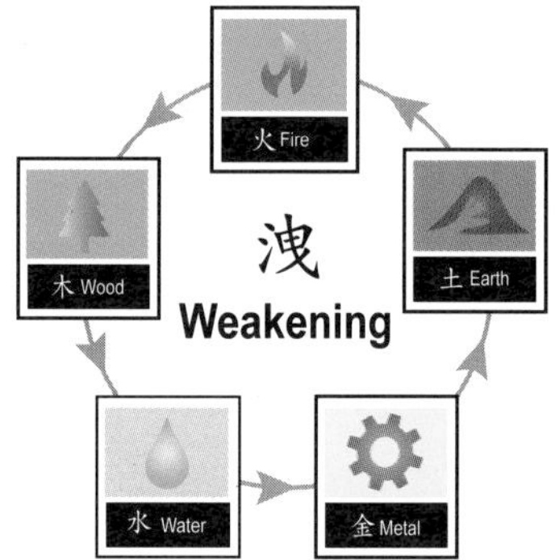

Five Element Productive, Controlling and Weakening Cycles.

This gentleman is Jia 甲 Wood is born in Chou 丑 (Ox) month. Chou 丑 (Ox) is the Winter season – in Winter, the Water element is strong. Water produces Wood. Now, notice that inside the Chou 丑 (Ox) and Chen 辰 (Dragon), what we call the Hidden Stems in BaZi, are roots of Water.

Hour 時	Day 日	Month 月	Year 年	
己 *Ji* Yin Earth	甲 *Jia* Yang Wood	辛 *Xin* Yin Metal	丙 *Bing* Yang Fire	Heavenly Stems 天干
巳 *Si* **Snake** Yin Fire	辰 *Chen* **Dragon** Yang Earth	丑 *Chou* **Ox** Yin Earth	寅 *Yin* **Tiger** Yang Wood	Earthly Branches 地支
庚 丙 戊	癸 戊 乙	辛 己 癸	戊 甲 丙	

Notice that this chart also has Bing 丙 Fire, which helps bring warmth to the chart. Fire is the Output of Wood. Fire produces Earth, which is the Wealth of Wood. Accordingly, we can see in this chart, that the Output Element is continuously producing the Wealth Element. The Wealth Element is supported by its source, indicating continuous growth.

The Day Master Element is strong, Wealth is strong and there is perfect use of Output star. This is a BaZi chart of a wealthy individual.

A Word on Wealth and Windfall

"Pennies do not come from Heaven – they must be earned here on Earth" – Margaret Thatcher

Many BaZi practitioners will tell you that in many consultations, people like to inquire about Pian Cai (偏財), or Wealth from the Heavens – better known as windfall gains. Usually, this relates to questions about the stock market or whether or not they can win money from gambling or the lottery.

I am no expert in stock broking. Asking any Destiny Code Analyst about stock broking is like asking a fishmonger how to write a computer program.

Stock picking is an art and a special skill. There are experts in this field and it requires much study and research. It is not that much just about luck alone.

It's the same with gambling. Winning at the casino is not just about a game of luck and chance. It's a game of statistics and probability.

People who win at gambling have very special charts or at least they go through very special 'timing' in their destiny. Not many people have such charts.

BaZi analysis of a person's wealth, is not about forecasting the ups and downs of the stock market, telling them what stocks to pick or whether they should buy a lottery ticket at 34. A BaZi analysis of a person's wealth is mainly about understanding his wealth amassing capacity, and through what fields or work can this be maximised.

BaZi is not an art specifically designed to predict trends of financial markets either. The Heavenly Star (Tian Xing 天星) method might be a better choice for this purpose. But that's not the topic of discourse here. BaZi is an art designed mainly to assess a person's destiny, not the market's destiny. Does the market have a date of birth? Is it a male of female? You get the point? If you want to pick stocks or play the market, you need a different kind of 'personal chart'!

So what about Warren Buffet or Li Ka Shing you might ask?

Stock picking is like any other profession – it has rules, it has skills and you need a talent for understanding the market, the complexity of the market and read the trends. Usually in BaZi, we look for the capacity of a person with regards to what we call Indirect Wealth. And of course, the right luck pillars do help.

You must have the correct BaZi chart (one that already has the capacity in its code) and the right supporting luck pillars in order to excel and win at the stock market or make windfall gains. In every market rise and fall, there are those who make money and those who don't. This is because there are those who go through wealth luck and those who do not.

BaZi is not specifically designed to help you gamble and make windfall profits. Though over the centuries, many people have been intrigued by the fact that there is a slight possibility that gambling can be 'calculated' with BaZi. I do not rule out this possibility, but definitely this is not an area of my expertise at the time of writing this book. And I personally do not endorse such practice. You can gamble for fun but I don't think you should gamble your fortunes away. It is definitely not a wise way to live and not a correct way to practice BaZi!

Chapter Nine:
Prince Charming and Ms Right – All About Romance

I think one of the main motivations in life for many people is to find that special someone to share their happiness and success with. Yet in this world, unfortunately, there are many who seem to succeed in everything but relationships.

It is common for BaZi consultations to sometimes be just about one thing: relationships. Women (although increasingly these days, Men) usually want to know … When will I have a relationship? When will I meet Mr/Ms Right or that Special Someone? When will I get married?

The Love Code: BaZi for Relationships

In some respects, evaluating your relationship through BaZi is like having marriage counseling – you're trying to find the source of a problem and understand what is wrong with your relationship. The advantage of BaZi is that you can use it to not only find out why your relationship or marriage is having difficulties, but also in the process, understand yourself and your personality better and thus, perhaps make changes to your attitude or your character that can make your relationships or marriage better.

Those of us who are more romantically inclined tend to think of relationships as an everlasting, till death do us part scenario. But like all things, in BaZi (and in the living world), nothing is permanent.

That is not to say that you can never be happy with just one person – but that relationships, like all things in life, have their ups and downs. Passion, commitment, love are not constant in this life or in a BaZi chart. It is for this very reason that BaZi is so useful when it comes to relationships matters.

View BaZi analysis as an education, offering solutions to the issues we encounter when dealing with the opposite sex. But remember also that when you are evaluating your BaZi, you need to think in an objective, unbiased way.

Admittedly, this is difficult so perhaps when it comes to evaluating relationships or marriage, get a friend to look at your chart rather than try to analyse it entirely by yourself. Often an opinion from someone who is not deeply involved in your life can provide a different perspective regarding your specific concerns. An unbiased or independent view can sometimes be harsh but would eventually be the real "help" or advice you need. When you are trapped in a 'love' or emotional problem, it is often difficult to get out of the maze.

The Chinese say, 'To force, there is no happiness'.

Perhaps the most important thing in relationships is don't 'force' the situation. Remember that while love and relationships are important, so is leading a happy, healthy and vibrant life.

This is a very simplified way of looking at Relationships and Marriage through BaZi. There are other more complicated relationships such as Clashes, Punishments, Harms and Destructions but as this is a beginner's text, let's just keep things simple. Having said that, don't underestimate what you can discern with simple techniques of BaZi. Often, matters aren't as complicated as they appear. It is the people who complicate them.

Remember, the journey of a thousand miles begins with the first step.

Peach Blossom Appeal

One of the simplest ways to determine how you will fare in the game of relationships is to find out how 'attractive' you are. The best part is you don't need a mirror for this!

Ever wondered how some seemingly ugly (by objective standards) people are always the center of attraction? Or some people who are not bad-looking have difficulty attracting the opposite sex? Or how some politicians or artists seem to maintain their popularity despite being flawed characters?

The answer is in the Peach Blossom.

Peach Blossom is a type of flower in China that is culturally associated with romance. When someone says you're going through "Peach Blossom luck" (桃花運), they are in effect saying that you are having good romance luck.

"Peach Blossom Stars"(桃花星)is the name for certain group of Earthly Branches that may appear in a set of BaZi. You could call them 'attraction magnets'. They give a person charisma, a certain Mystery-X factor that draws people to them or gives them a magic touch when it comes to managing or influencing people.

The reference point for the Peach Blossom star is the Day Master's Earthly Branch. (see diagram on the following page).

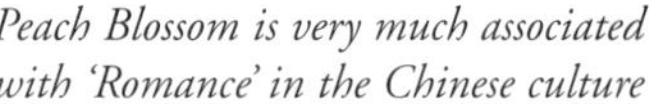

Peach Blossom is very much associated with 'Romance' in the Chinese culture

Day			Peach Blossom
寅 *Yin* **Tiger**	午 *Wu* **Horse**	戌 *Xu* **Dog**	卯 *Mao* **Rabbit**
巳 *Si* **Snake**	酉 *You* **Rooster**	丑 *Chou* **Ox**	午 *Wu* **Horse**
申 *Shen* **Monkey**	子 *Zi* **Rat**	辰 *Chen* **Dragon**	酉 *You* **Rooster**
亥 *Hai* **Pig**	卯 *Mao* **Rabbit**	未 *Wei* **Goat**	子 *Zi* **Rat**

Each person has an individual Peach Blossom star that is assigned to his or her Day Master's Earthly Branch. This Peach Blossom can manifest in 3 ways: it appears within the Eight Characters of your BaZi, or it appears in your Luck Pillar or in an Annual (Year) Pillar.

For example, if your Day Master's Earthly Branch is the Yin 寅 (Tiger), Wu 午 (Horse), or Xu 戌 (Dog), then your Peach Blossom star is Mao 卯 (Rabbit).

If your Day Master's Earthly Branch is the Si 巳 (Snake), You 酉 (Rooster) or Chou 丑 (Ox), then your Peach Blossom star is Wu 午 (Horse). If your Day Master's Earthly Branch is Shen 申 (Monkey), Zi 子 (Rat) or Chen 辰 (Dragon), then your Peach Blossom star is the You 酉 (Rooster).

If your Day Master Earthly Branch is the Hai 亥 (Pig), Mao 卯 (Rabbit) or Wei 未 (Goat) then your Peach Blossom is the Zi 子 (Rat).

Hour 時	Day 日	Month 月	Year 年

Day Master's Earthly Branch. Here is your reference point to find your Peach Blossom Star.

Example:

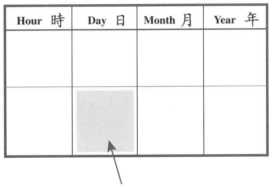

Hour 時	Day 日	Month 月	Year 年
	甲 Jia		
	申 Shen Monkey		

This example shows a lady born on the Jia 甲 (Yang Wood) Shen 申 (Monkey) Day. Her reference would be Shen 申 (Monkey). So her Peach Blossom star is the You 酉 (Rooster).

Check your BaZi chart now and find out WHICH animal sign is your Peach Blossom Star.

Evaluating Your Peach Blossom

If you have Peach Blossom Stars (and some people have more than one) as one of the Eight characters in your BaZi chart, you are someone who has a 'magic touch' with relationships. This can mean that you are very attractive to the opposite sex (or both sexes) or you have charisma that makes people want to gravitate towards you, but not necessarily in a boyfriend/girlfriend way. Politicians, movie stars, singers or speakers usually have Peach Blossom Stars – this is what gives them their public appeal, magnetism and charisma.

If you go through a luck pillar of your personal Peach Blossom star, in that ten years, your attractiveness towards the opposite sex will increase.

Hour 時	Day 日	Month 月	Year 年
	甲 *Jia*		
	申 *Shen* Monkey		

Year 2005
乙 *Yi*
酉 *You* Rooster

In the year 2005, year of Yi You 乙酉, (Wood Rooster) this lady born in the day of Jia Shen 甲申 (Wood Monkey) will meet with her personal Peach Blossom star. If she is still single in 2005, you can say that she will likely meet someone in the year of 2005.

Using the Peach Blossom Star method to check your attractiveness is the first and easiest way to analyse potential relationships. Of course, it is not the only way.

A word of caution, having Peach Blossom Star in your BaZi does not mean you are supermodel material. Sometimes, Peach Blossom Stars represent a potential attractiveness. This potential will only be realised in certain periods of time based on your cycle of luck. Sometimes this comes early in life and sometimes it doesn't come until a very old age. This is the luck factor in BaZi.

Are you the marrying kind?

Asian society places a great deal of importance on conformity and doing what everybody else is doing. It has become commonplace for us to define 'normality' through our stereotypes of how people should behave, what they should do with their lives and as far as relationships go, get married, have 2 or 3 children, a dog and house.

The unfortunate truth is that the determination to fit into the stereotype of 'normal' has not had the effect of creating a more 'normal' society, in fact it is quite the opposite. Divorces, broken families, misfit children or children with issues caused by their poor family background seem to be on the rise these days.

When you are evaluating the issue of relationships, specifically marriage, it is important (if you wish to make full use of the knowledge that comes from BaZi) to ask yourself this one very pertinent question: are you really the marrying kind?

The truth is that as far as Destiny Analysis goes, some people are better off being single. While some people may find their lives improve upon marriage, others may find marriage is not all that it is cut out to be.

Some people have excellent luck with relationships because their BaZi indicates they will have enjoyable and fruitful love lives. But it's also a fact that VERY FEW PEOPLE have it all.

What is 'having it all'?

A good love life. A good career. Good wealth luck. Respect. Status. Power. Harmonious family. Filial children. And a good end to their life.

The perfect life. Hassle free. Only happiness and no sorrow.

Now wouldn't this be ideal? But like there is Yin and Yang, so the world is incredibly unfair (all those people with good charts) and incredibly fair (no charts are forever good, or forever bad, or good in every single aspect equally).

Some good looking people flit from relationship to relationship, finding no satisfaction in any one. How is it the school geek seems happily married? When it comes to your Destiny and relationships, some people meet their soul-mate early in life, some late in life, some meet no one and some only can admire from afar.

Whatever you have in your chart or do not have in your chart, remember that it's not about the hand you're dealt, but how you play the game.

Finally, timing is one very important and crucial factor in BaZi. So sometimes you have to wait for your turn. Trying to 'win' the game early may be a temporary gain but could ultimately lead to a 'loss'.

Evaluating Your Marriage Luck

The idea of living with someone you love and sharing your success, indeed your life, together, is a very precious thing - not something that many people would turn down.

But yet, you have probably heard about the guy (or lady) who despite being very attractive just keeps falling in love with the wrong person or the wrong type. Or people you know who are trapped in terrible relationships but just don't seem to be able to get out of those relationships.

You may be the marrying kind, but have you got the Marriage Luck? Does your Destiny support your romantic or personal aspiration?

There are people out there with beautiful Destiny charts that give them not just the chance, but the certainty of such a life with someone special. And there are people out there with more money than they can ever spend in two lifetimes, trying to get out of their marriages.

Hour 時	Day 日	Month 月	Year 年	
己 *Ji* Yin Earth	壬 *Ren* Yang Water	己 *Ji* Yin Earth	乙 *Yi* Yin Wood	**Heavenly Stems 天干**
酉 *You* **Rooster** Yin Metal	辰 *Chen* **Dragon** Yang Earth	卯 *Mao* **Rabbit** Yin Wood	未 *Wei* **Goat** Yin Earth	**Earthly Branches 地支**
辛	癸 戊 乙	乙	乙 己 丁	

In the above example, we have a lady who has had a very unhappy marriage and is now divorced. What is the cause of her relationship woes?

She is Ren 壬 Water (Yang Water) born in Mao 卯 (Rabbit) month, which is the peak of Spring. Now, Wood is the strongest element in Spring and Wood absorbs Water so this Water Day Master is pretty weak. Her Day Master needs to be a bit stronger, which means she favours her Resource and Companion Elements.

Unfortunately, her Day Master has little support from the branches or stems in her chart. Not even the Metal in the You 酉 (Rooster) Branch of her Hour Pillar is enough to strengthen her Ren 壬 Water Day Master.

Now, ladies, remember that when your Day Master element is weak, you do not like to be controlled by another element. Thus, this Weak Ren 壬 Water does not like her Influence

Element, Earth. (Quick reminder: Earth controls Water in the Five Element cycle).

Accordingly, Earth is now an Unfavourable Element for her. In the study of BaZi, for a lady, the element that controls her Day Master element is called the Husband Star. Thus in the above chart, her Husband Star is an Unfavourable Element. Now, imagine if your Unfavourable Element is your Husband Element – what would you make of her relationship with her husband?

The obvious answer would be bad of course. The more she tries to force a marriage, the more the Unfavourable Element affects her. She has to wait for the time in her luck pillars where a certain Favourable Element appears to alleviate this flaw. When that time comes, her marriage or relationships will work out naturally.

De-Coding Relationship Luck Through BaZi

Generally, there are two methods for evaluating a person's Marriage Luck

- Evaluating the Spouse Palace
- Evaluating the Quality of the Wealth Element (for men) or Influence Element (for women)

Using these two methods, we are trying to ascertain if this person will have a good or bad relationship with their spouse but also, whether marriage is favourable or unfavourable. This is also sometimes used to evaluate if early or late marriage is preferable for a person.

The Spouse Palace

The Spouse Palace represents your relationship with your spouse. This Palace is located directly under your Day Master.

Hour 時	Day 日	Month 月	Year 年

Spouse Palace

In a majority of cases, if you have a Favourable Element located in your Spouse Palace, you will enjoy a good marriage in the sense that your relationship with your spouse will generally be good. You and your partner will enjoy your marriage to each other, have a loving relationship and will be committed to each other. Chances are that as long as you are not an unreasonable spouse or put needless pressure on your relationship, you will have a good marriage.

However, if in this palace you have an Unfavourable Element, then you might not feel that you would have a wonderful relationship with your spouse.

Hour 時	Day 日	Month 月	Year 年
	Unfavourable Element		

Having an Unfavourable Element in the Spouse Palace indicates unsatisfactory relationship with spouse.

This does NOT mean you will not get married. It may simply mean that in the duration of the marriage, you do not feel satisfied with the relationship for some reason or you are simply not as 'lovey-dovey' as some couples are.

So what do you do if this is the case? As commonplace and trite as the answer is, you simply have to work harder at your relationship.

I think I am by no means saying anything revolutionary when I say that people do have to work at their relationships, marriage or otherwise. People with Favourable Elements in their Spouse Palace simply don't have to put in as much effort as those who have an Unfavourable Element in their Spouse Palace.

This does not mean they do not have to work at maintaining their relationship (ie: keeping the spark, maintaining the zing in the marriage, appreciating their other halves – you know the drill).

Indeed, it may well be the case that people who do not take their marriage for granted (or know from their BaZi that their marriage luck is not so good) would do better simply because they make the effort. They go the extra mile to make their marriages work.

Now, I'm sure it probably seems a bit depressing to see all these less than good marriage charts. So let's take a look at what the chart of someone with good marriage luck looks like.

Hour 時	Day 日	Month 月	Year 年	
庚 *Geng* Yang Metal	乙 *Yi* Yin Wood	丙 *Bing* Yang Fire	己 *Ji* Yin Earth	Heavenly Stems 天干
辰 *Chen* **Dragon** Yang Earth	巳 *Si* **Snake** Yin,Fire	子 *Zi* **Rat** Yang Water	丑 *Chou* **Ox** Yin Earth	Earthly Branches 地支
癸 戊 乙	庚 丙 戊	癸	辛 己 癸	

This is the BaZi of a lady named Mrs. Chan, who enjoys a happy marriage. Mrs. Chan is Yi 乙 Wood, born in Zi 子 (Rat) month, which is the Winter month.

In my next books on BaZi, when I cover the Combinations, you will learn that Zi 子 (Rat) and Chou 丑 (Ox) is known as a 'half Winter' directional combination. This means that the Water element in this chart is strong. Now, with half of Winter in the chart, obviously this Bazi is also quite cold.

To keep the analysis simple, this is how you read this chart at the present level. In Winter, the Water element is strong. Water of course grows Wood. So we can say Wood is strong in this chart. Strong Wood usually requires Output to reduce the strength of the Wood and balance the chart – Wood's Output is Fire.

Now, look and see where the Fire Element is to be found? Smack inside her Spouse Palace is the Si巳 (Snake) which contains (in the hidden stems of the Earthly Branches) the favourable Bing丙 Fire element.

Hour 時	Day 日	Month 月	Year 年	
	乙 *Yi* Yin Wood			Heavenly Stems 天干
	巳 *Si* **Snake** Yin Fire			Earthly Branches 地支
	庚 丙 戊			

Mrs. Chan has her Favourable Fire element IN her Spouse Palace. A Favourable Element in the Spouse Palace usually indicates satisfying relationship with spouse.

The Untouchable Palace

Every relationship has its ups and downs. Some couples argue throughout their life together but still remain together. Some couples go through huge arguments then break up on a small issue. Some couples suddenly find after 20 years of marriage, they don't like each other.

By using BaZi, you can actually try to spot or foresee these arguments and conflicts and in some instances, stave off the 'break-up'.

Remember I asked you to memorize the Six Clashes 六沖? In case you haven't committed them to memory, here they are again.

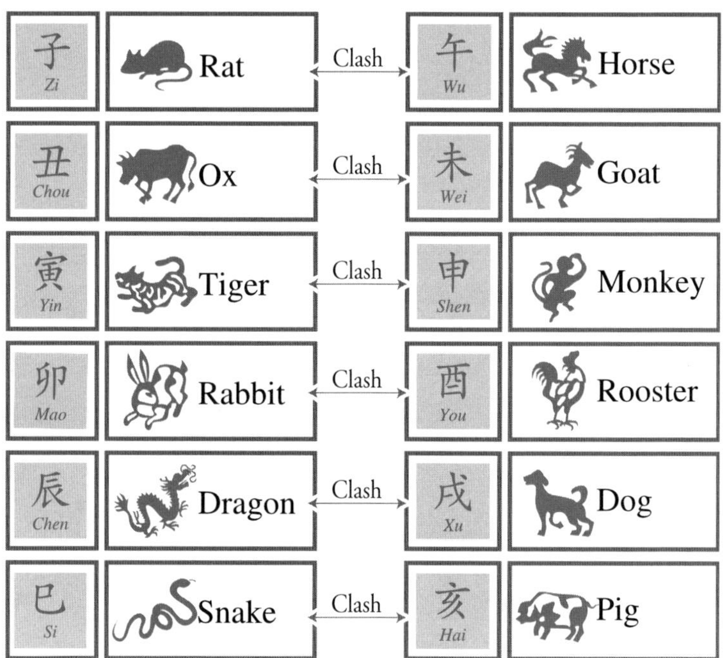

In BaZi, a person's spouse palace is SACRED. I call it the Untouchable Palace. Ideally, you don't want this palace to be clashed. A clash in the Spouse Palace usually denotes a problem associated with your relationship with your spouse.

There are major clashes and minor clashes. Pay attention to major ones (such as a clash due to a Luck Pillar) as these are the ones that hit a relationship hard. Minor ones (such as a clash from a Year Pillar) are not as bad.

Now, let's look at an example of how to evaluate the impact of a Clash in terms of relationships or marriage.

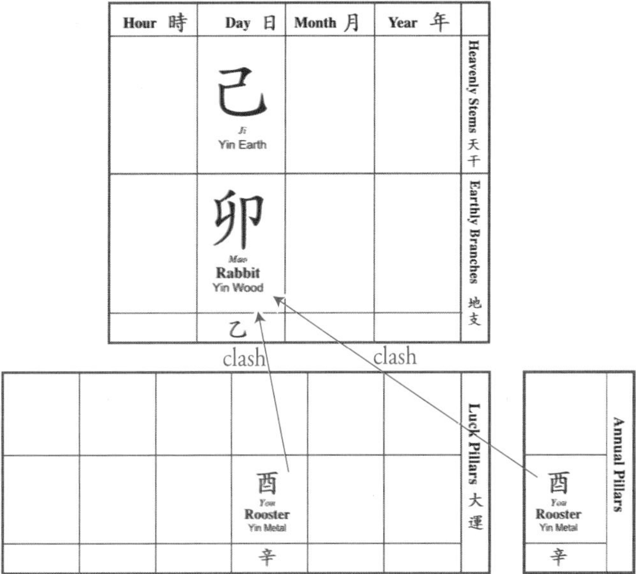

This chart belongs to a Ji 己 Earth lady. Her Influence element, which represents her Husband is Wood.

When she enters the 10 Year luck pillar of the You 酉 (Rooster) and in the Year of the You 酉 (Rooster) within those 10 years, a serious threat to her relationship can be expected.

Why? Because You 酉 (Rooster), which is Metal, clashes with her Mao 卯 (Rabbit), which is of a Wood Element. This Clash occurs in the Day Master's Earthly Branch, which is her Spouse Palace. When both the Luck Pillar and the Annual Pillars pose a double whammy into the Spouse Palace, this normally indicates an extremely strong likelihood of a turbulent period when it comes to the marital relationship.

Looking at Wealth and Influence

Remember in earlier chapters, I talked about the Husband Star and the Wealth Star? To the men, their Wealth Star represents their wife (remember, wealth is what your Day Master controls in the Five Element cycle) and to the women, their Influence Star represents their husband (since it is what controls your Day Master in the Five Element cycle).

Just a quick pointer here: the term 'stars' here is merely a term used by BaZi practitioners to describe what a specific element represents. Don't focus too much on the names or terms at this point. We are in the beginner's book remember? So let's keep things simple!

Now, so far we have learnt that if these are Favourable Elements to the person with regard to their Day Master, chances are, the quality of marriage for the person would be quite good. If these elements are Unfavourable, these usually belong to people who have a hard time enjoying their marriage or have a bad marriage. To analyse the quality of a marriage, you also can look at the quality of the Wealth or Influence Star and I'll show you how to do that in subsequent examples.

You may be curious to know: what does a REALLY good marriage chart look like?

One thing that you must remember: BaZi readings for relationships are based on what some people may regard as a bit of an old-fashioned viewpoint on marriage and relationships. In today's world of the working career woman and the age of the house husband, the idea of what is an ideal marriage has probably changed since the time of Grand Master Xu Zi Peng (from the Five Dynasty Era, about a thousand years ago)!

Grand Master Xu Zi Peng is the founding father of Zi Ping BaZi system, the system of Chinese Astrology we are using now to decode a person's Destiny Code.

Of course, what you believe to be an ideal marriage is an individual opinion but for now, let's focus with what BaZi considers to be the ideal marriage. (I will deal with the modern view of marriage in my next book).

Traditionally, a good marriage is a tall order. The woman is a good loving wife who takes care of her husband. Her husband is reasonably rich and takes care of their children and their home. The children are reasonably successful and filial. Finally, she will have the opportunity to see her grandchildren married before she dies.

Hour 時	Day 日	Month 月	Year 年	
丁 *Ding* Yin Fire	癸 *Gui* Yin Water	戊 *Wu* Yang Earth	丁 *Ding* Yin Fire	**Heavenly Stems** 天干
巳 *Si* **Snake** Yin Fire	卯 *Mao* **Rabbit** Yin Wood	申 *Shen* **Monkey** Yang Metal	未 *Wei* **Goat** Yin Earth	**Earthly Branches** 地支
庚 丙 戊	乙	戊 庚 壬	乙 己 丁	

This lady (BaZi Chart above) was in her 80s when she died. She was married to her husband for more than 60 years. At her funeral were her grandchildren and great grandchildren, along with hundreds of family members and friends.

This lady was Gui 癸 Water born in Shen 申 (Monkey) month, the Autumn season where Metal is the strongest. Metal produces Water, so her Water is reasonably strong. Now, her Influence Element is Earth. Where is her husband star then? Right next to her, in her Month Pillar! See the Wu 戊 (Yang Earth) in the Month Pillar's Heavenly Stem?

What makes this lady's marriage luck good is that her Day Master 'combines' with her husband star. In Advanced BaZi, Wu 戊 and Gui 癸 are a called a Heavenly Stem Combination – this means her husband loves her a lot.

Now, her Husband Star in this chart is no slouch either. He is well supported by the Fire elements in her chart (Fire produces Earth). So both her Self Element (Gui 癸) and her Husband Star (Wu 戊) are reasonably balanced.

What about her children? The children of Gui 癸 are the Wood element (Water produces Wood remember?). In this lady's chart, Wood is located right below her. Picture this – a gentle rain sprinkling down on the plants. In BaZi, this is a beautiful picture.

Hour 時	Day 日	Month 月	Year 年	
丁 *Ding* Yin Fire	癸 *Gui* Yin Water	戊 *Wu* Yang Earth	丁 *Ding* Yin Fire	Heavenly Stems 天干
巳 *Si* **Snake** Yin Fire	卯 *Mao* **Rabbit** Yin Wood	申 *Shen* **Monkey** Yang Metal	未 *Wei* **Goat** Yin Earth	Earthly Branches 地支
庚 丙 戊	乙	戊 庚 壬	乙 己 丁	

Now, emotional state is very important for a good marriage. This lady has no clashes, harms, punishments or destruction in her chart, indicating a stable personality and a balanced emotional state.

What does a chart that indicates a bad marriage look like? Take a look below:

Hour 時	Day 日	Month 月	Year 年	
乙 *Yi* Yin Wood	庚 *Geng* Yang Metal	甲 *Jia* Yang Wood	丙 *Bing* Yang Fire	Heavenly Stems 天干
酉 *You* **Rooster** Yin Metal	子 *Zi* **Rat** Yang Water	午 *Wu* **Horse** Yang Fire	午 *Wu* **Horse** Yang Fire	Earthly Branches 地支
辛	癸	丁 己	丁 己	

This lady was born in 1966. She has been married twice – presently she is single but is in a relationship.

She is Geng 庚 Metal, born in the month of Wu 午 (Horse) which is the height of Summer. Now, look at her BaZi – you will notice she has TWO Wu 午 (Horse) – so she has two Ding 丁 Fire. Look at the Hidden Stems underneath these Earthly Branches to find the two Ding 丁 Fire. Both these Ding 丁 Fires are strong as there is also a Bing 丙 Fire Heavenly Stem appearing in the Year pillar. This indicates the Fire element is excessively strong.

Now using what I like to call the 'Secret Art of Common Sense', we will know that Fire that is too strong will automatically hurt the Geng 庚 Metal Day Master. So, her Favourable Elements are Metal (to strengthen the Day Master) and Water, to cool the Fire.

The Zi 子 (Rat) contains Gui 癸 (Yin Water) which will be helpful in cooling her chart down. It is located in her Spouse Palace. Unfortunately, the Zi 子 (Rat) clashes with the Wu 午 (Horse) in the Month pillar.

Hour 時	Day 日	Month 月	Year 年	
乙 *Yi* Yin Wood	庚 *Geng* Yang Metal	甲 *Jia* Yang Wood	丙 *Bing* Yang Fire	Heavenly Stems 天干
酉 *You* **Rooster** Yin Metal	子 *Zi* **Rat** Yang Water	午 *Wu* **Horse** Yang Fire	午 *Wu* **Horse** Yang Fire	Earthly Branches 地支
辛	癸	丁 己	丁 己	

Most important element in this BaZi

Ding 丁 Fire is the Influence Element of this Geng Metal Day Master lady and thus, represents her Husband Star.

What causes this lady to have a bad marriage or bad husband luck in her life? In decoding a person's Destiny, like any other science, more than one indication of a problem, usually suggests that there is going to be a problem.

Hour 時	Day 日	Month 月	Year 年	
乙 *Yi* Yin Wood	庚 *Geng* Yang Metal	甲 *Jia* Yang Wood	丙 *Bing* Yang Fire	Heavenly Stems 天干
酉 *You* **Rooster** Yin Metal	子 *Zi* **Rat** Yang Water	午 *Wu* **Horse** Yang Fire	午 *Wu* **Horse** Yang Fire	Earthly Branches 地支
辛	癸	丁 己	丁 己	

Husband Star

In this lady's case, firstly, her Spouse Palace has a Clash. Secondly, this Clash involves her Husband Element (Fire) and her Spouse Palace, which is the Zi 子 (Rat) Earthly Branch. Thirdly, Fire element, which is the element that represents her Husband is her Unfavourable Element.

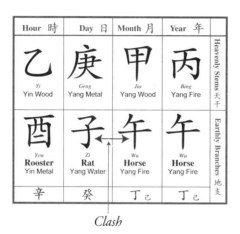

Hour 時	Day 日	Month 月	Year 年	
乙 *Yi* Yin Wood	庚 *Geng* Yang Metal	甲 *Jia* Yang Wood	丙 *Bing* Yang Fire	Heavenly Stems 天干
酉 *You* **Rooster** Yin Metal	子 *Zi* **Rat** Yang Water	午 *Wu* **Horse** Yang Fire	午 *Wu* **Horse** Yang Fire	Earthly Branches 地支
辛	癸	丁 己	丁 己	

Clash

Finally, you will also notice that ALL her four branches are Peach Blossom Stars. Now, remember that in BaZi, we are always striving for balance. A bit of Peach Blossom is good to enhance one's attractiveness but too many Peach Blossom Stars is not good for relationships and especially for women when it comes to ensuring a stable marriage.

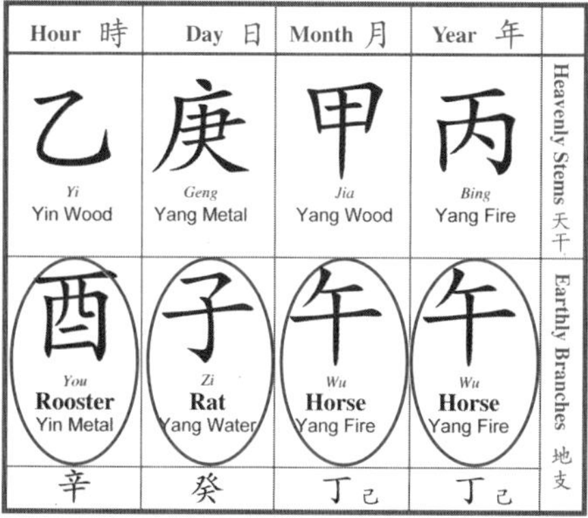

Hour 時	Day 日	Month 月	Year 年	
乙 *Yi* Yin Wood	庚 *Geng* Yang Metal	甲 *Jia* Yang Wood	丙 *Bing* Yang Fire	Heavenly Stems 天干
酉 *You* **Rooster** Yin Metal	子 *Zi* **Rat** Yang Water	午 *Wu* **Horse** Yang Fire	午 *Wu* **Horse** Yang Fire	Earthly Branches 地支
辛	癸	丁 己	丁 己	

All four branches are Peach Blossom Stars in this BaZi

As your knowledge of BaZi increases, come back and study this chart again. You will see that this lady's relationship issues are also caused by Self Punishment and Destruction in the branches of her BaZi, denoting emotional instability, the main cause of her relationship woes.

Giving the Right 'Love' Prescription

Of course, when people come for a BaZi consultation that relates to their relationship, they aren't just looking for the good news (or bad news) as it were. They want some advice.

In the course of my practice of BaZi (and I have done readings both locally and overseas), the "cultural" context is very important.

In countries and societies where divorce is commonplace, acceptable or not too difficult to undertake, you tend to get more people asking when is the right time to get a divorce rather than whether their marriage will be good.

In Asian societies, divorce is usually the last resort in terms of advice given by a BaZi practitioner. It is usually only suggested when the relationships is abusive or tormenting. This is because in Asian society, it is generally expected that couples will stay together for the sake of their children or the family, although I should add, this is changing.

How do you use BaZi then to 'plan' the decisions that relate to your relationships and marriage? All things considered, personal happiness is at stake here for most people.

Here are a few scenarios where BaZi can help you make a decision on how to handle your relationships.

Waiting for the Right Person

Your BaZi chart may indicate that you have more than one relationship possibility but the 'real' relationship (the Right Person as it were) only comes later in life.
What then do you do?

If you chose the first person who comes along, there is the possibility of running the risk that when the Real Ms or Mr Right comes along, the earlier relationship runs into difficulty or problems, of the Third Person kind.

Hitting the Clash

What do you do when your BaZi reveals a clash with your Luck Pillar and your Spouse Palace?

When you are in a relationship, 2-3 bad years might seem like an eternity, much less 10 years. It is often at these points that people contemplate the path of divorce. If your BaZi tells you that your marriage is going to hit a rough patch at that point, then you can make use of that knowledge to get around the problem. Perhaps you just need to tolerate your other half more. Or close an eye to some of the difficulties. Or attend counseling.

Perhaps your spouse or yourself may consider working overseas for a period – as they say, absence makes the heart grow fonder. Also temporary separation through overseas work can help 'fulfill' a BaZi chart clash in a controlled manner. Some families I know have weathered through the 'tough years' of their relationship period, almost threatening to divorce, but didn't choose that route.

Whatever it is, there is a solution at hand if you CHOSE to take action. And since you KNOW what is the cause of your difficulties, it would seem silly not to do something right?

It's all about the Right Time

If you have failed dismally in relationships or always end up picking the wrong person, it is likely that you have a certain negative element in your BaZi, especially in your spouse palace. In a majority of the cases, it's all the timing. If you are fortunate, this 'time of your life' comes early in life. For the rest of us, this 'time' come a little later.

For some people, a late marriage is better than an early marriage as this will ensure their relationship with their spouse will be positive rather than unfavourable. If you know that your early years (until say, 35) are likely to be unfavourable to marriage, it MIGHT seem wise not to walk up the altar at an early age.

It is wise to wait till it comes. In the meantime, try working in areas where you will achieve much better results. Work with your BaZi chart, not against it. Your time could be spent more productively doing something which has a good chance of achieving results or that we are good at.

Commitment when a person is ready.

One of the situations where a marriage turns sour is when people are 'forced' to commit to marriage when they are not ready. Sometimes this is psychological. Most of the time, it's in their BaZi. They are just not ready to take on the relationship.

千山易改，本性難移

A thousand mountains can be moved but to change a person's character, it is not possible – Chinese Saying

It is often easier to move mountains than to change a person's character. The only way is to wait until that person comes to a point in life where 'commitment' is a priority. Some people have this luck earlier in life, while some, much later. Hence the need to understand and accept these factors in life. Neither party should be forced into a situation that they don't want to be in.

Whose Problem is it?

Now, I realise this is a book about BaZi, with a little bit of Feng Shui thrown in so it seems a bit odd to sound like a marriage counselor. BUT, many people often refuse to acknowledge that sometimes, their marital problems are caused by their own attitudes.

In the many professional BaZi readings I've done, often I encounter clients who think the problem is with their partners or spouses, never with THEM! It's amazing how human nature is – others are always wrong and we always think or feel we are right.

Men who find their wives are naggy or a pain in the butt or who feel their marriages have lost that 'loving feeling' as it were sometimes don't realise that their spouses have not changed – they have simply not kept up their end of the bargain or not bothered with the relationship or they have changed!

Before people put the blame at the door of their spouses, they should first evaluate their own BaZi to see if perhaps the problem is THEM. (if it's not, then you check your spouse's chart).

If your Influence Element is what is causing your chart to be unbalanced, then it is probably your work that is putting a strain on your marriage. The answer – work harder at putting in quality time at home, even if it means you have to be a bit more organised.

If your Output Element is dominant in your chart, your problem is likely due to your overly high standards or demanding attitude. The answer? Expect less from your spouse and you'll be happier.

Admittedly, it is not easy to undertake some of these changes, easy as they seem. To change a person's attitude, indeed, approach to life is very difficult and requires a lot of effort. So you must ask yourself at the end of the day – if this relationship matters to me, can I do what it takes to make it work?

If You Believe in Soul-Mates

And there are few of us who don't believe in the existence of someone special, someone just right for us.

Then let Fate and Destiny (Yuan Fen缘份) to do its job.

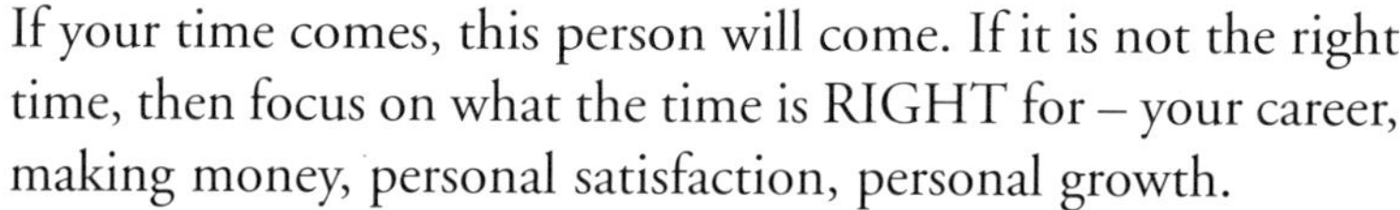

If your time comes, this person will come. If it is not the right time, then focus on what the time is RIGHT for – your career, making money, personal satisfaction, personal growth.

BaZi, above all, is about taking the right action, at the right time. Taking advantage of your luck. For some of us, missing that moment is missing the boat forever! Your next chance comes, well, in your next lifetime!

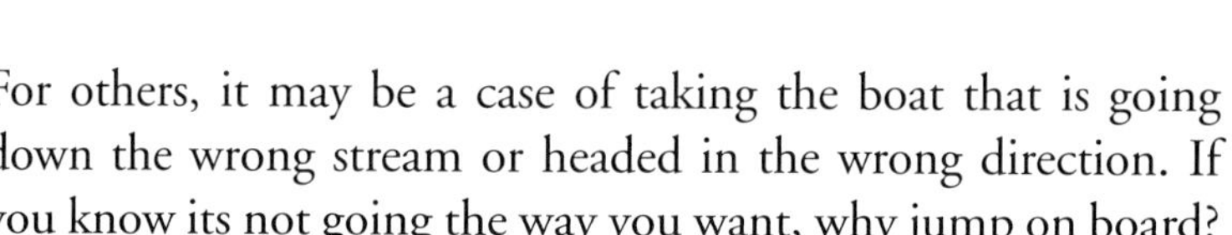

For others, it may be a case of taking the boat that is going down the wrong stream or headed in the wrong direction. If you know its not going the way you want, why jump on board?

Chapter Ten:
The Power of BaZi

八字

A lot has happened since we've started from Chapter One. By now, you would have grasped the basic idea of decoding your Destiny through BaZi. You have begun to understand YOUR Destiny Code.

You should be able to tell at this point, by reading your own chart, if you are enjoying good luck or suffering bad luck. This is achieved through the analysis of Favourable and Unfavourable Elements.

Once I taught a class, a student came up to me and said – okay, we have learnt BaZi. We have de-coded our own Destiny Code. Now what do we do with it?

Knowing one's Destiny Code through BaZi helps us understand ourselves better and enables us to make better decisions, decisions based on our true capacity and ability. BaZi reveals to us our potential and our capabilities. Make good use of the knowledge you have gained from your understanding of your Destiny Code to make informed decisions.

But the essence of BaZi is in our action. It is not good enough to just *know*, one must make use of what one has learnt and understood about oneself, and then take the right action. When one has all the information that is needed to make an informed decision, the question ultimately is: *what are you going to do about it?*

Taking action is important follow up to decoding your destiny. Perhaps you need to capitalise on opportunities or keep a low profile as you are in turbulent times. A change in your attitude and behaviour may be needed to improve your relationships – these are some examples of the empowerment that comes with unlocking the Destiny Code.

Fulfillment in life is sometimes about living our lives in accordance with our true identities and true selves.

It's difficult to encapsulate in just one chapter what we can learn from BaZi and how we can maximise the knowledge we derive from our BaZi to help us in life. What I'd like to do in this chapter is give you a few simple examples and illustrations of how BaZi can provide us with invaluable information that in turn can help us to make better decisions in life.

Health is the Greatest Wealth

Look at all the health products and health equipment available in the market nowadays. Undeniably, health is the greatest concern of many people today.

Many of the participants at my public seminars ask me about identifying health problems from a BaZi chart. Of course this is never an easy question to answer. Not because it is difficult to ascertain this information from the BaZi, but because it is difficult to teach someone in a quick discussion how to figure out what are his or her potential health problems! There are so many ways to help ascertain a person's potential health problems or ailments. Let me share with you a few simple techniques for identifying health issues from a person's BaZi.

One quick way of identifying health problems is by evaluating the strength of your Day Master, as was done in Chapter Six, and then finding out your Unfavourable Element.

Your Unfavourable Element is likely to be your 'problem' area or health threat. This is the case with a majority of cases. In BaZi studies, the Unfavourable Element is known as the Ji Shen 忌神 or the Negative God. This element is usually the cause of bad fortunes or more specifically, poor health or certain health ailments in an individual's life.

Your personal Unfavourable Element will determine the type of problems or the possible weak spots in your body. Here is a short quick summary of how the Elements relate to various types of health problems or parts of the body.

Element	Ailments / Area of Concern
火 Fire	Heart-related illnesses. Visual problems or problems with eyes.
土 Earth	Stomach or abdomen-related. Digestive systems. Cells and flesh.
金 Metal	Lungs and Intestines-related. Breathing problems and illnesses such as asthma
水 Water	Sexual Organs, Sexual diseases. Blood related problems, urinary disease or problems.
木 Wood	Liver and limbs related. Veins and arteries.

Hour 時	Day 日	Month 月	Year 年	
癸 *Gui* Yin Water	癸 *Gui* Yin Water	丁 *Ding* Yin Fire	壬 *Ren* Yang Water	Heavenly Stems 天干
丑 *Chou* **Ox** Yin Earth	未 *Wei* **Goat** Yin Earth	未 *Wei* **Goat** Yin Earth	午 *Wu* **Horse** Yang Fire	Earthly Branches 地支
辛 己 癸	乙 己 丁	乙 己 丁	丁 己	

This is the BaZi chart of a lady suffering from stomach cancer. She is Gui 癸 Water born in the Wei 未 (Goat) month. As Wei 未 (Goat) is a Summer month, Fire is very strong. We can also see that there are many Earth elements in the Earthly Branches – the Wei 未 (Goat) and the Chou 丑 (Ox). Therefore, we can conclude that her chart has a lot of Fire and Earth. Accordingly, her Gui 癸 Water Day Master is extremely weak.

Hour 時	Day 日	Month 月	Year 年	
癸 *Gui* Yin Water	癸 *Gui* Yin Water	丁 *Ding* Yin Fire	壬 *Ren* Yang Water	Heavenly Stems 天干
丑 *Chou* **Ox** Yin Earth	未 *Wei* **Goat** Yin Earth	未 *Wei* **Goat** Yin Earth	午 *Wu* **Horse** Yang Fire	Earthly Branches 地支
辛 己 癸	乙 己 丁	乙 己 丁	丁 己	

This earth is dry and it will contaminate Gui 癸 water

Her Unfavourable Element is Earth. We know that the Earth element corresponds with the stomach region so we can already see that her health problems are likely to relate to her stomach. What kinds of problems are related to the stomach? The Wei 未 (Goat) and Chou 丑 (Ox) contain Ji 己 Earth inside (Hidden Stems). Ji 己 Earth is mud, soil and dirt. Ji 己 Heavenly Stem also represents stomach and diaphragm. What happens when you mix dirt into water? It becomes contaminated and dirty. In BaZi, contaminated water is an image of poison. In reality this usually denotes malignancies. Hence, this suggests stomach cancer.

From this example, you can see how BaZi can help us understand our potential health problems and health conditions. This allows us to plan ahead by recognising problem areas in our health and health weaknesses and enabling us to prepare for problems (by knowing which areas will need attention) when age catches up. It is extremely advantageous to have early knowledge of prospective health problems so early treatment and appropriate medical attention can be sought.

Understanding Personal Relationships

One of the main uses of BaZi is to help us understand our relationships with the people around us. Often human beings behave, react and respond differently to different people around them. Even with the same person, sometimes we behave differently. The elemental effect from the time factor (Luck Pillars, Annual Pillars and Month Pillars) all play a role in shaping how we relate to others at different points in our lives, or even different months of the year.

By looking at the relationship between the elements in your BaZi chart, it is possible to ascertain what your relationship will be with someone or something.

There are generally TWO important perspectives that can be used to evaluate BaZi in terms of relationships with others. The first method is to look at the pillars as Palaces (宮位).

This method enables you to evaluate the nature of your relationships with something (such as your career) or someone (spouse, parents, children).

The second method for reading a BaZi is through the Ten Gods(十神). This is a slightly more sophisticated method that requires we delve more deeply into the Five Elements and the ten different stars(星), commonly known as the Ten Gods(十神). We will focus on the Palace Method, which is quicker and easier to apply, in this book.

In the Palace Method, each Pillar in the BaZi represents one of the following:

1. Grandparents, extended family members
2. Parents or superiors
3. Spouse or home
4. Children or subordinates

Hour 時	Day 日	Month 月	Year 年
Children	Self Spouse	Parents	Grand Parents

The Palace method of assessing your BaZi is the easiest and quickest way of assessing the above 4 types of relationship.

Now, let's say if in a particular luck cycle, there is a clash with the element in your Month Pillar. Immediately, you can ascertain that the problem might involve your relationship with your parents or your superiors.

If for example, you have an Unfavourable Element in your Year Pillar, then this indicates that your grandparents will not be very helpful to you in life or that you do not have much affinity with them. It may also indicate a less than good family background (ie: a broken family or perhaps, a dispersed family) or that you or your parents will have to be 'self-made' as you or your parents do not have anything inherited from your grandparents for you or your parents to gain a head-start in life.

Hour 時	Day 日	Month 月	Year 年
			Unfavourable Element

Unfavourable Element at the Year Pillar

If your Favourable Element is in your Children Palace, this indicates that your affinity with your children will be good – they are likely to be filial children or have a good relationship with you. Conversely if you have an Unfavourable Element in your Children Palace, then this indicates that you will not have good affinity with your children.

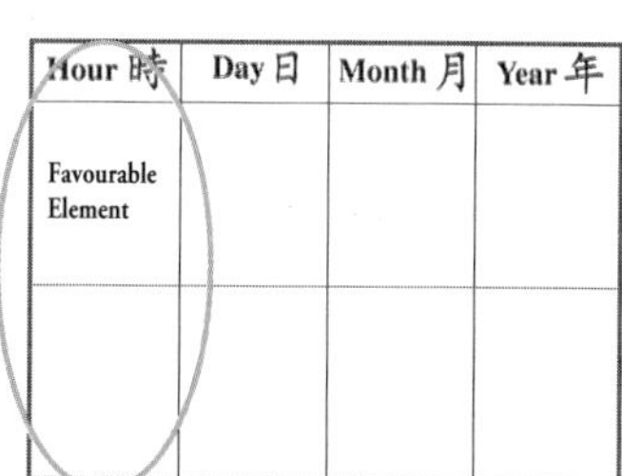

Favourable Element at the Year Pillar

What is affinity? It is difficult to translate this concept into English – in Chinese, it is known as "Yuan 緣"

Poor affinity can mean many things – it may mean separation by distance, it may mean that many obstacles or hindrances have to be overcome before you can be together. Poor affinity with your children might mean that you are separated by distance (you live in different countries) or in particularly bad cases, it may mean miscarriages or the early death of a child. In a mild case, it may simply mean that you and your child have different outlooks or perceptions about life. In extreme instances, parent and child simply cannot get along with each other.

The Grandparents Palace, besides representing your relationship with your Grandparents, can also represent your extended family members or older family members. Your Parents Palace represents not only your parents, but also your superior/boss or your mentor. Your Spouse Palace, besides representing your relationship with your spouse, also represents your home and living conditions. Your Children Palace does not only represents your children but also your subordinates and people under your care.

This is a quick and fast method to establish what your relationship or affinity with various individuals in your life will be like, using the relationship between the elements and your Day Master.

This is Your Life

The Palace Method also can be used to provide a general picture of your life in Four Phases – Young Age, Youth, Middle Age, Old Age.

Hour 時	Day 日	Month 月	Year 年
60 to old	36 - 60	17 - 35	0 - 17

Here's a quick method of checking to see if you can expect smooth sailing or rough waters through the different life phases. Where your Favourable Elements are located can tell you a lot about a person's life path. Whether they are good starters and good finishers or bad starters but good finishers in life all can be easily read just by looking at the position of the Favourable Element.

If your Favourable Element is in your Day or Hour Pillars (particularly in the Earthly Branches) this indicates that the older you get, the better your life gets. This is of course a good sign. It is always better to have a 'good ending' in life than to suffer a terrible fate. The Chinese believe that life should be bitter first, then sweet. So, a bad start and good finish is a blessed life. A good start and a pathetic finish is not considered good at all.

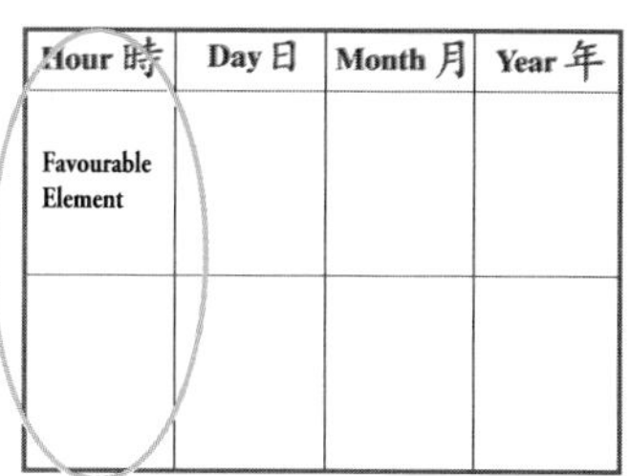

Favourable Element at the Year Pillar

Similarly, if you have Unfavourable Elements in your Year Pillar, this suggests a difficult or hard childhood. Unfavourable Elements in your Month Pillar indicate that life truly gets better for you after 40 and that your early life might be hard, tough or bumpy.

Individuals who enjoy good fortune from young age usually have Favourable Elements in their Year and Month pillars.

BaZi For Crisis Management

危機

'When written in Chinese, the word 'crisis' is composed of two characters – one represents danger, and the other represents opportunity,' – John F. Kennedy.

BaZi is not just about knowing the good things in life, but also about bracing yourself for the not-so-pleasant events in life. From a person's BaZi, we can anticipate the kinds of difficulties or obstacles a person may face.

How do you see what kind of 'trouble' is approaching from your BaZi? And what happens if you see 'trouble' heading your way in BaZi?

Take a look at the BaZi below:

Hour 時	Day 日	Month 月	Year 年	
甲 *Jia* Yang Wood	癸 *Gui* Yin Water	庚 *Geng* Yang Metal	丁 *Ding* Yin Fire	**Heavenly Stems 天干**
寅 *Yin* **Tiger** Yang Wood	丑 *Chou* **Ox** Yin Earth	戌 *Xu* **Dog** Yang Earth	巳 *Si* **Snake** Yin Fire	**Earthly Branches 地支**
戊 甲 丙	辛 己 癸	丁 戊 辛	庚 丙 戊	

2004

What can this person expect in the Year 2004, which is the year of Jia Shen 甲申 (Wood Monkey)?

This gentleman is Gui 癸 Water born in the Xu 戌 (Dog) month. Xu 戌 (Dog) month is the Autumn season - Metal is strong and Water is reasonably strong. This is because Metal produces Water, that's why in the Metal season, Water can be strong. The Geng 庚 Metal beside him and the hidden Water roots found in the Chou 丑 (Ox) makes this Gui 癸 Water a strong Day Master.

What element then is needed in this BaZi? Remember, our objective in BaZi is to have a balanced chart. You do not want any particular element to be too strong or too weak. The Gui 癸 Water is strong AND since this person is born in Autumn, the Fire element, which is this person's Wealth Element is accordingly weak.

Hour 時	Day 日	Month 月	Year 年
	癸 *Gui* Yin Water		
		Autumn	

This Day Master needs fire

Let's take the analysis a bit deeper. His Day Master is strong and it can easily control the weak Fire element. But take a closer look at the chart. Don't you think the chart is a little bit cold? This chart needs a little bit more Fire to help bring some warmth and life to the chart. This is called the Regulating Useful God Selection Technique(調候用神), which we will explore in later books.

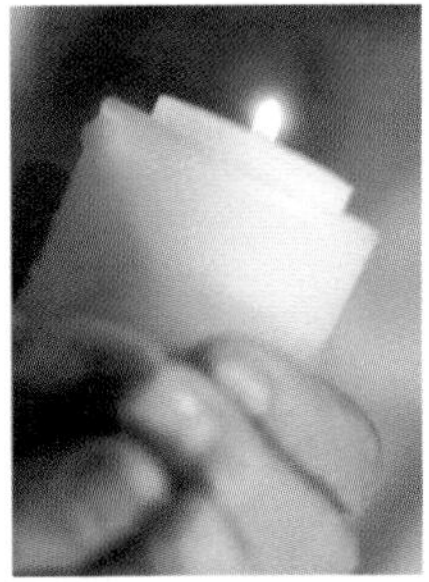

Now, where can we find the Fire needed to warm up the chart? It is found in the Ding 丁 Fire (the Year Pillar's Heavenly Stem) and the hidden Bing 丙 Fire (found inside the Si 巳 (Snake) of the Year Pillar's Earthly Branch). So, we can say that to this gentleman, his Year Pillar is extremely important to his BaZi.

The arrival of the Jia Shen 甲申 year brings about two events: The Shen 申 (Monkey) **clashes** with the Yin 寅 (Tiger) branch in the Hour Pillar and **combines** with the Si 巳 (Snake) in his Year Pillar. In BaZi, besides Clashes 沖 there are also Combinations 合 involving the Earthly Branches.

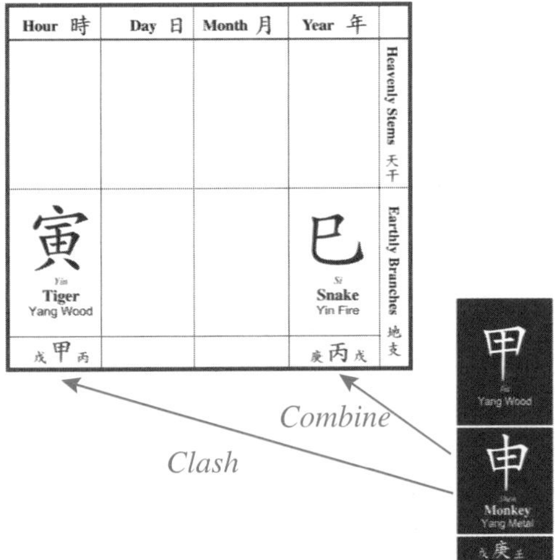

Now, a Clash or Combination does not always denote trouble. How do we know it will be trouble? By looking at what the elements that are clashed or combined represent and what the combination itself represents.

Inside the Si巳(Snake) is the Day Master Gui(癸) Water's Wealth Element, Bing丙Fire. Now, we know that the Wealth Element denotes wife/spouse or girlfriend. When Shen申(Monkey) comes in to combine with the Si巳(Snake), the Si巳(Snake) is combined away. In advanced BaZi, you will learn that a combination results in something being taken away or removed. In other words, the wife, spouse or girlfriend is removed or disappears from the picture.

Hour 時	Day 日	Month 月	Year 年	
				Heavenly Stems 天干
			巳 Si Snake Yin Fire	Earthly Branches 地支
			庚 丙 戊	

丙

Si巳 contains Bing丙 fire, the Wealth Element to a Gui癸 Water man.

What compounds the situation? The fact that the Si巳(Snake) and the Ding丁Fire in the Year Pillar are extremely important to this person's BaZi as they help to balance his BaZi chart. It is a needed element in the chart that keeps the BaZi balanced. If they are gone, the chart could fall apart.

Now, everyone has relationship troubles – the question is: will this relationship problem be a minor hassle or a tormenting pain that hurts and affects the person significantly?

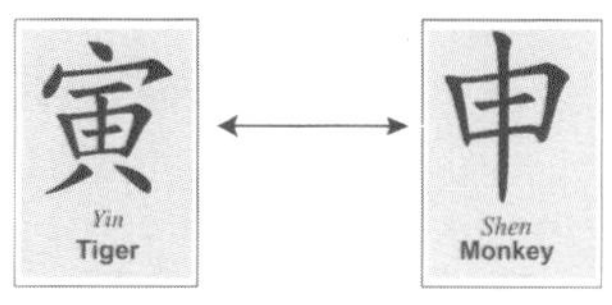

Emotional Clash

Yes, because the Yin寅(Tiger) and Shen申 (Monkey) clash is known as an 'Emotional Clash' (Duo Qing Zhi Chong 多情之沖). So, this is likely to be an agonising heartbreak or relationship problem. As the Yin寅(Tiger) Wood element represents Gui癸 Water's Output - his thoughts and thinking – this clash disrupts his life and causes disharmony and distraction.

Accordingly for this gentleman, we can say that the Jia Shen 甲申year is likely to bring emotional problems that affect his work and the source of the emotional problems is a break-up with his girlfriend or spouse.

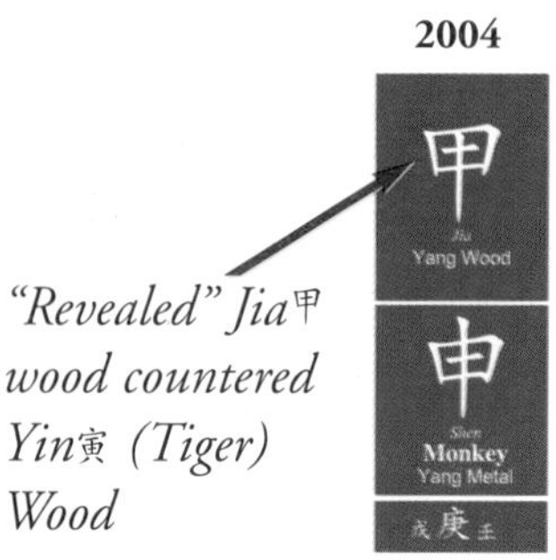

As this situation is revealed in the Heavenly Stems – this means that it is obvious to all since it's exposed on the Stems that it is emotional problems. Obvious to all here means that all his friends and people who know him will know about his problem. If the clash or combination is 'hidden', that means no one knows about it.

Now, you may be thinking – every 12 years, a Monkey year rolls around. Surely this gentleman cannot expect that every 12 years there will be a break up right? Remember, the Annual Heavenly Stem and the person's Luck Pillars also impact on the situation so, no, the next Monkey Year will not necessarily herald another break-up for this person yet again.

Forewarned is Forearmed

It's one thing to know what's going to happen but it's another thing to deal with the situation. While BaZi can help you 'see' what is coming, you can't always do something about the situation unfortunately. Why? Well, you can exert all your Man-Luck and will power to try to avoid the situation but sometimes, that is just not enough. So, if you can't avoid or side-step a problem, the best thing is to be mentally and psychologically prepared for it – brace for the impact! You can't always 'change' your Destiny entirely but you can surely soften the impact.

Dealing with an obstacle, hindrance or crisis that is coming is like getting ready for an examination. What do you do? You prepare of course! And *IF* you are prepared, 'chances' are you'll come out of it better than if you did not prepare yourself at all. Knowing your BaZi is like having a "cheat sheet" with you during your exam, you already know the 'questions' before the test!

Another analogy of BaZi is it is a bit like checking the weather forecast. If you know there will be showers tomorrow morning, you'd probably go out armed with an umbrella.

BaZi is not at all about fortune telling in this modern day and age. I prefer to view it as a tool that helps us prepare for events and situations and guides us on what is a suitable recourse or action to take.

Here's a personal example of how BaZi can be used to avoid obstacles, hindrances or hassles, when applied properly!

Last year, I was interviewed by a journalist about my teaching work in London. The interview was very cordial and I personally thought it had gone very well.

Two months later, the article comes out and the phone didn't stop ringing. The content of the article was accurate but it also gave the impression that I was an arrogant person with a seriously inflated ego who had made certain comments that could be misconstrued as offensive or critical of others. Obviously not an ideal outcome and did not quite reflect what I had meant in the context of our earlier interview.

Now, my BaZi at that time was being affected by a very strong 7 Killings or Influence Element. This combination indicated trouble caused by misunderstandings or miscommunications. Surprise surprise!

What would have been the solution then to this problem?

In Bazi, 'cures' come in the form of action. In my case, knowing that my BaZi was being influenced significantly by an overly strong 7 Killings element , it would probably be wise to have been very careful with the way I spoke to the journalist, or perhaps, to have my secretary on hand for the interview to ensure that the wrong message was not conveyed.

Action is the Cure

To understand how 'action' is the cure in BaZi, you need to have a good understanding of the Five Elements cycle, as is seen in the chart below.

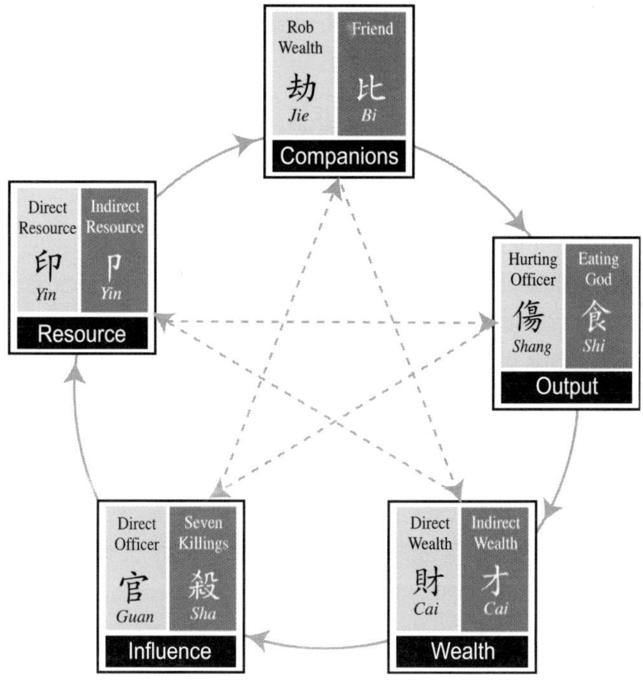

This chart 'translates' the Five Elements into human actions. In effect, the way to resolve or counter a problem that is 'revealed' by your BaZi is simply to take the right action in accordance with the Five Elements.

In Feng Shui, a cure involves using the forces of nature, your environment or Earth luck. In BaZi studies, it is about actions and decisions.

Let's say a chart has the problem of too much of the Wealth Element. Remember, having too much Wealth Elements in a chart is a problem because it causes imbalance in the BaZi. So what is the solution or cure?

Refer to the diagram on the previous page - based on the Control Cycle, what do you think controls the Wealth Element? The Companion Element of course!

The Companion Element helps Wealth. In Chinese we call this Bi Jian Fen Cai (比肩分財) meaning, Companions help share the Wealth. By helping you share the Wealth, they also at the same time lend your Day Master strength to control the Wealth Element. So, it's a win-win situation.

So how do you use the Companion Element? The key is to find out what the Companion Element represents. In most cases, the Companion Element represents your friends, your siblings or someone very close to you. If a person is troubled by excessive Wealth Element, then the advice is to seek a business partner or work with a sibling or friend.

What if a Day Master is strong or excessively strong and thus can control the wealth? Then these people do not need Companion elements and usually will be people who cannot participate in joint-venture opportunities or business partnerships.

Take a look at this example:

Hour 時	Day 日	Month 月	Year 年	
乙 *Yi* Yin Wood	壬 *Ren* Yang Water	丁 *Ding* Yin Fire	丙 *Bing* Yang Fire	**Heavenly Stems** 天干
巳 *Si* **Snake** Yin Fire	午 *Wu* **Horse** Yang Fire	酉 *You* **Rooster** Yin Metal	申 *Shen* **Monkey** Yang Metal	**Earthly Branches** 地支
庚 丙 戊	丁 己	辛	戊 庚 壬	

This BaZi chart belongs to a Male, born on September 12, 1956 in the Si 巳 (Snake) hour.

Let's start by evaluating the strength of the Day Master. This gentleman is a Ren 壬 Water, born in the You 酉 (Rooster) Month. You 酉 (Rooster) is an Autumn month and is part of the Metal season. In Autumn, the Water element is strong. The presence of a Geng 庚 Metal inside the Shen 申 (Monkey), the Year Pillar's Earthly Branch also helps to strengthen the Day Master. So clearly, this is a strong Ren 壬 Water.

To a Water person, Fire is the Wealth Element. In this chart the Fire elements are pretty strong. How do we know they are strong? The Ding 丁 and Bing 丙, seen on the Heavenly Stems are rooted in Si 巳 (Snake) and Wu 午 (Horse).

Fire = Wealth Element in this chart. Fire is rooted in the Day and Hour Branch.

In previous chapters, I talked about roots in a BaZi, which are the Hidden Stems. Rooted means that a particular Heavenly Stem has the same element in the Earthly Branches. When an element is rooted, it has a steady, strong and proper foundation – like a tree has roots. An element will have a truly strong presence in a person's chart if it is not only present in the Heavenly Stems but is also rooted in the Earthly Branches.

Where the Day Master is strong and Wealth element is strong, you will know that it belongs to someone who has considerable financial capacity. Why? Because the Day Master is strong enough to control the strong Wealth.

What makes this chart also exceptional is that there is only one visible Water element. And it is a strong Water element too. What does this mean? It means that all the Wealth in the chart is not shared with others.

Hour 時	Day 日	Month 月	Year 年	
	壬 Ren Yang Water			Heavenly Stems 天干
				Earthly Branches 地支

The only visible Water element.

This also demonstrates how the quantity of the elements in a person's chart does not always tell the whole story. It's much more important to look at the quality of the element.

Here in lies the difference in reading. If a person's Day Master is strong because of the presence of Companions, it means there potentially will be people who share in your wealth. If on the other hand, a person's Day Master is strong because of Resource Elements, then this person will not have to share his or her Wealth with others since Resource will never participate in sharing of the wealth. What's the Favourable Element in this BaZi? The Yi 乙 Wood. Why? Strong water needs to release its strength, so it is best

used to produce Wood. Why not chose the Wealth or Influence Elements? This BaZi can utilise Wealth and Influence as well, so the trick is to pick the best Favourable Element. Remember we are looking for good flow of Qi.

Water producing Wood and Wood then produces Fire is the most natural and smooth flow of Qi, since this follows the Five Elements Production Cycle to the hilt. Hence, it is best to first favour Wood over all the other possible Favourable Elements.

Now, 'what' or 'who' is the Wood element to this person? Wood is an Output Element. Output represents talents, arts and performance. In advance study of BaZi, the Yi 乙 Wood to a Ren 壬 Water Day Master is called a Hurting Officer (Shang Guan 傷官). The Hurting Officer Star represents expressive talents. Hurting Officer also represents perfectionists especially when the Hurting Officer is Yi 乙 Wood.

Hour 時	Day 日	Month 月	Year 年	
乙 Yi Yin Wood	壬 Ren Yang Water			Heavenly Stems 天干
				Earthly Branches 地支

Favourable Element is this chart.

You may be curious about the identity of this exceptional individual. His name is Leslie Cheong, a talented Hong Kong movie star and singer. Following his recent death, it was revealed that he had left behind a substantial fortune.

Riding the Luck with BaZi

"Those who fail to plan, plan to fail"

BaZi moves in luck cycles. Once the luck cycle has passed, it is over. This means your failures and hardships in the past will not repeat itself in the future. BUT, it also means your present success will not 'happen again'.

To decide what you want in life, and to know what is preventing you from getting it, you need precise information. To take the right action, you need precise instructions.

BaZi helps you plan for the future and at the same time, learn to take action that goes with the flow. Be it lying low when luck is bad, or being aggressive and opportunistic when luck is good, BaZi helps you plan your actions appropriately.

Self Improvement Through BaZi

Many of us would like to improve ourselves. How else can one explain the dearth of motivational books, tapes, seminars and life coaches, all out to help people improve their lives and 'take control'? Yet, people are sometimes uncertain as to what changes they need to make. It's understandable – how many of us can really look at our flaws objectively? Or even see our own flaws?

BaZi is, in that sense, a mirror that helps reflect back to us, our flaws, our weaknesses and our strengths, thus enabling us to make improvements or changes to improve things.

By understanding the elements that cause you to react or behave in a certain way, do your best to consciously change your actions and your decisions to change the way you feel about yourself, change how other people perceive you and change the way you feel about someone.

Taking the Stress out of Life

BaZi is also about being realistic. Yes, there are some things you can work hard at changing or improving but also some things which you cannot. It's good to be hopeful and optimistic. But don't be positively bluffing yourself when you place your hopes and dreams too high, to the point where it is beyond your BaZi capacity, then you are only paving the way for disappointments.

八字命理

Parents will save themselves a lot of angst and heartache if they recognised their child's abilities (or inabilities) early on and rather than trying to push them one way or another, guide them in the right direction.

How many books are out there looking to help people find the right job? Or change jobs? BaZi takes the stress out of this in some respects by helping you identify not just what kind of jobs you will be good at, but what kinds of industries will attract you and what kind of positions you can excel at.

I hope that by now you've gained considerable insights into the wonderful art of BaZi.

Your Destiny Code that reveals your LIFE. I hope that you will be able to use BaZi to make a difference in your life and in the lives of those around you.

In the next book on the Destiny Code ...

We will explore more techniques for analysis, concepts such as special relationships between Heavenly Stems and Earthly Branches, structures and formations, and delve deeper into how BaZi can help you determine your potential, unlock your talents and capabilities, make better decisions and in turn, achieve fulfillment and happiness in life by living life according to what we are able, capable, born to and destined to do and achieve.

This is the beginning of your journey into the Destiny Code.

About Joey Yap

Joey Yap is the founder and Master Trainer of the Mastery Academy of Chinese Metaphysics, a global organisation devoted to the worldwide teaching of Feng Shui, BaZi, Mian Xiang and other Chinese Metaphysics subjects. Joey is also the CEO of Yap Global Consulting, a Feng Shui and Chinese Astrology consulting firm offering audit and consultation services to corporations and individuals all over the world.

Joey received his formal education in Malaysia and Australia. He has combined the best of Eastern learning and Western education systems in the teaching methodology practiced at the Academy. Students of the Mastery Academy study traditional syllabuses of Chinese Metaphysics but through Western-style modular programs that are structured and systematic, enabling individuals to easily and quickly learn, grasp and master complex Chinese Metaphysics subjects like Feng Shui and BaZi. These unique structured learning systems are also utilized by Mastery Academy instructors all over the world to teach BaZi and Feng Shui.

The Mastery Academy is also the first international educational organisation to fully utilize the benefits of the Internet to promote continuous education, encourage peer-to-peer learning, enable mentoring and distance learning. Students interact with each other live, and continue to learn and improve their knowledge.

Despite his busy schedule, Joey continues to write for the Mastery Journal, a monthly eZine on Feng Shui and Astrology devoted for world-wide readers and the production of the world's first bilingual "Ten Thousand Year Calendar". He is also the best selling author of "Stories and Lessons on Feng Shui", "Mian Xiang- Discover Face Reading", "Tong Shu Diary" and "BaZi - The Destiny Code". Besides being a regular guest of various radio and TV talk shows, Joey is also a regular columnist for a national newspaper and various new magazines in Malaysia, as well as being the host of "*Discover Feng Shui with Joey Yap*" on national 8TV , a popular program which focuses on education in Feng Shui and Chinese Metaphysics studies.

Author's personal website: www.joeyyap.com

EDUCATION

The Mastery Academy of Chinese Metaphysics: the first choice for practitioners and aspiring students of the art and science of Chinese Classical Feng Shui and Astrology.

For thousands of years, Eastern knowledge has been passed from one generation to another through the system of discipleship. A venerated Master would accept suitable individuals at a young age as his disciples, and informally through the years, pass on his knowledge and skills to them. His disciples in turn, would take on their own disciples, as a means to perpetuate knowledge or skills.

This system served the purpose of restricting the transfer of knowledge to only worthy honourable individuals and ensuring that outsiders or Westerners would not have access to thousands of years of Eastern knowledge, learning and research.

However, the disciple system has also resulted in Chinese Metaphysics and Classical Studies lacking systematic teaching methods. Knowledge garnered over the years has not been accumulated in a concise, systematic manner, but scattered amongst practitioners, each practicing his/her knowledge, art and science, in isolation.

The disciple system, out of place in today's modern world, endangers the advancement of these classical fields that continue to have great relevance and application today.

At the Mastery Academy of Chinese Metaphysics, our Mission is to bring Eastern Classical knowledge in the fields of metaphysics, Feng Shui and Astrology sciences and the arts to the world. These Classical teachings and knowledge, previously shrouded in secrecy and passed on only through the discipleship system, are adapted into structured learning, which can easily be understood, learnt and mastered. Through modern learning methods, these renowned ancient arts, sciences and practices can be perpetuated while facilitating more extensive application and understanding of these classical subjects.

The Mastery Academy espouses an educational philosophy that draws from the best of the East and West . It is the world's premier educational institution for the study of Chinese Metaphysics Studies offering a wide range and variety of courses, ensuring that students have the opportunity to pursue their preferred field of study and enabling existing practitioners and professionals to gain cross-disciplinary knowledge that complements their current field of practice.

Courses at the Mastery Academy have been carefully designed to ensure a comprehensive yet compact syllabus. The modular nature of the courses enables students to immediately begin to put their knowledge into practice while pursuing continued study of their field and complimentary fields. Students thus have the benefit of developing and gaining practical experience in tandem with the expansion and advancement of their theoretical knowledge.

Students can also choose from a variety of study options, from a distance learning program, the Homestudy Series, that enables study at one's own pace or intensive foundation courses and compact lecture-based courses, held in various cities around the world by Joey Yap or our licensed instructors. The Mastery Academy's faculty and make-up is international in nature, thus ensuring that prospective students can attend courses at destinations nearest to their country of origin or with a licensed Mastery Academy instructor in their home country.

The Mastery Academy provides 24x7 support to students through its Online Community, with a variety of tools, documents, forums and e-learning materials to help students stay at the forefront of research in their fields and gain invaluable assistance from peers and mentoring from their instructors.

TM

MASTERY ACADEMY
OF CHINESE METAPHYSICS

www.masteryacademy.com

19-3, The Boulevard, Mid Valley City,
59200 Kuala Lumpur, Malaysia.
Tel: +603-2284 8080, +603-2284 8318
Fax: +603-2284 1218
Email: info@masteryacademy.com
Website: www.masteryacademy.com

Represented In:
Australia, Austria, Brazil, Canada, China, Cyprus, France, Germany, Greece, Hungary, India, Japan, Indonesia, Italy, Malaysia, Mexico, Netherlands, New Zealand, Philippines, Russian Federation, Poland, Singapore, South Africa, Switzerland, Turkey, U.S.A., Ukraine, United Kingdom

Mastery Academy around the world

YAP GLOBAL CONSULTING SDN. BHD

• Feng Shui Estate Design and Planning • Land Selection • Feng Shui f Residences • Feng Shui for Offices • Feng Shui for Corporate Headquarters Feng Shui for Commercial Properties • Date Selection for Official Openings Business Transactions • Date Selection for Individuals • BaZi/ Destiny Analys for Corporations • BaZi/Destiny Analysis for Individuals • BaZi/Desti Analysis for Career • BaZi/Destiny Analysis for Relationships • Corpora Seminars • Private Seminars • Public Talks

Yap Global Consulting is the foremost international Feng Shui and Ba consulting firm, offering professional confidential consultations and audits f individuals and corporations. We benchmark our services against the standar of international consulting firms, bringing a distinctly professional approach BaZi/Destiny Analysis and Feng Shui auditing and consulting.

Yap Global Consulting's CEO and Principal Consultant, Mr. Joey Yap, is Master Trainer for the Mastery Academy of Chinese Metaphysics, the worl first learning organisation dedicated to the study of Chinese Metaphysics. C global reach is supported by an international team of professional and hig experienced Senior Consultants. No matter where you are located in the wor Yap Global Consulting has experienced and professional consultants availa to conduct BaZi consultations and Feng Shui audits and consultations for you.

For more details or to make an appointment,
visit www.joeyyap.com or contact us at:

Tel : +603-2284 1213
Fax : +603-2284 2213
Email : consultations@joeyyap.com

Or you may visit our office by appointment at

19-3, The Boulevard,
Mid Valley City,
59200 Kuala Lumpur, Malaysia.

www.joeyyap.com

Accelerate Your Face Reading Skills With Joey Yap's Face Reading Revealed DVD Series

Face Reading Revealed – DVD 1

Introduction to Face Reading

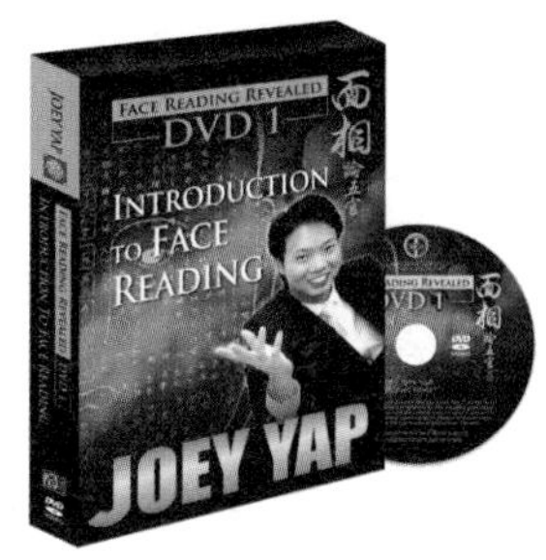

Mian Xiang, the Chinese art of Face Reading is an ancient form of physiognomy and entails the use of the face and facial characteristics to evaluate key aspects of a person's life, luck and destiny. In this Introduction to Face Reading DVD, Joey Yap shows you how the eyes, ears, mouth, nose and eyebrows reveal a wealth of information about a person's luck, destiny and personality.

Face Reading Revealed – DVD 2

12 Palaces of the Face

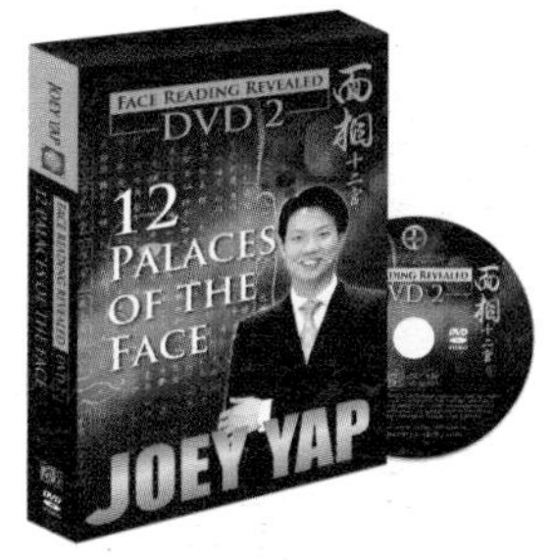

Mian Xiang reveals not just a person's destiny and fortune, but talents, quirks and personality. Did you know that just by looking at a person's face, you can ascertain a wealth of information about their health, wealth, relationships and career? In this DVD, Joey Yap shows you how the 12 Palaces can be utilised to reveal a person's inner talents, personality quirks and much more.

Face Reading Revealed – DVD 3

100 Positions of the Face - Ages 1 to 30

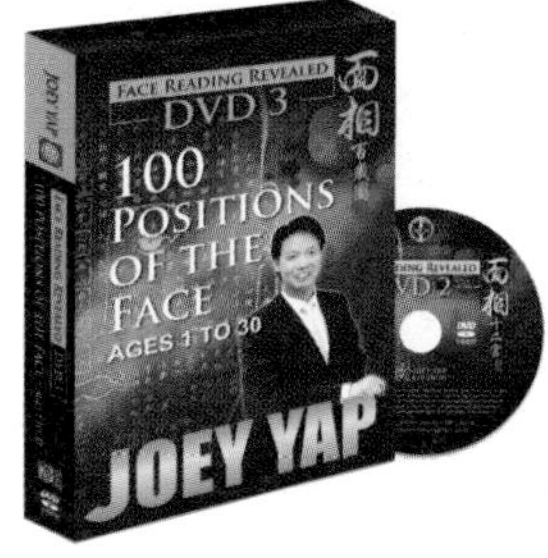

Each facial feature on the face represents one year in a person's life. Joey Yap guides you through the 100 year map of the face and shares with you which features on your face govern your luck between the ages of 1 to 30. Also, learn how to deploy Fixed Position Face Reading and Multiple Position Face Reading techniques in this lively, entertaining and educational DVD.

Accelerate Your Face Reading Skills With Joey Yap's Face Reading Revealed DVD Series

Face Reading Revealed – DVD 4

100 Positions of the Face - Ages 31 to 100

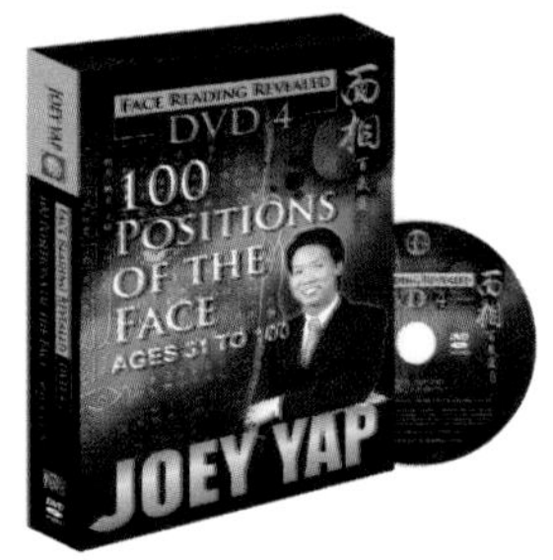

Your face is a 100 year map of your life but each position not only reveals your fortune and destiny for that age, but also reveals insights and information about your personality, skills, abilities and destiny. Delve deeper into the 100 year map of the face and discover, with Joey Yap, what facial features determine your luck between the ages of 31-100.

Face Reading Revealed – DVD 5

How to Read Face Shapes

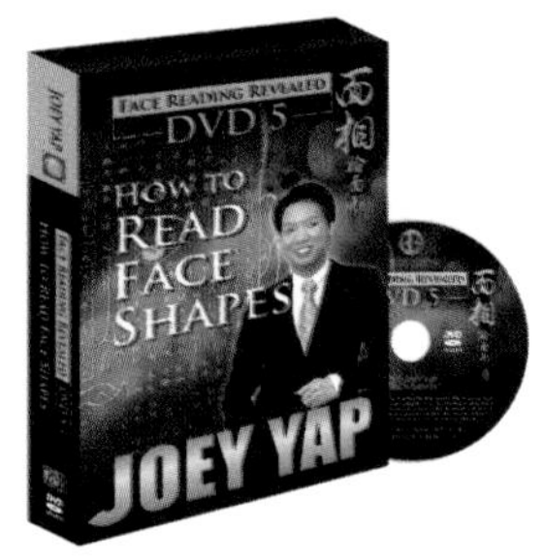

This highly entertaining and insightful DVD shows you how just by evaluating the shape of a person's face, you can learn about their abilities, inclinations, personality and capacity in life. What does a Water face person excel in? What is the personality of a Metal faced person? Let Joey Yap show you the differences between the 10 character faces and how to discern the 5 basic element face shapes in this fun, entertaining and educational DVD.

Face Reading Revealed – DVD 6

The Significance of Moles, Hair and Birthmarks

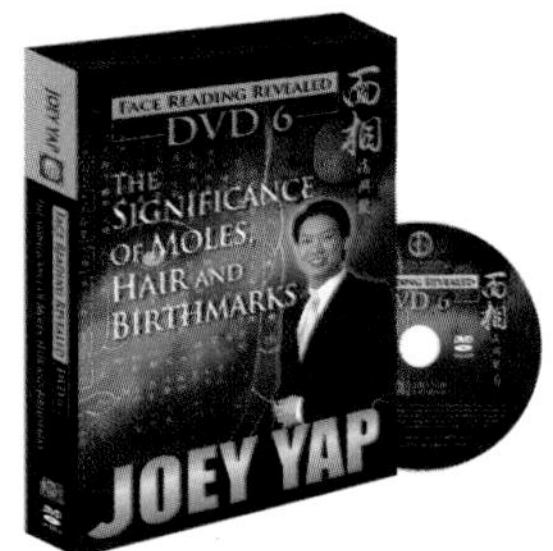

Do moles have meanings? Yes they do and in Face Reading, moles, birthmarks and even, the type of hair on your head, can reveal a lot about a person. Find out the meaning of moles on the face, what kinds of moles are favourable and unfavourable and whether or not you should remove certain moles with Feng Shui, Chinese Astrology and Face Reading Master Trainer Joey Yap.

Continue Your Journey with Joey Yap's Books

The Ten Thousand Year Calendar

The Ten Thousand Year Calendar or 萬年曆 Wan Nian Li is a regular reference book and an invaluable tool used by masters, practitioners and students of Feng Shui, BaZi (Four Pillars of Destiny), Chinese Zi Wei Dou Shu Astrology (Purple Star), Yi Jing (I-Ching) and Date Selection specialists.

JOEY YAP's Ten Thousand Year Calendar provides the Gregorian (Western) dates converted into both the Chinese Solar and Lunar calendar in both the English and Chinese language.

It also includes a comprehensive set of key Feng Shui and Chinese Astrology charts and references, including Xuan Kong Nine Palace Flying Star Charts, Monthly and Daily Flying Stars, Water Dragon Formulas Reference Charts, Zi Wei Dou Shu (Purple Star) Astrology Reference Charts, BaZi (Four Pillars of Destiny) Heavenly Stems, Earthly Branches and all other related reference tables for Chinese Metaphysical Studies.

Stories and Lessons on Feng Shui

Stories and Lessons on Feng Shui is a compilation of essays and stories written by leading Feng Shui and Chinese Astrology trainer and consultant Joey Yap about Feng Shui and Chinese Astrology.

In this heart-warming collection of easy to read stories, find out why it's a myth that you should never have Water on the right hand side of your house, the truth behind the infamous 'love' and 'wealth' corners and that the sudden death of a pet fish is really NOT due to bad luck!

BaZi - The Destiny Code

Leading Chinese Astrology Master Trainer Joey Yap makes it easy to learn how to unlock your Destiny through your BaZi with this book. BaZi or Four Pillars of Destiny is an ancient Chinese science which enables individuals to understand their personality, hidden talents and abilities as well as their luck cycle, simply by examining the information contained within their birth data. The Destiny Code is the first book that shows readers how to plot and interpret their own Destiny Charts and lays the foundation for more in-depth BaZi studies. Written in a lively entertaining style, the Destiny Code makes BaZi accessible to the layperson. Within 10 chapters, understand and appreciate more about this astoundingly accurate ancient Chinese Metaphysical science.

Continue Your Journey with Joey Yap's Books

Mian Xiang - Discover Face Reading

Need to identify a suitable business partner? How about understanding your staff or superiors better? Or even choosing a suitable spouse? These mind boggling questions can be answered in Joey Yap's introductory book to Face Reading titled 'Mian Xiang – Discover Face Reading'. This book will help you discover the hidden secrets in a person's face.

Mian Xiang – Discover Face Reading is comprehensive book on all areas of Face Reading, covering some of the most important facial features, including the forehead, mouth, ears and even the philtrum above your lips. This book will help you analyse not just your Destiny but help you achieve your full potential and achieve life fulfillment.

Xuan Kong - Flying Stars Feng Shui

Xuan Kong Flying Stars Feng Shui is an essential introductory book to the subject of Xuan Kong Fei Xing, a well-known and popular system of Feng Shui, written by the International Feng Shui Master Trainer Joey Yap.

In his down-to-earth, entertaining and easy to read style, Joey Yap takes you through the essential basics of Classical Feng Shui, and the key concepts of Xuan Kong Fei Xing (Flying Stars). Learn how to fly the stars, plot a Flying Star chart for your home or office and interpret the stars and star combinations. Find out how to utilise the favourable areas of your home or office for maximum benefit and learn 'tricks of the trade' and 'trade secrets' used by Feng Shui practitioners to enhance and maximise Qi in your home or office.

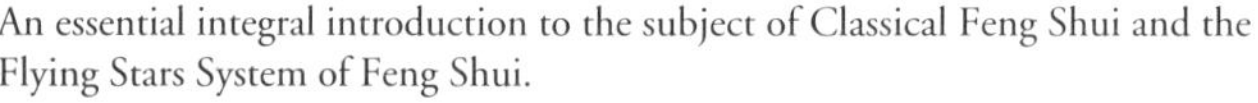

An essential integral introduction to the subject of Classical Feng Shui and the Flying Stars System of Feng Shui.

Feng Shui and Astrology for 2006

The Annual influences of each year play a crucial role in determining the Feng Shui of your property as well as your Destiny for the year 2006. Learn all about what 2006 holds in store for you with best selling author Joey Yap's new book - Feng Shui & Astrology for 2006.

This book will reveal the Feng Shui path ahead by charting out the Annual and Monthly Flying Stars, and explaining the influence the various sectors have on the occupants of the property. Based on your Chinese Zodiac animal sign, you will also be able to plan ahead using the Astrological guide for the year.

Discover the monthly guide to the Feng Shui of your home and learn how to manage it on a monthly basis as Joey Yap guides you with a clear explanation on what the effects will be and what you can do to mitigate them. Date selection is also a breeze with the auspicious dates for important activities already pre-selected in this book.

Elevate Your Feng Shui Skills With Joey Yap's Home Study Course And Educational DVDs

Xuan Kong Vol.1

An Advanced Feng Shui Home Study Course

Learn the Xuan Kong Flying Star Feng Shui system in just 20 lessons! Joey Yap's specialised notes and course work have been written to enable distance learning without compromising on the breadth or quality of the syllabus. Learn at your own pace and learn the same material students in a live class would learn. The most comprehensive distance learning course on Xuan Kong Flying Star Feng Shui in the market. Xuan Kong Flying Star Vol. 1 comes complete with a special binder for all your course notes.

Xuan Kong 10-Day Video Coaching Program

In 10 days and just 10 lessons, learn step-by-step from Joey Yap himself the fundamentals of Xuan Kong Flying Star Feng Shui. Comes complete with a Journal for students to record important notes and reference key diagrams and charts. It's like being in class with Joey, in the comfort of your own living room.

Feng Shui for Period 8 - (DVD)

Don't miss the Feng Shui Event of the next 20 years! Catch Joey Yap LIVE and find out just what Period 8 is all about. This DVD boxed set zips you through the fundamentals of Feng Shui and the impact of this important change in the Feng Shui calendar. Joey's entertaining, conversational style walks you through the key changes that Period 8 will bring and how to tap into Wealth Qi and Good Feng Shui for the next 20 years.

Xuan Kong Flying Stars Beginners Workshop - (DVD)

Take a front row seat in Joey Yap's Xuan Kong Flying Stars workshop with this unique LIVE RECORDING of Joey Yap's Xuan Kong Flying Stars Feng Shui workshop, attended by over 500 people. This DVD program is an effective and quick introduction of Xuan Kong Feng Shui essentials for those who are just starting out in their study of classical Feng Shui. Learn to plot your own Flying Star chart in just 3 hours. Learn 'trade secret' methods, remedies and cures for Flying Stars Feng Shui. This boxed set contains 3 DVDs and 1 workbook with notes and charts for reference.

BaZi Four Pillars of Destiny Beginners Workshop - (DVD)

Ever wondered what Destiny has in store for you? Or curious to know how you can learn more about your personality and inner talents? BaZi or Four Pillars of Destiny is an ancient Chinese science that enables us to understand a person's hidden talent, inner potential, personality, health and wealth luck from just their birth data. This specially compiled DVD set of Joey Yap's BaZi Beginners Workshop provides a thorough and comprehensive introduction to BaZi. Learn how to read your own chart and understand your own luck cycle. This boxed set contains 3 DVDs, 1 workbook with notes and reference charts.

BaZi Mastery Series™

LIVE COURSES (MODULES ONE TO FOUR)

BaZi Mastery – Module One

Intensive Foundation Course

This Intensive One Day Foundation Course provides an introduction to the principles and fundamentals of BaZi (Four Pillars of Destiny) and Destiny Analysis methods such as Ten Gods, Useful God and Strength of Qi. Learn how to plot a BaZi chart and interpret your Destiny and your potential. Master BaZi and learn to capitalize on your strengths, minimize risks and downturns and take charge of your Destiny.

BaZi Mastery – Module Two

Practical BaZi Applications

BaZi Module Two teaches students advanced BaZi analysis techniques and specific analysis methods for relationship luck, health evaluation, wealth potential and career potential. Students will learn to identify BaZi chart structures, sophisticated methods for applying the Ten Gods, and how to read Auxiliary Stars. Students who have completed Module Two will be able to conduct professional BaZi readings.

BaZi Mastery – Module Three

Advanced Practitioners Program

Designed for the BaZi practitioner, learn how to read complex cases and unique events in BaZi charts and perform Big and Small assessments. Discover how to analyze personalities and evaluate talents precisely, as well as special formulas and classical methodologies for BaZi from classics such as Di Tian Sui and Qiong Tong Bao Jian.

BaZi Mastery – Module Four

Master Course in BaZi

The graduating course of the BaZi Mastery Series, this course takes the advanced practitioner to the Masters' level. BaZi M4 focuses on specialized techniques of BaZi reading, unique special structures and advance methods from ancient classical texts. This program includes techniques on date selection and ancient methodologies from the Qiong Tong Bao Jian and Yuan Hai Zi Ping classics.

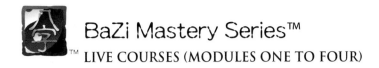

XUAN KONG MASTERY SERIES™

LIVE COURSES (MODULES ONE TO THREE)

*** Advanced Courses For Master Practitioners**

Xuan Kong Mastery – Module One

Advanced Foundation Program

This course is for the experienced Feng Shui professionals who wish to expand their knowledge and skills in the Xuan Kong system of Feng Shui, covering important foundation methods and techniques from the Wu Chang and Guang Dong lineages of Xuan Kong Feng Shui.

Xuan Kong Mastery – Module Two A

Advanced Xuan Kong Methodologies

Designed for Feng Shui practitioners seeking to specialise in the Xuan Kong system, this program focuses on methods of application and Joey Yap's unique Life Palace and Shifting Palace Methods, as well as methods and techniques from the Wu Chang lineage.

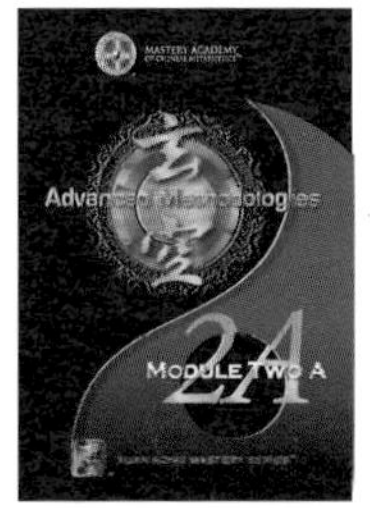

Xuan Kong Mastery – Module Two B

Purple White

Explore in detail and in great depth the star combinations in Xuan Kong. Learn how each different combination reacts or responds in different palaces, under different environmental circumstances and to whom in the property. Learn methods, theories and techniques extracted from ancient classics such as Xuan Kong Mi Zhi, Xuan Kong Fu, Fei Xing Fu and Zi Bai Jue.

Xuan Kong Mastery – Module Three

Advanced Xuan Kong Da Gua

This intensive course focuses solely on the Xuan Kong Da Gua system covering the theories, techniques and methods of application of this unique 64-Hexagram based system of Xuan Kong including Xuan Kong Da Gua for landform analysis.

MIAN XIANG MASTERY SERIES™

LIVE COURSES (MODULES ONE AND TWO)

Mian Xiang Mastery – Module One

Basic Face Reading

A person's face is their fortune – learn more about the ancient Chinese art of Face Reading. In just one day, be equipped with techniques and skills to read a person's face and ascertain their character, luck, wealth and relationship luck.

Mian Xiang Mastery – Module Two

Practical Face Reading

Mian Xiang Module Two covers face reading techniques extracted from the ancient classics Shen Xiang Quan Pian and Shen Xiang Tie Guan Dau. Gain a greater depth and understanding of Mian Xiang and learn to recognize key structures and characteristics in a person's face.

Walking the Mountains! Learn Feng Shui in a Practical and Hands-on Program.

Feng Shui Mastery Excursion Series™ : CHINA

Learn landform (Luan Tou) Feng Shui by walking the mountains and chasing the dragon's vein in China. This Program takes the students in a study tour to examine notable Feng Shui landmarks, mountains, hills, valleys, ancient palaces, famous mansions, houses and tombs in China. The Excursion is a 'practical' hands-on course where students are shown to perform readings using the formulas they've learnt and to recognize and read Feng Shui Landform (Luan Tou) formations.

Read about China Excursion here:
http://www.masteryacademy.com/Education/schoolfengshui/fengshuimasteryexcursion.asp

Mastery Academy courses are conducted around the world. Find out when will Joey Yap be in your area by visiting **www.masteryacademy.com** or call our office at +603-2284 8080 or +603-2284 8318.